An inveterate traveller, **Alexander Stewart** has walked, trekked and tramped in more than 30 countries around the world. In the course of these trips he has researched and written guidebooks for several publishers, including for Trailblazer: *New Zealand – The Great Walks*; *Inca Trail, Cusco and Machu Picchu*, and *The Walker's Haute Route*. As a freelance travel writer and photographer he has also contributed articles and photographs to various newspapers and magazines.

When he isn't escaping the city, he lives in London and works for Stanfords, the renowned map and travel specialist, wondering where to go next.

Peddars Way and Norfolk Coast Path
First edition: 2011

Publisher
Trailblazer Publications
The Old Manse, Tower Rd, Hindhead, Surrey, GU26 6SU, UK
Fax (+44) 01428-607571, info@trailblazer-guides.com
www.trailblazer-guides.com

British Library Cataloguing in Publication Data
A catalogue record for this book is available from the British Library

ISBN 978-1-905864-28-7

Editor: Anna Jacomb-Hood
Layout: Nick Hill
Proof-reading: Jane Thomas
Photographs (flora): © Bryn Thomas
Photographs (birds): © Roderick Leslie & Derek Moore OBE
Cover photograph: © Alex Stewart
All other photographs: © Alex Stewart
Cartography: Nick Hill
Index: Anna Jacomb-Hood

The maps in this guide were prepared from out-of-Crown-copyright Ordnance Survey maps amended and updated by Trailblazer.

Warning: **long distance walking can be dangerous**
Please read the notes on when to go (pp24-6) and outdoor safety (pp77-80). Every effort has been made by the author and publisher to ensure that the information contained herein is as accurate and up to date as possible. However, they are unable to accept responsibility for any inconvenience, loss or injury sustained by anyone as a result of the advice and information given in this guide.

Printed on chlorine-free paper by
D'Print (☎ +65-6581 3832), Singapore

Peddars Way

AND

NORFOLK COAST PATH

KNETTISHALL HEATH TO CROMER
planning, places to stay, places to eat,
includes 54 large-scale walking maps

ALEXANDER STEWART

TRAILBLAZER PUBLICATIONS

Dedication

For Katie, who has always been there, and Rory, who arrived during the creation of this book.

Acknowledgements

I'd like to thank the people all along the Peddars Way and Norfolk Coast Path who assisted me with the research for this book, showed me such hospitality and took time to answer my many, many queries.

As ever, thanks to the team at Trailblazer as well: Bryn Thomas for encouraging me to explore this stunning region and providing me with the opportunity to write and travel; Anna Jacomb-Hood for diligently editing and tying the text together to make this a better book; Nick Hill for interpreting my drawings and producing the maps; Roderick Leslie and Derek Moore OBE for the bird photos and Roderick Leslie for advising on the bird text.

A request

The author and publisher have tried to ensure that this guide is as accurate and up to date as possible. However, things change even on these well-worn routes. If you notice any changes or omissions that should be included in the next edition of this guide, please email or write to Trailblazer (address on p2). You can also contact us via the Trailblazer website (💻 www.trailblazer-guides.com). Those persons making a significant contribution will be rewarded with a free copy of the next edition.

Updated information will shortly be available on:
💻 **www.trailblazer-guides.com**

Front cover: Burnham Overy Tower Mill (see p142)

CONTENTS

INTRODUCTION

In that country of luminous landscapes and wide horizons where the wind runs in the reeds and the slow rivers flow to our cold sea, a man may still sense and live something of the older England which was uninhabited, free and natural.

Alan Savory, *Norfolk Fowler*

On the surface, the Peddars Way and Norfolk Coast Path seem unlikely companion routes. One is an ancient 'dry' route to the shoreline whilst the other is a more modern trail vulnerable to the vagaries of the North Sea. However, this marriage of convenience results in one of the most straightforward and enjoyable National Trails to walk.

It was Noel Coward in *Private Lives* who labelled Norfolk 'very flat', dismissing at a stroke Britain's fifth largest county as being rather dull. True, this is a peaceful, undramatic countryside without mountain ranges, valleys or major towns, yet it is littered with picturesque villages and is full of subtle charms.

Heading north across the historic landscape there's time to ponder the bewildering notion that the Romans who constructed the Peddars Way were far from the first to pass this way. Even then the route from Knettishall Heath to the coast, from the forested Suffolk–Norfolk border to the sea, was an ancient highway, a safe, dry chalk ridge above the treacherous mudflats, fens and marshes. There is a lazy roll to the fields and farmland, nothing too taxing for your lungs or legs, but enough to change the perspective thus concealing a windmill or church tower, hiding the remnants of Neolithic and Bronze Age civilisations, and delaying tantalising glimpses of the coast. This section of Norfolk has always had a raw deal and is rarely thought of in the same light as its more celebrated northern neighbour. As a result it is quieter and emptier, but no less magical. The landscape around Little Cressingham, Castle Acre and Sedgeford is frequently underrated but if you are willing to forgo a few urban pleasures for a couple of days this timeless stretch of Norfolk is very rewarding.

Dog-legs in the notoriously straight Roman road near Ringstead lead to the sea, where there is an unassuming meeting of the two paths at Holme. Nothing prepares you for the scale and beauty of the North Norfolk coast. From here on the Coast Path bears east and you enjoy brisk head-up walking over beach, bunker and boardwalk, through fragile dunes and past salt-marshes, crumbling cliffs, and creeks of fast-filling, fast-emptying tidal water. Along this stretch there is a constant blurring of sea, salt, sand and sky, but rather than making the area too similar the coastline has an ever-changing beauty.

The western half of the coast path enjoys vast expanses of beach and dunes with plenty of sand and space between amenities, whilst the eastern end is a little tamer and tidier, with the sand succumbing to shingle and traditional fishing communities giving way to the charms of faded Victorian seaside towns such as Wells, Sheringham and finally Cromer. Nonetheless there are still some unmissable villages such as Stiffkey, Morston, Blakeney and Cley containing little more than a glorious church and a cluster of cottages centred on a pub serving outstanding food and local real ale, as well as some of the best nature reserves and wildlife or bird-spotting sites in the country.

This is a walk to saunter along and savour in every respect; the many gastro pubs and restaurants boast some of the finest, freshest ingredients that Britain has to offer. Ecclesiastical remains all along the route are indicative of the wealth and status the region once enjoyed; the churches built on the profits of a thriving medieval wool trade are almost always worth a visit as are the grand Palladian-style houses. Spend time exploring this landscape with its simple lines and succumb to its many and varied charms.

About this book

This guidebook contains all the information you need. The hard work has been done for you so you can plan your trip from home without the usual pile of books, maps, guides and tourist brochures. It includes:

- All standards of accommodation from campsites to luxurious guesthouses
- Walking companies if you want an organised tour
- Suggested itineraries for all types of walkers
- Answers to all your questions: when to go, degree of difficulty, what to pack and how much the whole walking holiday will cost

When you're packed and ready to go, there's comprehensive information to get you to and from the coast path and 54 detailed maps (1:20,000) and town plans to help you find your way along it. The route guide section includes:

- Walking times
- Reviews of campsites, hostels, B&Bs, inns and guesthouses
- Cafés, pubs, tea shops, takeaways, restaurants and shops for buying supplies
- Rail, bus and taxi information for all the villages and towns along the path
- Street maps of the main towns and villages: Thetford, Castle Acre, Old Hunstanton, Hunstanton, Burnham Deepdale, Wells-next-the-Sea, Cley next the Sea, Sheringham and Cromer
- Historical, cultural and geographical background information

Minimum impact for maximum insight

Everybody needs a break; climb a mountain or jump in a lake.

Christy Moore, *Lisdoonvarna*

Why is walking in wild and solitary places so satisfying? Partly it is the sheer physical pleasure: sometimes pitting one's strength against the elements, sometimes relaxing on the springy turf or sand. The beauty and wonder of the natural world restore our sense of proportion, freeing us from the stresses and strains of everyday life.

All this the countryside gives us and the least we can do is to safeguard it by supporting rural economies, local businesses and environmentally sensitive forms of transport, and low-impact methods of farming and land use. In this book there is a detailed and illustrated chapter on the wildlife and conservation of Pembrokeshire and a chapter on minimum impact walking with ideas on how to tread lightly in this fragile environment. By following these principles we can help to preserve our natural heritage for future generations.

PLANNING YOUR WALK 1

The Peddars Way & Norfolk Coast Path

HISTORY

The route of the **Peddars Way** is a combination of the historic and the more modern, the old and the purposely created. First used by migrating animals and then the hunters who pursued them, the remnants of ancient travellers are visible as shards of worked flint and Bronze Age tumuli. The path as we now know it was developed around AD61, when the Romans established routes across East Anglia in the wake of the defeat of the Iceni (a Celtic tribe who inhabited areas covered by modern-day Norfolk between the 1st century BC and the 1st century AD) and Queen Boudica (also written as Boudicca and Boadicea). The military route that was to become the Peddars Way, established between the Roman garrison at Colchester and the heart of Iceni land, was meant to offer access to all areas of the region and allow troops to police the rebellious territory. As with most Roman roads it was built in a straight line and constructed from locally sourced material.

It wasn't until the 15th or 16th centuries though that it was dubbed the Peddars Way in respect to the pilgrims who would walk the route to the coast and the religious centre at Walsingham. In fact it is just the best known of several 'Peddars Ways' which developed at this time, which may simply be a generic term or reference to a frequently walked path. Although the Romans had long since left, the Way remained as a landmark and defining feature of the landscape, used to mark boundaries, connect communities and transport goods.

In contrast, the **Norfolk Coast Path** is a deliberately constructed route, made up from a series of existing footpaths and sections of trail created to link them. The two routes were connected to form a Long Distance Path, a title officially bestowed on them in 1986, when the route was opened by The Prince of Wales in a ceremony on Holme beach. Five years later the Long Distance Paths became National Trails (see box p75), and the pair were duly accorded this status.

HOW DIFFICULT ARE THE PATHS?

Neither of these is a technically demanding walk and most people with a reasonable level of fitness ought to be able to complete either or both without any problems. However, do not underestimate the

distances or Norfolk's seemingly flat landscape; there are still gradients to tackle and the path can stretch ahead interminably if you are not well prepared.

Although more isolated, the Peddars Way is more straightforward; the going on grassy tracks, green lanes (unsurfaced country ways often with hedges either side and sometimes quite old) and metalled roads is easy and the gradients gentle. However, the distances between villages are greater and there are extended sections without the opportunity to replenish supplies of water or food. Once on the coast, the gradients are more pronounced, the sand and shingle underfoot are more enervating, and the path is more exposed to the elements. Always be aware of the ever-present danger of cliff edges, and take care on the broad expanses of beach, especially as the tide turns. Be aware of steeply shelving beaches, treacherous currents and a strong undertow, especially at Cley and Weybourne. The marshes also pose a potential threat and should be approached with caution. Accidents often happen later in the day when people lose their footing or their bearings as fatigue sets in. Be aware of your level of ability and plan your day accordingly. Do not attempt to do too much in a single stretch, instead go slowly, relax and take in everything around you.

ROUTE FINDING

This should be straightforward since the entire path is clearly visible, well trodden and marked with clear signage. Fingerposts marked with an acorn symbol show the direction of the path at most junctions. The Peddars Way is perfectly straight in many places and can be seen arrowing across the countryside, whilst the Coast Path largely follows the North Norfolk shoreline, occasionally detouring inland.

GPS

Whilst modern Wainwrights will scoff, more open-minded walkers will accept that GPS technology can be an inexpensive, well-established if non-essential navigational aid. In no time at all a GPS receiver with a clear view of the sky will establish your position and altitude in a variety of formats, including the British OS grid system, to within a few metres. However, a GPS is not a replacement for a map and compass. Although modern units are robust and durable, it only takes a flat battery to render them useless. You should view the two systems as compatible and use both older and newer technologies together. A GPS will prevent you from making exaggerated errors when navigating and will reduce the time it takes to correct mistakes if you do stray off the path.

Using GPS with this book is an option. Without it you could end up ambling confidently along the wrong path. With it you can quickly establish your position and work out how to return to your last known position on the trail.

Using GPS with this book

It is not expected that you will walk along checking off the GPS waypoints found throughout the book, since the detailed maps and route descriptions are more than sufficient for finding your way on the Peddars Way and Norfolk Coast Path most of the time. Only when you are unsure of your position or need reassurance as to which way to go might you feel the need to reach for your GPS for confirmation.

The maps in the route guide include numbered waypoints; these correlate to the list on pp184-5, which gives the latitude/longitude position in a decimal minute format as well as a description. Where the path is vague, or there are several alternatives, you will find more waypoints. Typically landmarks or other significant features are also waymarked. Waypoints are less common in towns or villages but can still be found to help you pin down the path ahead or identify a junction.

You can manually key the nearest presumed waypoint from the list into your GPS as and when the need arises. Alternatively, with less room for error when inputting the co-ordinates, download the complete list for free as a GPS-readable file (that doesn't include the text descriptions) from the Trailblazer website. You'll need the correct cable and adequate memory in your unit (typically the ability to store 500 waypoints or more). The file as well as instructions on how to interpret an OS grid reference can be found on the Trailblazer website: 💻 www.trailblazer-guides.com.

It's also possible to buy state-of-the-art digital mapping to import into your GPS unit, assuming that you have sufficient memory capacity, but it's not the most reliable way of navigating and the small screen on your pocket-sized unit will invariably fail to put places into context or give you the 'big picture'. This is also a far more expensive option than buying the traditional OS paper maps which, whilst bulkier, are always preferable.

Bear in mind that the vast majority of people who tackle the Peddars Way and Norfolk Coast Path do so perfectly successfully **without** a GPS unit. Instead of rushing out to invest in one, consider putting the money towards good-quality waterproofs or footwear instead. That said, a GPS unit may assist in the odd dicey decision, and if used correctly in tandem with this book's waypoints might just see you safely to the next pub or overnight stop that much more quickly.

HOW LONG DO YOU NEED?

This depends on your fitness and level of ability. If you are new to multi-day trekking do not try to travel too far in one day. The Peddars Way is 46 miles long, the Norfolk Coast Path 47 miles. With the short section from the end of the Peddars Way at Holme to the official start of the Coast Path in Hunstanton, you will walk 96 miles if you cover the entire route described here. Although it can be completed in as little as three days, most people comfortably complete the walk in around eight days and still have time to explore the villages and towns along its length. If you want to enjoy the beaches, explore some of the historic churches and houses or loiter in the seaside towns longer allow closer to ten days. Similarly, if you wish to make side trips or build in excursions to see the seals on Blakeney Point (see box p160) or the birds, particularly along the coast, factor in a couple more days.

If you are camping don't underestimate how much longer it will take you to carry a full pack and all your gear the same distance. Rather than yomping across the countryside, consider travelling more slowly; by taking it easy more of the area's subtle delights and secrets will become apparent. On pp28-30 there are some suggested itineraries for people walking at different speeds. If you only have a long weekend or a couple of days concentrate on the best bits; there is a list of recommended day and weekend walks in the box on pp34-5.

❑ Peddars Way and Norfolk Coast Path certificate

The National Park authority is offering free completion certificates to walkers who finish either the Peddars Way, Norfolk Coast Path, or indeed the whole trail. Simply visit the website (🖳 www.nationaltrail.co.uk/PeddarsWay) and click on 'Planning a trip' and then on 'Badges and completion certificates' to download a feedback form. Either complete the form online, email your responses or post them, and they will send you a certificate as a thank you.

As a memento of your trip you can also buy woven cloth badges from the official website. Simply send a cheque for £3.50 made payable to Norfolk County Council to The National Trail Office, The Old Courthouse, Baron's Close, Fakenham, Norfolk NR21 8BE.

Practical information for the walker

ACCOMMODATION

Accommodation is available along the length of the Peddars Way and Norfolk Coast Path. However, there is not a lot of choice along the Peddars Way, which passes through a thinly populated part of the county, and on occasions there are just one or two options each night. In these instances you may find it difficult to pick and choose something appropriate for your budget so may opt to detour from the path to one of the more substantial, nearby villages or towns, where you will generally find a wider range of places to stay. Once you arrive on the coast there is more choice, from campsites to luxury hotels. The route guide (Part 4) includes a full selection of places to stay both on the trail and in the nearby villages.

Book all accommodation in advance, especially during the high season (Easter to September). Pre-planning is crucial, particularly for barren areas such as the start of the Peddars Way. Also take into account the fact that although there are fewer people on the trail outside the summer season there are, however, fewer beds as some establishments shut down over the winter months.

Camping

Camping is an excellent way of immersing yourself in a landscape and there is a great deal of satisfaction to be gained from spending both the day and night in the great outdoors. Technically wild camping is not permitted anywhere along the Peddars Way or Norfolk Coast Path although a friendly farmer or landowner may allow you to pitch a tent in a field (see p74). However, there are several official campsites, with basic facilities such as shower and toilet blocks, charging £5-14.50 per person, making this the cheapest and most economical way of walking the path.

You may find that you need alternative accommodation as well if you are planning short days as the campsites are not spaced evenly along the path. Equally at certain times of year you may find them closed, so will have to make alternative arrangements.

Hostels

Youth hostels are good places to meet like-minded fellow walkers and allow you to travel on a budget without having to carry additional camping gear. Prices range from £13.95 to £15.95 (£10.50-11.95 for under 18s) per night. There are two comfortable, modern YHA hostels along the Coast Path, in Wells-next-the-Sea and Sheringham. However, there aren't any on the Peddars Way, so you will need to find alternative accommodation.

Both the youth hostels provide bedding so there is no need to carry a sleeping bag. In addition to traditional dorm rooms they also offer comfortable, lockable private rooms with en suite facilities. The hostels are generally self-catering and have well-equipped kitchens, but some also provide meals for an extra charge. There's also a lounge and communal area as well as toilet and washing facilities and a drying room for wet gear. Most also have a small shop on site selling basic groceries and supplies. Booked beds are usually saved until 6pm on the day, so it's worth phoning ahead if you are running late or are unlikely to arrive before this time.

Youth Hostels (YHAs) are, despite their name, for anyone of any age. You can join the Youth Hostels Association of England and Wales (☎ 0800-019 1700 or ☎ 01629-592700, 🖳 www.yha.org.uk) at either of the hostels on the route, or over the phone or online, for £15.95 per year for an individual (£22.95 for two people living at the same address or a family, £9.95 for people aged under 26 and under); there is a 10% discount if paying by direct debit. Children under the age of 18 travelling with either or both of their parents are covered on their parents' membership card. If you aren't a member you can still stay at the hostels but must pay a £3 supplement for each night's stay.

In addition to the YHA hostels there is an **independent hostel** at Burnham Deepdale; it has the same advantages as a YHA hostel in that it offers affordable accommodation in dormitory or private rooms (some with en suite facilities), provides bed linen and has a fully equipped kitchen, but it is more informal and has fewer regulations. Rates are similar too with a dorm bed costing just £9.50. The Old Red Lion in Castle Acre has dorm beds (including breakfast) for £22.50 as well as private rooms and effectively operates as an independent hostel.

There is also a **bunkhouse** barn at Courtyard Farm, just outside Ringstead. Although the accommodation is more basic, the barn is full of character and well worth visiting, if only for one night. Excellent value at just £10, the drawback is that you will need to bring your own bedding and cooking equipment.

By using YHA hostels on the Norfolk Coast Path and a combination of independent hostels or bunkhouse barns and B&Bs on the Peddars Way you cut the need to pack any bed linen altogether, thereby significantly lightening your load and keeping your costs down.

Bed and Breakfasts (B&Bs)

B&Bs are a great British tradition, and Norfolk boasts some excellent examples of this type of accommodation. They vary greatly in terms of style and quality, and also in price, but usually consist of a bed in someone's house and a substantial cooked breakfast to start the day. For visitors from outside the UK it can provide an insight into the daily routines and workings of a family home.

What to expect Most walkers are after a hot bath and a comfortable bed after a day on the trail. The B&Bs featured in this guide are selected because of their proximity to the path and therefore their usefulness to the walker.

Rooms are often en suite, but some rooms share bathroom facilities. These tend to be slightly cheaper. Few places have **single rooms** so if you are walking on your own you are likely to have to pay a single occupancy supplement to stay in a twin or double room. **Twin** and **double rooms** are often confused, but a twin usually contains two single beds whilst a double has just the one double bed. **Family rooms** are for three or more people and usually contain a combination of single and double beds but sometimes have bunk beds.

Breakfast (see opposite) is usually included in the price of the room, and you may find that the owners also offer an evening meal or packed lunch for the following day, if asked for in advance.

Tariffs B&Bs vary in price from £25 per room for two sharing for the most rudimentary accommodation to £110 in rather more luxurious establishments. Most charge around £60-80 for two sharing. Single occupancy of a double or

❑ Booking accommodation

You should always book your accommodation. In summer there can be a lot of competition for beds and in winter some of the properties shut.

YHA hostels can be booked through the centralised reservation system over the phone (☎ 0800-019 1700 or ☎ 01629-592700), but can also be booked online (💻 www.yha.org.uk, or through 💻 www.hihostels.com) and may provide instant confirmation.

B&Bs, hotels and pubs can also often be booked online via their website or that of an agency, but you'll be able to check details more carefully and get an instant response by phoning instead. Usually you will have to pay a deposit or the full charge at the time of booking. If you are unable to keep your reservation make sure you let the establishment know so they can offer it to someone else instead.

Many B&Bs and hotels, particularly along the route, are happy to accommodate dogs and/or young children, but make sure that you check in advance as not all do.

If you don't want to book all your accommodation yourself some of the walking companies listed on pp19-22 might do it. Alternatively, the tourist information centres (see box p41) offer a bed-booking service. They charge a £3 fee plus 10% of the first night's accommodation; the latter is deducted from the final bill paid to the proprietor. Alternatively they can give you all the relevant contact details for places to stay.

twin room is usually available for a supplement of £5 to £10. Rates are often much lower during the winter months and you can cut costs further by asking to go without breakfast, which will usually result in a reduction of the rate.

At the time of research many places had not decided if they would change their tariffs bearing in mind the 2.5% increase in VAT in January 2011. Thus rates may differ from those quoted here.

Guesthouses, hotels, pubs and inns

One step up from B&Bs, guesthouses and hotels tend to be smarter and more sophisticated, with evening meals, a communal lounge and a bar for guests. Pubs and inns generally offer bed-and-breakfast-style accommodation, again with a bar within easy stumbling distance. Most along the route are high quality and relatively restrained, but you may find that noisy, tipsy neighbours are a problem if you are after an early night. Rates generally range from £60 to £100 for two sharing.

Hotels are usually less well equipped for walkers and the higher rates (£100 to well over £150 for two sharing) may put off the cash-conscious traveller. However, there are some good-value places to stay and you may well want to treat yourself in the course of your trip, particularly since there are some wonderful hostelries along the route.

Holiday cottages

If you are part of a small group or are considering basing yourself in one place for an extended period of time consider a holiday cottage. This can be an effective way of exploring a section of the Norfolk Coast Path for instance using public transport (see pp45-8), travelling to and from a start and finish point each day.

A good base for this type of trip would be one of the attractive villages along the coast, which are well served by the Coasthopper bus (see p45).

Prices for cottages start around £120 per person for a week based on four to six sharing, but vary considerably according to season, size of property and location. Cottages haven't been included in this book; contact the tourist information centre (see box p41) in the area for details of what's available. The Landmark Trust (💻 www.landmarktrust.org.uk) also have a couple of properties in Norfolk including Appleton Water Tower near Sandringham and Houghton West Lodge in Houghton.

FOOD AND DRINK

Breakfast and lunch

If staying in B&B-style accommodation **breakfast** tends to be a hearty, substantial cooked meal with many ingredients sourced from local produce. The amount of food may be more than you are used to or indeed want; ask for a lighter continental or vegetarian version if you'd rather. Alternatively if you want an early start or prefer no breakfast ask if you can have a packed lunch instead of breakfast. Most hostels also offer breakfast.

A number of the B&Bs and hostels along the path can also provide you with a packed **lunch** if given enough notice, at an additional fee. This is particularly useful on the Peddars Way where some stages pass though sections of countryside without access to places at which to buy food en route; check the route guide in Part 4 to make sure that you don't inadvertently go hungry. Alternatively, along much of the path there are bakeries or small shops where you can buy the ingredients to make your own. Cafés and pubs also often offer lunches, be it sandwiches or more substantial dishes.

Evening meals

Hotels and guesthouses usually offer an evening meal. Some B&Bs and YHA hostels also do although you'll often have to book in advance and eat at a set time. All the hostels have self-catering facilities and some provide meals. Most B&Bs are close enough to pubs or restaurants for you to have some choice in the evening. The proprietors of those that aren't may offer to run you to and from the nearest pub for supper.

The North Norfolk region is blessed with some outstanding **pubs** and inns, which will provide just the motivation for you to complete each daily section. Most offer both lunch and evening meals; some even open early to provide breakfast. The standard varies from hearty pub grub to be eaten in the bar to very high quality à la carte meals served in tasteful dining rooms. Although you might be happy with whatever is put in front of you after a hard day's walk, you'd do well to treat yourself occasionally to the best the region has to offer.

In many of the towns there are also excellent **restaurants**, with seasonal menus often influenced by the proximity of the sea and the local farmland. The larger seaside towns also have takeaway joints and cheap fast-food options as well as the ubiquitous fish and chips vans. Open later than most restaurants, often till after 11pm, they can come in handy if you finish your day late.

Buying camping supplies

If you are camping, food, fuel and outdoor equipment become important considerations. There aren't many equipment shops along the route so come prepared with whatever you think you'll need. During the summer you can usually buy fuel from campsite shops as well as general stores in the larger towns. Remember though that these may be shut during the winter months or only open for a reduced number of hours. Check the services details in Part 4 for more information. The Peddars Way is particularly barren when it comes to trying to source supplies of any kind.

Drinking water

The exposed North Norfolk countryside and wide open beaches can get very hot during the summer months, therefore you may need to drink as much as two to four litres of water a day. If you're feeling lethargic it may be that you are dehydrated, so force yourself to consume some water, even if you don't feel thirsty. Avoid drinking directly from streams and waterways that run alongside or cross the path; the water tends to have flowed across farmland and is unlikely to be safe to drink.

Drinking-water taps and water fountains are marked on the maps in the route guide. Where they are sparse you could ask a shopkeeper or pub landlord for a glass of water or to fill your bottle from their tap.

❑ Local food

Norfolk has a strong tradition of farming and walkers will soon see the benefits when sampling the local produce. Being stuck out of the way has meant that Norfolk eateries have also had to strive to attract attention. The result is that the region is now known for its fantastic local produce and there are scores of good-quality restaurants, pubs and delis, making it an ideal destination for foodies.

Drawing on the bountiful reserves right on its doorstep, each of the coastal villages has developed a **seafood** speciality: Brancaster its mussels, Stiffkey its cockles (see p156), Wells its whelks, Sheringham its lobsters and Cromer its crabs. Head to the **Smokehouse** in Cley (see p165) to pick up umpteen delicious varieties of seafood preserved using a traditional process.

The grain fields and coastal marshes shelter a mass of **game**: partridge, quail, woodcock, wild duck and pheasant. The area is also known for its Norfolk Black turkeys, famous for their distinctive, gamey flavour. Hare also frequently appears on menus, as does rare-breed pork, organic lamb and naturally reared beef. Venison from the grounds of Houghton Hall is also available in butchers and restaurants.

The main **seasons** for seafood and game are: mussels – best in 'ber' months ie September to December; crabs – late March to early October; lobsters – July to October; cockles – January to April; whelks – June to September; partridge – September to February; quail – year-round but best June to September; woodcock – October to January; wild duck – September to January; pheasant – October to February.

Cheese-making is another skill associated with the area. Catherine Temple, of Mrs Temple's Cheeses close to Wells, makes the finest in East Anglia: try the simple Wighton; mature, crumbly, Cheshire-style Walsingham; or the creamy, semi-soft Binham Blue. Elsewhere look for Norfolk Dapple, a hard cheddar-style cheese with a distinctive dappled rind, Norfolk Tawny, which is bathed in Norfolk strong dark ale; and Norfolk White Lady, a soft, slightly sharp sheep's milk cheese.

The fields around Norwich are also full of brilliant yellow mustard seed, used to produce hot English **mustard**. The name Colman is synonymous with the stuff. Originally a flour miller, Jeremiah Colman began to mill mustard seed in 1814 and the Colman factory still produces mustard to this day.

Samphire (see also p65), sometimes referred to as glasswort or more colloquially as poor man's asparagus, is a wild, succulent sea vegetable that can be harvested all along the coast. The season starts in June and lasts until about August; samphire can be cooked like French beans or pickled, as was popular in Victorian times. During the season bundles are often for sale from stalls outside houses in the villages adjacent to the sea. Delicious organic vegetables are widely available as well.

Norfolk is as famous for its **treacle tart** as the North East, although both versions differ slightly; the Norfolk tart is sometimes referred to as Norfolk treacle custard tart but actually it's just a lighter and less dense version, with a subtle hint of lemon.

To pick up some of this fantastic produce head to **Marsh Larder** (see box p146) in the grounds of Holkham Hall, **Wells Deli** (see p150) in Wells-next-the-Sea, or **Picnic Fayre** (see p165) in the Old Forge in Cley.

❑ Local beers, ciders and liqueurs

The fields of barley seen during the summer also fuel the region's burgeoning micro-brewery business. In fact there are more than 30 breweries in the county, making it the second most prolific in terms of production. Each produces distinctive ales and distributes them to pubs and restaurants in the area. For the real ale devotee, the Norwich Beer festival (see p28), which takes place in October, is an essential stop.

Whilst walking the path though, try the following to pick up a flavour of the area: **Woodforde's** (🖳 www.woodfordes.co.uk), based in Drayton, are the county's leading brewer and produce award-winning bitters. Their signature beer, **Woodforde's Wherry** (3.8%) is fresh and zesty and widely available. Also worth trying are: **Nelson's Revenge** (4.5%), an amber-coloured rich bitter that's slightly sweet and citrusy; **Admiral's Reserve** (5%), a strong copper-coloured, fruit-flavoured beer that's dangerously drinkable; and **Sundew** (4.1%), a subtle, golden beer that's lighter and more refreshing. Alternatively, try **Mardler's** (3.5%), a nut-brown mild, or **Norfolk Nog** (4.6%), a smooth, rich, ruby-red ale with a velvety texture. The more adventurous might want to consider Woodforde's barley wines; the aptly named **Headcracker** (7%) is pale but strong and full-bodied, whilst **Norfolk Nip** (8%) is a dark mahogany drink with an intense flavour.

Competition comes from the **Brancaster Brewery** (🖳 www.brancasterbrewery.co.uk), a five-barrel brewery yards from the Jolly Sailors pub in Brancaster Staithe (see p139). Try their **Brancaster Best** (3.8%), a refreshing, hoppy pale ale; **Oyster Catcher** (4.2%), a fuller-bodied beer with a distinct flavour; **Malthouse Bitter** (4.4%), a pale amber ale; or a pint of **The Wreck** (4.9%), a malty, coffee-flavoured beer named after the wreck of the *SS Vina* which lies just off Brancaster Beach.

A relatively recent addition to the local brew world, **Tipples** (🖳 www.tipplesbrewery.com) have gained a good reputation for their classic English ales: **Redhead** (4.2%), an amber-coloured bitter with a slightly nutty flavour and **Hanged Monk** (3.8%), a deep-coloured, sweeter mild, are both worth keeping an eye out for.

In the village of Heacham, close to Hunstanton, is the **Fox Brewery** (🖳 www.foxbrewery.co.uk) which produces nine beers across all styles and strengths; check out their **Peddars Sway** (5%), a reddish, fruity beer available only during the summer months.

Cider drinkers should look out for **Whin Hill Cider** (🖳 www.whinhillcider.co.uk); the apples and pears for their ciders, perrys and apple juices are grown on their own orchards ten miles south-west of Wells and then pressed using equipment housed in old eighteenth-century barns and outbuildings adjacent to the main car park in town. There is also a shop in Wells (see p150; ☎ 01328-711033) selling their produce.

For something a little more potent, look out for **Nelson's Blood**, a rum liqueur made by the Lord Nelson pub in Burnham Thorpe (see box p143), the home town of one of England's most celebrated seamen. The actual recipe is a well-kept secret but consists of a unique blend of 100 proof Navy Rum and herbs and spices. The result is sold by the tot in the pub or by the bottle to take away.

MONEY

On some sections of the path, particularly the Peddars Way, there is a distinct lack of banks and ATMs. Although some Costcutter supermarkets and other independent shops offer 'cash back', where they advance you a sum of money against a debit or credit card; a minimum spend may be required. Some Link ATMs are also 'pay to use'; the charges for withdrawing money are clearly posted on the machine.

With this in mind, it is a good idea to carry plenty of cash with you, discretely stashed in a moneybelt for security. Although pubs, restaurants and hotels may allow you to pay by debit or credit card, smaller shops, B&Bs and campsites will often insist on cash. Some hostels accept debit/credit cards but cash is always safest. Cheques are increasingly unwelcome as a means of payment and are set to become obsolete in the future. Travellers' cheques can only be cashed at banks, foreign exchange offices and some large hotels.

See also p20 and the town and village facilities table, pp32-3.

Using the post office for banking

Several British banks have agreements with the Post Office to allow customers to make cash withdrawals using a chip-and-pin debit card over the counter at post offices throughout the country. Some post offices also have a free-to-use ATM. Although there are only a few post offices along the trail, they are a useful substitute for the walker. Visit 💻 www.postoffice.co.uk and click on 'Counter services', then 'Counter money services', then 'Pay in and withdraw money' under 'Use your bank account' for a full list of banks offering withdrawal facilities through post office branches and for a list of the branches with an ATM.

OTHER SERVICES

Most towns have at least one public telephone – note that most accept phone cards rather than cash. However, in the smaller villages, particularly in rural areas along the Peddars Way, the traditional red telephone boxes remain as heritage symbols, but have long since been disconnected. Towns and villages also usually boast a small shop and post office, which can be useful for withdrawing money (see above) or sending home unnecessary kit or equipment that is slowing you down. In Part 4 special mention is made of services relevant to the walker such as banks, cash machines, outdoor equipment shops, launderettes, internet access, pharmacies and tourist information centres; the latter can be used for finding and booking accommodation amongst other things.

WALKING COMPANIES

For people looking to make their trip as straightforward and hassle free as possible, there is a number of specialist companies who offer a range of services from accommodation booking to self-guided tours. At the time of writing no company provides a group/guided walking tour for this national trail.

Expect to pay upwards of £525 for a 6-day/7-night self-guided holiday and half as much again for treks lasting up to nine or ten days. These prices tend to be for two sharing a room. Walkers on their own may be charged a single supplement of £15-20 per night.

Baggage carriers

Walk Free (☎ 07500-196151, 💻 www.walk-free.co.uk, Wells-next-the-Sea, Norfolk) bag courier service will collect your luggage just after breakfast and deliver it to your next overnight stop; they aim to ensure it arrives before you do. They cover the Peddars Way from Castle Acre and the whole of the Coast Path. Prices are £10 for the first bag and £5 for each additional one transferred per day. The maximum weight per bag is 15kg.

Taxi firms can also provide a baggage-carrying service within a local area. Additionally, some **B&Bs** offer a similar service; where relevant, details are given in the route guide. See also Self-guided holidays below.

Self-guided holidays

These are generally all-in packages tailored for an individual or group, usually including detailed route advice, notes on itineraries, maps, accommodation booking, baggage transfer and transport to and from the start and finish of the walk. If you want a less comprehensive package most companies will simply offer accommodation booking and baggage transfer if you ask.

❑ Information for foreign visitors

• **Currency** The British pound (£) comes in notes of £100, £50, £20, £10 and £5, and coins of £2 and £1. The pound is divided into 100 pence (usually referred to as 'p', pronounced 'pee') which comes in silver coins of 50p, 20p, 10p, and 5p and copper coins of 2p and 1p.

• **Rates of exchange** Up-to-date rates of exchange can be found on 💻 www.xe.com/ucc, at some post offices, or at any bank or travel agent.

• **Business hours** Most **shops** and main **post offices** are open at least from Monday to Friday 9am-5pm and Saturday 9am-12.30pm but many choose longer hours and some open on Sunday as well. Occasionally, especially in rural areas, you'll come across a local shop that closes at midday during the week, usually a Wednesday or Thursday, a throwback to the days when all towns and villages had an 'early closing day'. Many **supermarkets** remain open 12 hours a day; the Spar chain usually displays '8 till late' on the door. **Banks** typically open at 9.30am Monday to Friday and close at 3.30pm or 4pm, but of course ATM machines are open all the time. **Pub** hours are less predictable; although many open daily 11am-11pm, often in rural areas opening hours are 11am-3pm and 6-11pm Mon-Sat, 11am/noon-3pm and 7-11pm on Sunday.

• **National holidays** Most businesses in Norfolk are shut on 1 January, Good Friday (March/April), Easter Monday (March/April), first and last Monday in May, last Monday in August, 25 December and 26 December.

• **School holidays** State-school holidays in England are generally as follows: a one-week break late October, two weeks over Christmas and the New Year, a week mid-February, two weeks around Easter, one week at the end of May/early June (to coincide with the bank holiday at the end of May) and five to six weeks from late July to early September. Private-school holidays fall at the same time, but tend to be slightly longer.

• **EHICs and travel insurance** Although Britain's National Health Service (NHS) is free at the point of use, that is only the case for residents. All visitors to Britain should be properly insured, including comprehensive health coverage. The European Health Insurance Card (EHIC) entitles EU nationals (on production of the EHIC card so ensure you bring it with you) to necessary medical treatment under the NHS while on a temporary visit here. For details, contact your national social security institution. However, this is not a substitute for proper medical cover on your travel insurance for unforeseen bills and for getting you home should that be necessary. Also consider

The following companies provide self-guided holidays:

- **British and Irish Walks** (☎ 01242-254353, 💻 www.britishandirishwalks.com; Cheltenham, Gloucestershire) Runs 6-day trips with baggage transfer on the Peddars Way and Norfolk Coast Path; they can also tailor-make walks.
- **Celtic Trails** (☎ 01291-689774, 💻 www.celtic-trails.com; Chepstow) Itineraries from 3 to 4 days on the Peddars Way, 3-5 days on the Norfolk Coast Path and 6-10 days combining the two from Knettishall Heath to Cromer.
- **Contours Walking Holidays** (☎ 017684-80451, 💻 www.contours.co.uk; Cumbria) Offers 7-, 8- and 9-night trips as well as the Peddars Way and Norfolk Coast Path in two separate sections: 4 and 5 nights, and 4-6 nights respectively.
- **HF Holidays** (☎ 0845 470 7558, 💻 www.hfholidays.co.uk; Herts) Provides 6-day trips from Hunstanton to Cromer.

cover for loss and theft of personal belongings, especially if you are camping or staying in hostels, as there will be times when you'll have to leave your luggage unattended.

- **Weights and measures** The European Commission is no longer attempting to ban the pint or the mile: so, in Britain, milk can be sold in pints (1 pint = 568ml), as can beer in pubs, though most other liquid including petrol (gasoline) and diesel is sold in litres. Distances on road and path signs will continue to be given in miles (1 mile = 1.6km) rather than kilometres, and yards (1yd = 0.9m) rather than metres. The population remains divided between those who still use inches (1 inch = 2.5cm), feet (1ft = 0.3m) and yards and those who are happy with millimetres, centimetres and metres; you'll often be told that 'it's only a hundred yards or so' to somewhere, rather than a hundred metres or so.

  Most food is sold in metric weights (g and kg) but the imperial weights of pounds (lb: 1lb = 453g) and ounces (oz: 1oz = 28g) are frequently displayed too. The weather – a frequent topic of conversation – is also an issue: while most forecasts predict temperatures in centigrade (C), many people continue to think in terms of fahrenheit (F; see the temperature chart on p25 for conversion equivalents).
- **Smoking** The ban on smoking in public places relates not only to pubs and restaurants, but also to B&Bs, hostels and hotels. These latter have the right to designate one or more bedrooms where the occupants can smoke, but the ban is in force in all enclosed areas open to the public – even if they are in a private home such as a B&B. Should you be foolhardy enough to light up in a no-smoking area, which includes pretty well any indoor public place, you could be fined £50, but it's the owners of the premises who carry the can if they fail to stop you, with a potential fine of £2500.
- **Time** During the winter, the whole of Britain is on Greenwich Meantime (GMT). The clocks move one hour forward on the last Sunday in March, remaining on British Summer Time (BST) until the last Sunday in October.
- **Telephone** From outside Britain the international country access code for Britain is ☎ 44 followed by the area code minus the first 0, and then the number you require. Within Britain, to call a landline number with the same code as the landline phone you are calling from, the code can be omitted: dial the number only. If you're using a mobile phone that is registered overseas, consider buying a local SIM card to keep costs down. See also p39.
- **Emergency services** For police, ambulance, fire brigade and coastguard dial ☎ 999.

• **Explore Britain** (☎ 01740-650900, 💻 www.xplorebritain.com; Co Durham) Self-guided 4-day/5-night treks from Thetford to Hunstanton and Hunstanton to Cromer. Alternatively combine the two in an 8-day/9-night trip. They can also tailor-make treks.
• **Load off your Back** (☎ 01282-814974, 💻 www.loadoffyourback.co.uk Skipton) Offer walks from 6 days/7 nights to 8 days/9 nights. Can tailor-make walks.
• **The Walking Holiday Company** (☎ 01600-718219, 💻 www.thewalkingholidaycompany.co.uk; Monmouthshire) A variety of itineraries for either or both the Peddars Way and the Norfolk Coast Path and can be tailored to your needs.

TAKING DOGS ON THE PEDDARS WAY & NORFOLK COAST PATH

Dogs should always be kept on leads whilst on the footpath to avoid disturbing wildlife, livestock and other walkers. Uncontrolled dogs can cause an animal stress, serious injury or even death. You should be particularly vigilant during the spring when young animals are being born and are least likely to be able to run away from an inquisitive dog. When passing through or close to nature reserves along the Coast Path you should keep the dog on a short lead. Dog excrement should always be cleaned up and not left to foul the path.

Conversely, domestic livestock can potentially cause you and your dog harm if they become agitated. In rare but particularly serious cases, people have been trampled to death by cattle, when these typically docile animals have become aggressive and charged in the course of defending their young. Usually the cattle are interested in the dog and not the walker, but can injure the person whilst attempting to get at the dog.

Wherever possible avoid walking through fields of livestock when out with dogs. However, if this is unavoidable, both the National Farmers Union and Ramblers (see box p41) advise that walkers release dogs from their leads when passing through a field of cows but that they be kept under strict control nonetheless. The dog can then run away if charged, whilst the person is generally ignored.

Bear in mind that during certain times of year dogs are banned from some of the North Norfolk beaches; from 1st May to 30th Sept inclusive you can not take dogs onto the main beaches at Wells, Sheringham or Cromer and they must be kept on a lead on promenades or stretches of coast adjacent to these areas. However, these restrictions do not pose any great obstacle to walkers with dogs since the path only occasionally crosses a beach, and where it does there is almost always an alternative (inland) route close by. For more information contact the Environmental Protection section of North Norfolk District Council (☎ 01263-516085, 💻 www.northnorfolk.org/environment/184.asp).

Remember when booking your accommodation to check whether your dog will be welcome; places that accept dogs are mentioned in the relevant place in the route guide; in some cases you may need to pay an additional charge (mostly £5 per dog per night but occasionally up to £12).

DISABLED ACCESS

Given Norfolk's reputation as a flat landscape it may come as no surprise to learn that sections of the Peddars Way and Coast Path are accessible by wheelchair. There are several sections where you can gain equal access to enjoy the countryside and coast although it's worth noting that the trail is frequently unsurfaced; along the sea walls at Sheringham and Cromer there is easy parking and a tarmac surface on which to explore. Elsewhere there are metalled surfaces and access to sections of board walk which may not be totally even but should be negotiable nonetheless. In this way it's possible to enjoy the saltmarsh and sea views at Holkham, Thornham and Blakeney. Between Old Hunstanton and Holme is a stretch of path that is alternately surfaced and unsurfaced but generally level and accessible. The unsurfaced path between Holkham Gap and Pinewoods to the north of Wells is also readily accessible at either end, and even enough to tackle. To the east of Weybourne the cliff paths would provide spectacular views and several miles of accessible track, although there is a short section of compacted shingle to negotiate before joining the unsurfaced path. Both Snettisham Bird Reserve and Cley Marshes Reserve have hides with wheelchair access. Sheringham Park on the outskirts of Sheringham has wheelchair-friendly waymarked paths leading to parkland views.

Budgeting

The amount of money that you spend completing the walk will depend on the standard of accommodation you use and the quality of meals you enjoy. If you carry a tent, camp and cook your own meals you can expect to get by cheaply with minimal expenses. However, most people prefer some sort of night out and even the hardy camper may be tempted to swap their canvas for something more substantial when the rain is falling.

CAMPING

If you use the cheapest sites and prepare all your own meals from staple ingredients you can survive on as little as £10-15 per person per day. However, if you want to factor in a meal out, a pint at the end of each day and a few unforeseen expenses along the route, it's more realistic to expect to spend £15-20 per day.

HOSTELS AND BUNKHOUSES

YHA hostels on the Norfolk Coast Path charge between £13.95 and £15.95 per adult (£10.50-11.95 per child under 18) per night whilst independent hostels cost £9.50-20 and the only bunkhouse costs £10. With the exception of the bunkhouse at Courtyard Farm, they each have their own self-catering kitchen allowing you to cook your own meals from ingredients that can be bought from local supermarkets or suppliers. Some hostels also provide breakfast for around £4.65, a packed lunch for about £4.50 and an evening meal for £6.50.

Occasionally you will need or want to eat out, which will increase your expenditure. Around £30-35 should cover accommodation and the odd meal and post-walk ale. If you're going to eat out more nights than not you ought to increase your budget to £40 per day.

B&Bs, INNS, GUESTHOUSES AND HOTELS

B&B prices can be as little as £25 per room per night (for two sharing) but are often two to three times as much, especially if walking on your own as most establishments will levy a single occupancy supplement. The rate includes breakfast though. Incorporate a packed lunch, pint, pub meal and other expenses to your budget and you'll spend around £40-60 person per day. If staying in a guesthouse or hotel, rates are likely to be higher; expect to pay £60-80 per day.

EXTRAS

Any number of forgotten items or last-minute expenses can eat into your budget so factor in a contingency fund for buses, ice-creams, beer, souvenirs, email access, postcards and stamps; it all adds up!

When to go

SEASONS

In general, Norfolk is dry in comparison to the rest of the UK, with Breckland (see p50) on the Norfolk–Suffolk border actually the driest part of the country. However, Norfolk is exposed to the full force of the weather sweeping in from the North Sea so expect conditions to be changeable and be prepared for rain or a strong wind at any time of year. Equally, the area enjoys a high percentage of clear, sunny days when temperatures can soar. Although there are no obvious best times to go, the main walking season is from Easter to the end of September.

Spring

The fresh spring days can be particularly pleasant on the Peddars Way; as the weather warms up and the days grow longer the surrounding countryside begins to come to life, wild flowers start to bloom and crops in the cultivated fields begin to grow. Animals start to establish territories and look for a mate whilst in March birds begin to migrate to their summer breeding grounds. You can still be caught by a cold snap or icy wind well into May though so be prepared for changeable conditions.

Summer

The popular tourist towns along the North Norfolk coast can get particularly busy during school holidays in July and August as the weather is at its warmest. Wildlife is also at its most visible, with juvenile animals beginning to appear and chicks that fledged the nest starting to search for their own food. By the end of the season birds become quieter as they moult their worn feathers, so head to the heathland or woodland to see the diverse flora instead.

Autumn

An attractive time of year with leaves changing colours and fruits, berries and nuts beginning to adorn the hedgerows. Birds begin to gather in preparation for their migration and animals start to look for suitable hibernation sites. By the end of the season, in October, summer migrant birds are replaced by winter migrants arriving from Scandinavia, Germany and Russia. This is also the rutting season for red and fallow deer, which fight to protect their territories and breeding females.

Winter

Many locals profess that this is their favourite time of year, with the crowds of visitors dispersed yet the weather cold and crisp enough to still crunch along a shingle beach or stroll through a nature reserve where the trees are bare so you stand a better chance of spotting secretive birds. The weather can vary from crisp bright days to snow, rain or hail. Throughout November thousands of geese arrive from their breeding grounds and seal pups are born.

TEMPERATURE

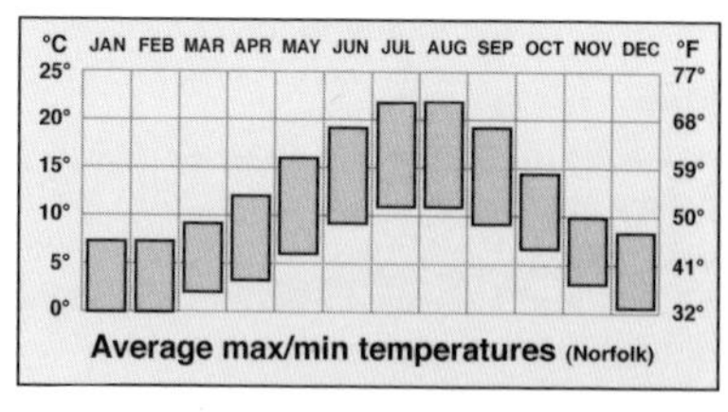

Average max/min temperatures (Norfolk)

Norfolk sits at the crossroads of four wind patterns, with easterlies coming off the continent, southerlies carrying warmer air, westerlies bringing temperate conditions and northerlies channelling colder winds. Generally though, the Norfolk climate is temperate and even in winter the air temperature is relatively mild. Consequently temperatures are generally quite comfortable at any time of year and on rare occasions the summer can actually get too hot for walking.

RAINFALL

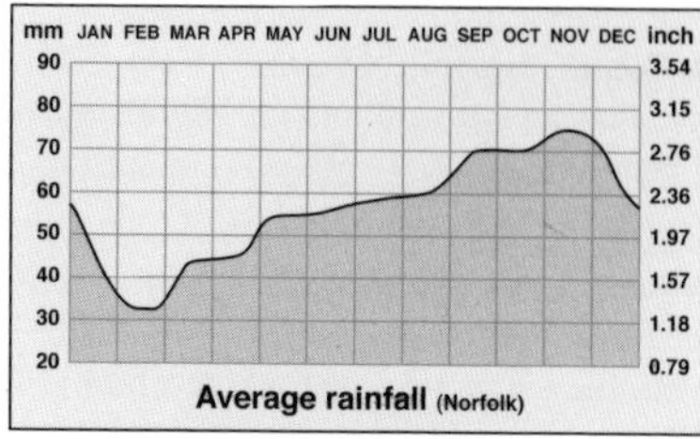

Average rainfall (Norfolk)

Norfolk is relatively dry for the UK but can still occasionally feel the force of the violent weather systems that sweep in from the North Sea. Most rainfall occurs from late summer and into winter, with spring being a drier period.

DAYLIGHT HOURS

If walking in autumn (particularly after the clocks have changed; see box p21), winter or early spring, you must take account of how far you can walk in the available light.

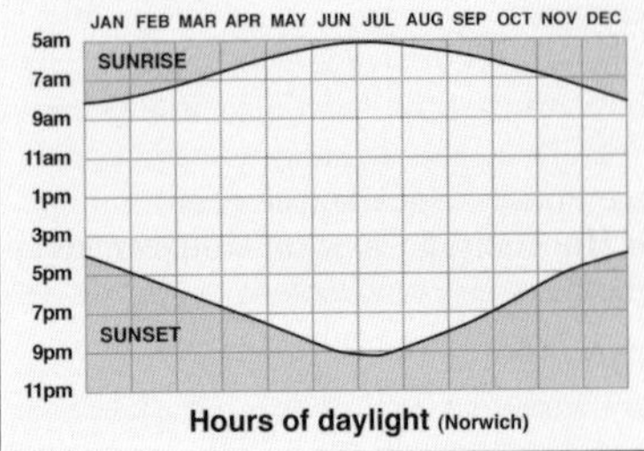

Hours of daylight (Norwich)

ANNUAL EVENTS

January

- **New Year's Day swim** – Takes place in a number of the coastal locations but most famously in the sea off Hunstanton (see p128).

February

- **World Wetlands Day** (🖳 www.enjoythebroads.com) – Events are held throughout the Broads, Britain's most important wetland, in the first week of the month, to commemorate the Convention on Wetlands in 1971.
- **UEA Spring Literary Festival** (☎ 01603-508050, 🖳 www.uea.ac.uk/litfest) – A bi-annual literary festival at the University of East Anglia in Norwich, showcasing work by many of Britain's finest writers and poets with talks taking place throughout the spring, and also in the autumn (see p28).

April

- **Spring Craft Fair** – Craft exhibition and sale typically held on the last Saturday of the month in the Queens Hall in Watton (see p94).

May

- **Poetry-next-the-Sea Festival** (🖳 www.poetry-next-the-sea.com) – Small poetry and literary festival based in Wells-next-the-Sea (see p150) on the second weekend in May, with people from around the world giving readings.
- **Crab and Lobster Festival** – Sheringham (see p171) and Cromer (see p179). A two-day celebration of community and heritage in late May that includes concerts, food demonstrations, the World Pier Crabbing Championship and a RNLI demonstration.
- **Houghton International Horse Trials** (🖳 www.houghtoninternational.co.uk) – Four-day event during the last week of May at Houghton Hall (see p112) with the world's leading riders competing. Also includes falconry displays and other events for non-equestrians.
- **North Norfolk Country Fair** (🖳 www.northnorfolkcountryfair.co.uk) – Traditional fair held outside Weybourne (see p167) on the last weekend in May, featuring stalls and craft sales as well as dog and bird displays.

June

- **Brancaster Midsummer Music** (🖳 www.brancaster-music.co.uk) – Classical concerts held in churches in Brancaster (see p139) and Thornham (see p134) with the signature event taking place at Houghton Hall (see box p112), where audience members can picnic on the lawn and walk in the walled gardens. Events are held at the end of May, June and early July.

- **Hunstanton Arts Festival** (🖳 www.princesstheatrehunstanton.co.uk) – Various events including music recitals held throughout the month, mostly at the Princess Theatre (see p128).
- **Hunstanton Carnival** – Street entertainment, music, games and activities on the Green in Hustanton (see p128), on the last Sunday of the month.

July

- **Holkham Country Fair** – Spectacular large-scale event with trade stands and performances celebrating the countryside, its traditions and its conservation, held every other year (odd-numbered years) in the grounds of Holkham Hall (see box p146) in mid-July.
- **Lobster Potty Morris Festival** – A gathering of around 20 teams of folk and morris dancers who perform their traditional steps on the first weekend of the month in Sheringham (see p171), using the Lobster Pub as the headquarters for the event.
- **Lifestyles Festival** (🖳 www.lifestylesfestival.co.uk) – Extreme sports festival on the beach at Hunstanton (see p128) in the second week of July includes national kitesurfing and windsurfing competitions and demonstrations by pro skaters and BMX riders, as well as 'come and have a go' sessions and workshops.
- **British Superbike Championship** (🖳 www.britishsuperbike.com/events/snetterton.aspx) – The UK road-racing superbike championship descends on the Snetterton Circuit in Thetford (see p82) in mid-July for a round of high-speed racing.

August

- **Wells Carnival** (🖳 www.wellscarnival.co.uk) – A traditional summer carnival taking place in the first week of the month, featuring processions, floats, fancy dress, competitions and activities for all. See p150.
- **British Touring Car Championship** (🖳 www.btcc.net) – the Snetterton Circuit in Thetford (see p82) plays host to a round of touring-car racing during the first week of the month.
- **Hunstanton Kite Festival and Classic Car Rally** (🖳 www.hunstanton-rotary.org.uk) – Displays of flying and acrobatics as well as other practical activities during the third week of the month with some glorious classic cars also on display.
- **Cromer Carnival** (🖳 www.cromercarnival.co.uk) – One of the largest carnivals in the county, takes place in the third week of the month with parades, competitions, fireworks and fancy dress. See p179.

September

- **North Norfolk Music Festival** (🖳 www.northnorfolkmusicfestival.com) – Classical concerts by leading musicians, performed in churches in South Creake and Burnham Norton during the first two weeks of the month.
- **Norfolk Food Festival** (🖳 www.norfolkfoodfestival.co.uk) – Food stalls, cookery demonstrations and tasting sessions as well as other village-fête fare

taking place during the third week of the month and early October, largely around Norwich.

October

- **Norwich Beer Festival** (🖳 www.norwichcamra.org.uk) – Week-long festival in Norwich's St Andrew's and Blackfriars' Hall at the end of the month, featuring more than 200 real ales from Britain's best independent breweries as well as a selection of bottled beers and ciders.
- **UEA Autumn Literary Festival** – see UEA Spring Literary Festival p26.

Itineraries

The route guide in this book has not been split into rigid daily stages. Rather, it has been structured to provide you with accessible information in order to plan your own itinerary. The Peddars Way and Norfolk Coast Path can be tackled in

CAMPING

	Relaxed pace		Medium pace		Fast pace	
Night	**Place**	**Approx distance miles/km**	**Place**	**Approx distance miles/km**	**Place**	**Approx distance miles/km**
0	Knettishall Heath*		Knettishall Heath*		Knettishall Heath*	
1	(Merton)*	14/22.5	(Merton)*	14/22.5	South Pickenham	17.5/28
2	South Pickenham	6.25/10	South Pickenham	6.25/10	Castle Acre	9.5/15
3	(Swaffham)	6.25/10	Castle Acre	9.5/15	Ringstead	17/27.5
4	Castle Acre	6.75/11	(Sedgeford)*	14/22.5	Burnham Deepdale	12.5/20
5	(Great Bircham)	12.5/20	Hunstanton*	8/13	Blakeney	18/29
6	Ringstead	6.25/10	Burnham Deepdale	12/19	Cromer*	17/27.5
7	Hunstanton*	5.5/9	Wells-next-the Sea*	10.5/17		
8	Burnham Deepdale	12/19	Cley next the Sea*	10.5/17		
9	Wells-next-the-Sea*	10.5/17	Cromer*	14/22.5		
10	Blakeney	8/13				
11	Sheringham*	10.5/17				
12	Cromer*	5/8				

NB Places in brackets are a short walk off the official Peddars Way/Norfolk Coast Path

* Alternative to specified accommodation option available

various ways, the most challenging of which is to do it all in one go. This requires around eight days.

Some people choose to complete the walk in two halves; Hunstanton, at the end of the Peddars Way and the start of the Norfolk Coast Path, is conveniently half-way from start to finish. Alternatively, people tackle the trek as a series of short walks, returning year after year to do the next section. Others just pick and choose the best bits, skipping those areas that don't interest them as much. Still others go on linear day walks along the coast, using public transport to return to their base.

To help you plan your walk see the planning map (opposite the inside back cover) and the table of village and town facilities on pp32-3; the latter provides a full rundown of the essential information you will need regarding accommodation, eating options and services.

SUGGESTED ITINERARIES

The suggested itineraries in the boxes opposite, below and on p30 may also be helpful; they are based on different accommodation types – camping, hostels and B&Bs – with each one then broken down into three alternatives according

STAYING IN HOSTELS/BUNKHOUSES

	Relaxed pace		Medium pace		Fast pace	
Night	Place	Approx distance miles/km	Place	Approx distance miles/km	Place	Approx distance miles/km
0	Knettishall Heath*		Knettishall Heath*		Knettishall Heath*	
1	(Thompson)*	10.5/17	Little Cressingham*	14.5/23.5	Little Cressingham*	14.5/23.5
2	Little Cressingham*	5.5/9	Castle Acre	11.5/18.5	Castle Acre	11.5/18.5
3	Castle Acre	11.5/18.5	Ringstead	17/27.5	Hunstanton*	23/37
4	(Great Bircham)*	12.5/20	Hunstanton*	5.5/9	Wells-next-the-Sea	22.5/36
5	Ringstead	6.25/10	Burnham Deepdale	12/19	Cromer*	24.5/39
6	Hunstanton*	5.5/9	Wells-next-the-Sea	10.5/17		
7	Burnham Deepdale	12/19	Sheringham	19/30.5		
8	Wells-next--the-Sea	10.5/17	Cromer*	5/8		
9	Blakeney*	8/13				
10	Sheringham	10.5/17				
11	Cromer*	5/8				

NB Places in brackets are a short walk off the official Peddars Way/Norfolk Coast Path

* Alternative to specified accommodation option available

STAYING IN B&B-STYLE ACCOMMODATION

	Relaxed pace		Medium pace		Fast pace	
Night	**Place**	**Approx distance miles/km**	**Place**	**Approx distance miles/km**	**Place**	**Approx distance miles/km**
0	Knettishall Heath		Knettishall Heath		Knettishall Heath	
1	(Thompson)	10.5/17	Little Cressingham	14.5/23.5	Little Cressingham	14.5/23.5
2	Little Cressingham	5.5/9	Castle Acre	11.5/18.5	Castle Acre	11.5/18.5
3	Castle Acre	11.5/18.5	Ringstead	17/27.5	Hunstanton	23/37
4	(Great Bircham)	12.5/20	Hunstanton	5.5/9	Wells-next-the-Sea	22.5/36
5	Ringstead	6.25/10	Burnham Overy Staithe*	12/19	Cromer	24.5/39
6	Hunstanton	5.5/9	Wells	10.5/17		
7	Brancaster	9.5/15	Cley next the Sea	10.5/17		
8	Burnham Overy Staithe*	6.25/10	Cromer	14/22.5		
9	Wells-next-the-Sea	6.75/11				
10	Blakeney	8/13				

NB Places in brackets are a short walk off the official Peddars Way/Norfolk Coast Path

* Closest accommodation is in Burnham Market (1.8 miles/3km away)

to how quickly you walk. These are only suggestions though; feel free to adapt them to your needs. You will need to factor in your travelling time before and after the walk too.

There is also a list of suggested linear day and weekend walks on pp34-5; these cover some of the best stretches of the trail and are well served by public transport. The public transport map and table are on pp46-8. With the aid of an Ordnance Survey map of the area and a basic sense of direction most of these linear walks can be extended and turned into circuits by breaking away from the coast and looping back to your start point inland.

Once you have worked out a schedule turn to Part 4 for detailed information on accommodation, places to eat and other services in each village and town both on the route and close to it. In Part 4 there are also summaries of the route to accompany the detailed trail maps.

WHICH DIRECTION?

Traditionally the Peddars Way is tackled south to north and then the Norfolk Coast Path west to east. This way you are drawn towards the sea and then able to explore the salt-marshes and nature reserves strung along the coast.

Some may choose to walk in the opposite direction, perhaps to get the busier sections of the path out of the way early. The maps in Part 4 give timings and since these are relevant in either direction the guide can easily be used in reverse or simply for day trips.

SIDE TRIPS

The Peddars Way and Norfolk Coast Path give a fairly thorough impression of what the region has to offer. However, there are some sections and highlights that are worth spending more time on, if you have additional days to spare.

The boat trips to Blakeney Point (see box p160) make a relaxing change to walking and provide an excellent excursion on a day off. A trip to Scolt Head Island (see p142) is also worth doing. If you are interested in wildlife then an additional day or two spent exploring the salt-marshes and wildlife reserves anywhere along the coast will not go amiss.

EXTENDING YOUR WALK

The Greater Ridgeway

If you want to extend the Peddars Way, consider starting your walk earlier on the Greater Ridgeway, which runs from Lyme Regis, on the west Dorset coast, all the way to Hunstanton. From Lyme Regis the **Wessex Ridgeway** goes to Marlborough, Wilts, from where it is an easy walk to join **The Ridgeway** (see p192) from Overton Hill to Ivinghoe Beacon; a series of green lanes, farm and forestry tracks and paths collectively known as the **Icknield Way** run along the chalk spine from Ivinghoe Beacon in the Chilterns to Knettishall Heath in Suffolk, passing through Baldock, Royston, Great Chesterford and Icklingham, to meet the **Peddars Way** and thus reach the coast at Hunstanton.

Other possibilities

For the similarly adventurous there is the 226-mile (363km) **Around Norfolk Walk** which connects the Nar Valley Way, Peddars Way, Norfolk Coast Path, Weavers' Way and Angles Way; the 34-mile (54km) **Nar Valley Way**, which starts in King's Lynn, runs through the watershed of the River Nar to cross the Peddars Way at Castle Acre, although it continues to its finish point at Gressenhall. At the other end of the Norfolk Coast Path, you can continue from Cromer to Great Yarmouth by tackling the 56-mile (90km) **Weavers' Way** which combines footpaths, disused railway lines and some sections of minor road to travel from the farmland and woodland of the north to the grazing marshes of the Broadland river valleys. The **Angles Way** is a 77½-mile (125km) route linking the Broads to the Brecks, joining Great Yarmouth with the Peddars Way at Knettishall Heath.

Alternatively, if you prefer a circuit to a linear walk, consider the **Iceni Way**, an 80-mile (129km) path which connects Knettishall Heath to Hunstanton via Thetford, Brandon, King's Lynn, Sandringham and Snettisham. By linking this and the Peddars Way it is possible to create an attractive circular loop.

VILLAGE AND

Place name (places in brackets area a short walk off the path)	**Distance from previous place** (approx miles/km)	**Cash machine/ bank** CB = cash-back only	**Post office**	**Tourist Information Centre (TIC) Point (TIP)**
Thetford		✔		TIC
Knettishall Heath				
Stonebridge/East Wretham	6.5/10.5	**CB**		
(Thompson)	4/6.5	✔	✔	
(Merton)	3.5/5.5 (5.3/8.5 to Stonebridge)			
(Watton)	3/4.5	✔	✔	TIP
Little Cressingham	3.0/5 (8/13 to Stonebridge)			
(Great Cressingham)	2.5/4			
South Pickenham	2.5/4 (3/4.5 to Little Cressingham)			
North Pickenham	2/3 (5/8 to Little Cressingham)			
(Swaffham)	3.75/6			TIP
(Sporle)	3.5/5.5 (4.4/7 to North Pickenham)			
Castle Acre	4.4/7 (7/11 to North Pickenham)	**CB**	✔	
(Great Massingham)	6.25/10			
(Harpley)	4/6.5 (7.5/12 to Castle Acre)			
(Great Bircham)	6.25/10 (12.5/20 to Castle Acre)			
(Snettisham)	6.25/10 (15.5/25 to Castle Acre)			
(Sedgeford)	3/4.5 (15.5/25 to Castle Acre)		✔	
Ringstead	3/4.5 (17/27 to Castle Acre)	**CB**		
Holme-next-the-Sea	3/4.5			
Old Hunstanton	1.5/2.5		✔	
Hunstanton	1.25/2	✔	✔	TIC
Thornham	5.3/8.5 (3.5/5.5 to Holme)			
Brancaster	4/6.25			
Brancaster Staithe	1.5/2.5			
Burnham Deepdale	0.6/1	**CB**		TIP
Burnham Overy Staithe	3.75/6			
(Burnham Market)	1.8/3			
(Holkham)	4.4/7 to Burnham Overy Staithe			
Wells-next-the-Sea	3.75/6 (6.25/10 to Burnham Overy Staithe)	✔	✔	TIC
Stiffkey	3.75/6		✔	
Morston	3/4.5			NT info centre
Blakeney	1.5/2.5	✔	✔	
Cley next the Sea	2.5/4			NWT centre
(Weybourne)	5.5/9		✔	
Sheringham	3.5/5.5 (8.5/13.5 to Cley)	✔	✔	TIC
(West Runton)	1.8/3			
Cromer	4.4/7 (5/8 to Sheringham)	✔	✔	TIC

Knettishall Heath to Cromer	90 miles	145km
including Holme to Hunstanton and back (6/9)	96 miles	154.5km

TOWN FACILITIES

Eating place ✔=one ✔✔=two ✔✔✔=3+	**Food store**	**Campsite**	**Hostels** (see below)	**B&B-style accommodation** ✔=one ✔✔=two ✔✔✔=three+	**Place name** (places in brackets are a short walk off the path)
✔✔✔	✔			✔✔✔	**Thetford**
					Knettishall Heath
✔					**Stonebridge/East Wretham**
✔				✔✔✔	**(Thompson)**
				✔	**(Merton)**
✔✔✔				✔✔✔	**(Watton)**
				✔	**Little Cressingham**
✔				✔✔	**(Great Cressingham)**
		✔*			**South Pickenham**
		✔			**North Pickenham**
✔✔✔		✔		✔✔✔	**(Swaffham)**
✔	✔			✔	**(Sporle)**
✔✔✔	✔	✔	H	✔✔✔	**Castle Acre**
✔	✔			✔	**(Great Massingham)**
				✔	**(Harpley)**
✔✔	✔	✔		✔	**(Great Bircham)**
✔				✔	**(Snettisham)**
✔				✔✔	**(Sedgeford)**
✔	✔	✔	B	✔	**Ringstead**
✔				✔✔	**Holme-next-the-Sea**
✔✔✔	✔			✔✔✔	**Old Hunstanton**
✔✔✔	✔			✔✔✔	**Hunstanton**
✔✔✔	✔			✔✔✔	**Thornham**
✔				✔	**Brancaster**
✔					**Brancaster Staithe**
✔✔	✔	✔	H	✔✔	**Burnham Deepdale**
✔					**Burnham Overy Staithe**
✔				✔✔✔	**(Burnham Market)**
✔		✔*		✔	**(Holkham)**
✔✔✔	✔		YHA	✔✔✔	**Wells-next-the-Sea**
✔✔	✔	✔*		✔	**Stiffkey**
✔✔		✔		✔✔	**Morston**
✔✔✔	✔	✔*		✔✔✔	**Blakeney**
✔✔✔				✔✔✔	**Cley next the Sea**
✔✔	✔	✔		✔✔	**(Weybourne)**
✔✔✔	✔		YHA	✔✔✔	**Sheringham**
		✔		✔	**(West Runton)**
✔✔✔	✔			✔✔✔	**Cromer**

* campsite is a short walk away
YHA = YHA hostel H = independent hostel B = bunkhouse

❑ THE BEST DAY AND WEEKEND WALKS

If you don't have time to walk the entire trail the following day and weekend walks highlight some of the best sections of the Peddars Way and Norfolk Coast Path. The Coast Path is particularly good for short walks as it is well served by the Coasthopper bus service (see pp45-8), which allows you to walk out in one direction and catch the bus back to your base or start point at the end of the day.

Day walks

• **The Great Eastern Pingo Trail** – 8 miles/13km Explore the eastern edge of the Brecks by making this circuit, which starts and finishes in Stow Beddon, just to the east of Thompson, and takes in Thompson Common, Thompson Water and the village itself. Much of the walk goes through wooded countryside and wetlands and incorporates a section of the Peddars Way.

• **Ringstead to Old Hunstanton** – 4miles/6.5km (see pp122-7) A chance to enjoy the transition from the county's wide open spaces to its coast at Holme, finishing with a gentle stroll along the dunes to an attractive town. This can be a circular route if you walk back along the narrow road running north-west/south-east between Ringstead and Old Hunstanton.

• **Holme to Thornham** – 3¼ miles/5.25km (see pp123-36) A wonderful introduction to the coast and the bird reserves that can be found amidst the beaches and marshes. Both ends are also stops on the Coasthopper bus route.

• **Brancaster to Burnham Deepdale** – 2¼ miles/3.5km (see pp136-42) A gentle linear walk along the edge of the salt-marshes that takes in the Roman fort at Branodunum and finishes in Burnham Deepdale where there is an excellent pub overlooking the marshes in which to relax. Both ends are also stops on the Coasthopper bus route.

• **Brancaster to Holkham Gap** – 10 miles/16km (see pp136-48) A longer walk that takes you from the salt-marshes onto the spectacular sands at Holkham where you can explore the pine-backed beach before accessing the main road and picking up the Coasthopper bus. For a shorter version consider the 4-mile/6.5km section of path between Burnham Overy Staithe and Holkham Gap instead.

• **Holkham Gap to Wells** – 3 miles/4.75km (see pp148-53) A short stroll that starts on Holkham Beach and means you have time to explore this superb stretch of sand before a pleasant and easy walk through an attractive forested stretch via the beach to the north of Wells and the causeway that leads to the town itself. Holkham, ¾-mile from Holkham Gap, is on the Coasthopper bus route, as is Wells.

• **Stiffkey to Cley** – 7 miles/11.25km (see pp153-65) A chance to meander along some of the most spectacular and scenic salt-marsh sections of the trail, past the best bird reserves in the region, with Blakeney Point dominating the horizon. Both ends are also stops on the Coasthopper bus route.

• **Blakeney Circular Walk** – 4½ miles/7.25km (see pp158-65) A fantastic circular walk along the sea defences from Blakeney to Cley, past the marshes and bird reserves, that returns to the start point via Wiveton and Blakeney Road. Both Blakeney and Cley are stops on the Coasthopper bus route.

• **Sheringham to Cromer** – 5½ miles/8.75km (see pp169-82) A chance to climb inland from the coast enjoying spectacular views from Beeston Bump before exploring the forested slopes surrounding the National Trust property at Roman Camp then looking back to the coast from Norfolk's highest point before finally descending once again to finish in a bustling town. You can complete a circuit by walking back along the beach to turn this into a 9-mile/14.5km loop. Both ends are stops on the Coasthopper bus route.

THE BEST DAY AND WEEKEND WALKS *(cont'd)*

Weekend walk

Much of the Norfolk Coast can be connected in two-day walks, taking in a variety of landscapes, villages and larger coastal resorts, all of which are connected by the Coasthopper bus. For ideas, consider combining some of the day trips outlined opposite.

- **Brancaster to Cley** – 23 miles/36.75km (see pp136-65) An outstanding two-day stretch that showcases the best of the coastal scenery and wildlife reserves and allows you to overnight in Wells. Both ends are also stops on the Coasthopper bus route.

❑ Alternatives to walking

If you want to explore the region but don't fancy doing so on foot, it is possible to access sections of the Peddars Way on bike and horseback. Most of the Peddars Way can be **cycled** as the route is largely classified as a bridleway, marked with blue arrows, or unsurfaced country road. Although there are short sections of public foot-path, for instance between Knettishall Heath and the A11 trunk road or from Fring to just south of Ringstead, there are alternative road links to bypass them. There are also a couple of places where the trail is classified as a footpath, but here it simply runs parallel to a tarmac road, usually on the grass verge; cyclists must use the road at these points. There is, however, no right to cycle on the Norfolk Coast Path. Instead, there is a specifically created cycleway (The Norfolk Coast Cycleway) which runs just inland from the coast between King's Lynn and Cromer, using National Cycle Network Route 1 between King's Lynn and Wighton to the south east of Wells and Regional Route 30 from here to Cromer and beyond to Great Yarmouth. A map (£2) is available from tourist information centres in the area.

Bike hire, which usually includes suggested routes and specific maps, is possible from the following: **Bircham Windmill Cycle Hire** (see p115; ☎ 01485-578393, 🖳 www.birchamwindmill.co.uk), Great Bircham, offers mountain bikes and tandems on an hourly or daily basis (they will also come and rescue you if you get lost or have a problem with your bike); **The Bike Shed** (see p173; ☎ 01263-822255, 🖳 www.the-bikeshed.biz), 28 Beeston Rd, Sheringham, offers mountain bikes for full-day hire only; booking in advance (available online) is recommended from June to August; **Pedal Revolution** (see p179; ☎ 01263-510039, 🖳 www.pedalrevolution.co.uk; Tue & Thur-Sat 9.30am-5.30pm), West St, Cromer, offers mountain bikes and tourers.

It is also possible to **ride** much of the Peddars Way on horseback although again you cannot follow the path where it is designated a public footpath, and must use alternative detours or stick to the tarmac road. Again, there is no right to ride on the Norfolk Coast Path.

What to take

Deciding how much to take with you can be difficult. Experienced walkers know that you should take only the bare essentials but at the same time you must ensure you have all the equipment necessary to make the trip safe and comfortable.

KEEP IT LIGHT

Carrying a heavy rucksack really can ruin your enjoyment of a good walk and can also slow you down, turning an easy seven-mile day into an interminable slog. Be ruthless when you pack and leave behind all those little home comforts that you tell yourself don't weigh that much really. This advice is even more pertinent to campers who have added weight to carry.

HOW TO CARRY IT

The size of your **rucksack** depends on where you plan to stay and how you plan to eat. If you are camping and cooking you will probably need a 65- to 75-litre rucksack which can hold the tent, sleeping bag, cooking equipment and food.

Make sure your rucksack has a stiffened back and can be adjusted to fit your own back comfortably. This will make carrying the weight much easier. When packing the rucksack make sure you have all the things you are likely to need during the day near the top or in the side pockets, especially if you don't have a bum bag or daypack. This includes water bottle, packed lunch, waterproofs and this guidebook (of course). Make sure the hip belt and chest strap (if there is one) are fastened tightly as this helps distribute the weight with most of it being carried on the hips. Rucksacks are decorated with seemingly pointless straps but if you adjust them correctly it can make a big difference to your personal comfort while walking.

Consider taking a small **bum bag** or **daypack** for your camera, guidebook and other essentials for when you go sightseeing or for a day walk.

Hostellers should find a 40- to 60-litre rucksack sufficient. If you have gone for the B&B option you will find a 30- to 40-litre day pack is more than enough to carry your lunch, warm- and wet-weather clothes, camera and guidebook.

A good habit to get into is to always put things in the same place in your rucksack and memorise where they are. There is nothing more annoying than having to pull everything out of your pack to find that lost banana when you're starving, or your camera when there is a seal basking on a rock ten feet away.

It's also a good idea to keep everything in **canoe bags**, **waterproof rucksack liners** or strong plastic bags. If you don't it's bound to rain.

FOOTWEAR

Boots

Your boots are the single most important item of gear that can affect the enjoyment of your trek.

In summer you could get by with a light pair of trail shoes if you're only carrying a small pack, although this is an invitation for wet, cold feet if there is any rain and they don't offer much support for your ankles. Some of the terrain can be quite rough so a good pair of walking boots is a safer bet. They must fit well and be properly broken in. It is no good discovering that your boots are slowly murdering your feet three days into a week-long trek. See p79 for more blister-avoidance advice.

Socks
The traditional wearing of a thin liner sock under a thicker wool sock is no longer necessary if you choose a high-quality sock specially designed for walking. A high proportion of natural fibres makes them much more comfortable. Three pairs are ample.

Extra footwear
Some walkers have a second pair of shoes to wear when they are not on the trail. Trainers, sport sandals or flip flops are all suitable as long as they are light.

CLOTHES

Experienced walkers will know the importance of wearing the right clothes. Don't underestimate the weather: Norfolk juts out into the North Sea so it's important to protect yourself from the elements. The weather can be quite hot in the summer but spectacularly bad at any time of the year. Modern hi-tech outdoor clothes can seem baffling but it basically comes down to a base layer to transport sweat from your skin; a mid-layer or two to keep you warm; and an outer layer or 'shell' to protect you from the wind and rain.

Base layer
Cotton absorbs sweat, trapping it next to the skin and chilling you rapidly when you stop exercising. A thin lightweight **thermal top** of a synthetic material is better as it draws moisture away keeping you dry. It will be cool if worn on its own in hot weather and warm when worn under other clothes in the cold. A spare would be sensible. You may also like to bring a **shirt** for wearing in the evening.

Mid-layers
In the summer a woollen jumper or mid-weight polyester **fleece** will suffice. For the rest of the year you will need an extra layer to keep you warm. Both wool and fleece, unlike cotton, have the ability to stay reasonably warm when wet.

Outer layer
A **waterproof jacket** is essential year-round and will be much more comfortable (but also more expensive) if it's also 'breathable' to prevent the build up of condensation on the inside. This layer can also be worn to keep the wind off.

Leg wear
Whatever you wear on your legs it should be light, quick-drying and not restricting. Many British walkers find polyester tracksuit bottoms comfortable. Polycotton or microfibre trousers are excellent. Denim jeans should never be worn; if they get wet they become heavy and cold, and bind to your legs.

A pair of **shorts** is nice to have on sunny days. Thermal **longjohns** or thick tights are cosy if you're camping but are probably unnecessary even in winter. **Waterproof trousers** are necessary most of the year. In summer a pair of windproof and quick-drying trousers is useful in showery weather. **Gaiters** are not really necessary but you may appreciate then when the vegetation around your legs is wet.

Underwear

Three changes of what you normally wear is fine. Women may find a **sports bra** more comfortable because pack straps can cause bra straps to dig painfully into your shoulders.

Other clothes

A **warm hat** and **gloves** should always be kept in your rucksack; you never know when you might need them. In summer you should also carry a **sun hat** with you, preferably one which also covers the back of your neck. Another useful piece of summer equipment is a **swimsuit**; some of the beaches are irresistible on a hot day. Also consider a lightweight super-absorbent microfibre travel **towel**, especially if you are camping or staying in hostels.

TOILETRIES

Only take the minimum: a small bar of **soap** in a plastic container (unless staying in B&Bs) which can also be used instead of shaving cream and for washing clothes; a tiny tube of **toothpaste** and a **toothbrush**; and one roll of **loo paper** in a plastic bag. If you are planning to defecate outdoors you will also need a lightweight **trowel** for burying the evidence (see p73 for further tips). In addition a **razor**; **deodorant**; **tampons/sanitary towels** and a high-factor **sun screen** should cover all your needs.

FIRST-AID KIT

Medical facilities in Britain are excellent so you only need a small kit to cover common problems and emergencies; pack it in a waterproof container. A basic kit should contain: **aspirin** or **paracetamol** for treating mild to moderate pain and fever; **plasters/Band Aids** for minor cuts; **Moleskin**, **Compeed**, or **Second Skin** for blisters; a **bandage** for holding dressings, splints or limbs in place and for supporting a sprained ankle; elastic knee support (tubigrip) for a weak knee; a small selection of different-sized **sterile dressings** for wounds; **porous adhesive tape**; **antiseptic wipes**; **antiseptic cream**; **safety pins**; **tweezers** and **scissors**.

GENERAL ITEMS

Essential

The following should be in everyone's rucksack: a one-litre **water bottle or pouch**; a **torch** (flashlight) with spare bulb and batteries in case you end up walking after dark; **emergency food** which your body can quickly convert into energy; a **penknife**; a **watch** with an alarm; and a **plastic bag** for packing out any rubbish you accumulate. A **whistle** is also worth taking; although you are very unlikely to need it you may be grateful of it in the unlikely event of an emergency (see pp77-9).

Useful

Many would list a **camera** as essential but it can be liberating to travel without one once in a while; a **notebook** can be a more accurate way of recording your impressions. Other things you may find useful include a **book** to pass the time on train and bus journeys; a pair of **sunglasses**, particularly in summer; **binoculars** for observing wildlife; a **mobile phone** (though reception is patchy, particularly on the Peddars Way) or a **phone card** to use in public phone boxes; a **walking stick** or pole to take the shock off your knees and a **vacuum flask** for carrying hot drinks. Although the path is easy to follow a 'Silva' type **compass** and the knowledge of how to use it is a good idea in case you do lose your way.

SLEEPING BAG

A sleeping bag is only necessary if you are camping or staying in one of the bunkhouses on the route. Campers should find that a two- to three-season bag will cope but obviously in winter a warmer bag is a good idea.

CAMPING GEAR

Campers will need a decent **tent** (or bivvy bag if you enjoy travelling light) able to withstand wet and windy weather; a **sleeping mat**; a **stove** and **fuel** (there is special mention in Part 4 of which shops stock fuel); a **pan** with frying pan that can double as a lid/plate is fine for two people; a **pan handle**; a **mug**; a **spoon**; and a wire/plastic **scrubber** for washing up.

MONEY

There are not many banks or cash machines along the Peddars Way in particular so you will have to carry most of your money as **cash**. A **debit card** is the easiest way to withdraw money from banks or cash machines and a **credit card** can be used to pay in larger shops, restaurants and hotels.

A **cheque book** is very useful for walkers with accounts in British banks as a cheque will often be accepted where a card is not, though some supermarkets no longer accept cheques and they are gradually set to be phased out as a means of payment. However, you may have to have a debit card to act as a guarantee.

MAPS

The hand-drawn maps in this book cover the trail at a scale of 1:20,000; plenty of detail and information to keep you on the right track.

For those after a traditional paper map, you will need five Ordnance Survey maps (☎ 0845-605 0505, 💻 www.ordnancesurvey.co.uk, or for online map shop 💻 http://leisure.ordnancesurvey.co.uk) to cover the entire route.

The OS Explorer maps (with an orange cover) you'll need are: No 229 (Thetford Forest in the Brecks); 236 (King's Lynn, Downham Market & Swaffham); 250 (Norfolk Coast West – King's Lynn & Hunstanton); 251 (Norfolk Coast Central – Wells-next-the-Sea & Fakenham); and 252 (Norfolk Coast East – Cromer & North Walsham), all at a scale of 1:25,000. Laminated, waterproof Active Map editions are also available.

Enthusiastic map buyers can reduce the cost of purchasing a full set: members of the Backpackers' Club (see box opposite) can purchase maps at a significant discount through their map service. Alternatively, members of the Ramblers (see box opposite) can borrow up to 10 maps from their library for a period of four weeks at 50p per map (£1 for weatherproof maps) plus post and packing.

RECOMMENDED READING

Most of the following books can be found in the tourist information centres in Norfolk as well as good bookshops elsewhere in Britain.

General guidebooks

Both Rough Guides and Lonely Planet produce books to *England* and *Great Britain* that cover Norfolk to a small degree. *East Anglia*, published by Crimson in their 'Best of Britain' series, is a more comprehensive look at the region. The Time Out guide to *Norfolk & Suffolk* is the best of the bunch though.

There are two guides to the architecture of the region in the Pevsner Architectural Guides series currently published by Yale University Press: Volume 1 covers *Norwich and North-East Norfolk*, whilst the more immediately relevant Volume 2 deals with *North-West and South Norfolk*.

Walking guidebooks

Pub Walks along the Peddars Way & Norfolk Coast Path and *Pub Walks in Norfolk*, both by Liz Moynihan, published by Countryside Books, contain 20 circular walks varying in length from three to eight miles.

Jarrold Publishing produces a guide to short *Norfolk Walks* in their Pathfinder series as well as a list of itineraries along the coast in their *Norfolk into Suffolk* Short Walks guide. The AA also produces a guide to *50 Walks in Norfolk*, each between two and ten miles long.

General reading

There isn't a great deal of writing on the part of the country the Peddars Way and Norfolk Coast Path pass through. In 1883 Clement Scott wrote an article for the Daily Telegraph newspaper entitled 'Poppyland' that described the North Norfolk Coast and was responsible for bringing the region to the attention of the London literati. For a flavour though look out Paul Theroux's *Kingdom by the Sea*, in which the caustic travel writer travels clockwise around the coast of Britain in 1982 to see what the country and its inhabitants were really like. Robert Macfarlane's beautiful eulogy, *The Wild Places,* contains a description of Blakeney Point and a night spent sleeping rough on the shingle.

The naturalist Richard Mabey grew up on the coast at Cley and there are references to Norfolk in many of his books, including *Beechcombings*. Mark Cocker's *Crow Country* is a detailed examination of the rooks and jackdaws that flock around the author's home in remote Norfolk.

For a fictional idea of the area, Arthur Conan Doyle's *The Hound of the Baskervilles* is based on the legend of Black Shuck, a ghost dog who terrorises the marshes off the North Norfolk coast, and Baskerville Hall was reputed to be inspired by a visit to Cromer Hall, a country house located a mile south of Cromer on Hall Rd. The present Grade II listed building was built in 1829 by architect William Donthorne in the Gothic style after the original structure burnt down. The hall is not open to the public but can be seen clearly from Hall Road.

❑ SOURCES OF FURTHER INFORMATION

Trail information The Peddars Way and Norfolk Coast Path National Trail website (🖳 http://www.nationaltrail.co.uk/peddarsway) has a wealth of useful information about the trails and the area in general.

When actually on the trail look out for copies of the free *Norfolk Coast Guardian* newspaper, which contains news and features about the Norfolk coast of interest to both tourists and locals as well as an events calendar. It is distributed in many of the shops, places of interest and tourist information centres along the trail.

For general information on footpaths, bridleways and byways for walkers, cyclists and horse riders visit 🖳 www.countrysideaccess.norfolk.gov.uk.

Tourist information

• **Tourist information centres (TICs)** TICs are based in towns throughout Britain and can provide all manner of locally specific information as well as an accommodation-booking service (see box p14). The TICs relevant to this route are in **Thetford** (p83), **Hunstanton** (p128), **Wells-next-the-Sea** (p150), **Sheringham** (p172) and **Cromer** (p179).

There is also a well-equipped information service at Deepdale Backpackers in **Burnham Deepdale** (p141) which fulfills a similar function. In addition, there are information points in **Watton** (p94) and **Swaffham** (p101). These are generally staffed by volunteers and don't have the full range of services.

For further information visit 🖳 www.visitnorthnorfolk.com to see what's available to do, where you can stay, where you can eat out and for information on everything you need to put together a holiday itinerary.

Organisations for walkers

• **The Backpackers' Club** (🖳 www.backpackersclub.co.uk) A club aimed at people who are involved or interested in lightweight camping through walking, cycling, skiing, canoeing, etc. They produce a quarterly magazine, provide members with a comprehensive advisory and information service on all aspects of backpacking, organise weekend trips and also publish a farm-pitch directory. Membership is £12/15/7 per year for an individual/family/anyone under 18 or over 65.

• **The Long Distance Walkers' Association** (LDWA; 🖳 www.ldwa.org.uk) An association of people with the common interest of long-distance walking. Membership includes a journal, *Strider*, three times per year giving details of challenge events and local group walks as well as articles on the subject. Information on over 730 paths is presented in their *UK Trailwalkers' Handbook*. Individual membership is £13 a year whilst family membership for two adults and all children under 18 is £19.50 a year.

• **Ramblers** (formerly Ramblers' Association; ☎ 020-7339 8500, 🖳 www.ramblers.org.uk) Looks after the interests of walkers throughout Britain. They publish a large amount of useful information including their quarterly *Walk* magazine (£3.40 to non-members), the *Walk Britain* yearbook (£5.99 to non-members), and *Walk Britain's Great Views* (£14.99), a guide to Britain's top 50 viewpoints. Membership costs £29.50/39.50 individual/joint.

Film and TV

In addition to the literary titles that have come out of Norfolk, a great many films and television series have been shot in the area, taking advantage of its scenery and photogenic appearance. For instance the beach at Holkham starred in the final scenes of *Shakespeare in Love*, whilst farmland at Burnham Deepdale was transformed into a North Korean paddy field for the James Bond film, *Die Another Day*.

The films *A Cock and Bull Story*, *The Eagles have Landed*, *Great Expectations* and *The Duchess* all feature Norfolk, as did the television series *Dad's Army* and *Kingdom*, the fictional central town of which is a composite of Swaffham and the quayside in Wells. *The Go-Between* by LP Hartley featured a central character who spent the summer of 1900 in Norfolk. The film adaptation by Harold Pinter was filmed at Melton Constable and Heydon both of which are close to the Norfolk Coast path.

Flora and fauna field guides

To get the best of Norfolk's birdwatching pick up a guide to the avifauna of the area. *Where to Watch Birds in East Anglia* (Helm), by Peter Clarke, is a comprehensive guide to where to go to see the different species that visit the region. It also contains site accounts, plans, maps, lists of birds and advice on planning birdwatching trips. *Birds of Norfolk* (Helm) written by a team of experts, provides detailed species' accounts and overviews of each of the birds to be found here.

The *Best Birdwatching Sites in Norfolk* (Buckingham Press) by Neil Glenn is a light, readable guide to a range of sites that also includes forecasts as to which birds can be seen during which season. For a good general identification book look out the *Collins Birds Guide* by Lars Svensson, Killian Mullarney, Dan Zetterstrom and Peter Grant.

Getting to and from the Peddars Way and Norfolk Coast Path

A quick look at a map of Britain will show that Norfolk is relatively accessible and well connected to the rest of the country. The fact that it is within a fairly short hop of London and all the transport options available there means that sections of the county at least have become popular weekend retreats for city folk. In reality, although there are good road and rail links with the region, the start of the Peddars Way is poorly serviced. Public transport, in the form of trains and coaches will get you to Thetford or Bury St Edmunds easily enough, but there is no public transport service to Knettishall Heath where the trail actually starts. Instead you must use a dial-a-ride service (see p45), call for a taxi (see p83) or settle for a bus (Simonds No 338) from Bury St Edmunds to Coney Weston (see p48), from where you must walk around two miles to Knettishall Heath, initially along Norwich Lane.

❑ Getting to Britain

• **By air** Most international airlines serve London Heathrow and London Gatwick. In addition a number of budget airlines fly from many of Europe's major cities to the other London terminals at Stansted and Luton. Norwich International Airport (🖳 www.norwichairport.co.uk) is four miles north of Norwich city centre and has connections to a number of European destinations, often via Amsterdam. There are frequent bus services to the city centre. Alternatively it is a short taxi ride.

• **From Europe by train (with or without a car)** **Eurostar** (🖳 www.eurostar.com) operate a high-speed passenger service via the Channel Tunnel between Paris and London, and Brussels and London. Trains arrive at and depart from St Pancras International Terminal, which also has good underground links to other railway stations. For more information about rail services between Europe and Britain contact your national rail operator or Railteam (🖳 www.railteam.eu). **Eurotunnel** (🖳 www.eurotunnel.com) operates a shuttle train service for vehicles via the Channel Tunnel between Calais and Folkestone taking 35 minutes to cross between the two.

• **From Europe by ferry (with or without a car)** Numerous ferry companies operate routes between the major North Sea and Channel ports of mainland Europe and the ports on Britain's eastern and southern coasts as well as from Ireland to ports both in Wales and England. For further information see websites such as 🖳 www.directferries.co.uk.

• **From Europe by coach** **Eurolines** (🖳 www.eurolines.com) have a huge network of services connecting over 500 cities in 25 European countries to London.

Despite the lack of straightforward public transport access, you are still better off using one of these combinations than driving to the start of the trail. Although there is a car park at Knettishall Heath it is not supervised or secure. Since the walk is a linear route you will also end up a long way away from your vehicle. Overall then, public transport makes sense: there's no undue worry about your vehicle whilst walking, there are no logistical issues getting back to it when you are finished and it's obviously one of the biggest steps you can take towards minimising your ecological footprint.

In contrast, the end of the Norfolk Coast Path at Cromer is much better connected, with both regular rail and National Express coach services leaving from the town.

NATIONAL TRANSPORT

By rail

For those walking the entire trail, the closest train stations are at Thetford (15 miles from the start of the Peddars Way at Knettishall Heath) and Cromer, where the Norfolk Coast Path concludes.

National Express East Anglia (🖳 www.nationalexpresseastanglia.com) operate frequent services to Thetford from both Cambridge and Ely. They also have services from London Liverpool St to Cambridge. However, First Capital Connect's services from London King's Cross to Cambridge are quicker.

Cross Country (🖳 www.crosscountrytrains.co.uk) have direct services to Ely from Birmingham New St with hourly departures for the 2½hr journey.

Alternatively you can catch a train to Bury St Edmunds, via Ipswich or Cambridge if coming from London, and take Simonds No 338 bus service to Coney Weston, around two miles from the trailhead (see p89).

Other points on the path that can be reached by rail include Sheringham and Cromer, which are both stops on the Bittern Line (💻 www.bitternline.com) from Norwich. National Express East Anglia (see p43) operates from London (Liverpool St) to Norwich. The Bittern Line offers a regular, reliable almost hourly service, with good-value fares. The Bittern Line Rover offers unlimited train travel between Norwich and Sheringham and includes bus travel on the Coasthopper bus service (see opposite). Tickets are available from the conductor on Bittern Line trains.

All timetable and fare information can be found at National Rail Enquiries (☎ 08457-484950, 💻 www.nationalrail.co.uk). Tickets can be booked online through the relevant rail operators (see p43), or through 💻 www.thetrainline.com and 💻 www.qjump.co.uk.

Other rail services in the area include: **North Norfolk Railway/Poppy Line** (see pp171-2), a full-size steam and diesel railway which runs between Sheringham and Holt, and **Wells and Walsingham Light Railway** (see p150), which is the longest 10½-inch gauge steam railway in the world.

By coach

National Express (☎ 0871-781 8178, lines open 8am-10pm daily; 💻 www.nationalexpress.com) is the main coach (long-distance bus) operator in Britain. Tickets can also be booked through the North Norfolk tourist information centres (see box p41). Coach travel is generally cheaper (non-refundable 'funfares' are available online for as little as £5 one way but expect to pay closer to £15 one way if you want more flexibility) but takes longer than travel by train.

National Express's NX490 (daily 7/day) operates from London Victoria to Norwich via Thetford and the NX496 (daily 1/day) runs between London Victoria and Cromer via Swaffham, Holt, Sheringham, West Runton and East Runton.

If you wish to approach the trail via Bury St Edmunds the NX497 (daily 3/day) calls there en route between London Victoria and Great Yarmouth. National Express's NX308 operates from Birmingham to Great Yarmouth via Coventry, Leicester, King's Lynn and Swaffham.

At present there are no National Express services to Hunstanton.

By car

Norfolk has good links to the national road network; the A17 runs into Norfolk from Lincolnshire whilst the A47 links Norfolk with Peterborough and Leicester, providing straightforward routes from the A1 and M1. The M11 and A12 provide links to London and the south-east. Thetford can be reached via the A11, which joins the M11 just south of Cambridge, or the A134 which links Bury St Edmunds to King's Lynn.

From Thetford it is a five-mile drive east on the A1066 (Rushford to Knettishall) road. There is a car park immediately opposite the start point of the Peddars Way. However, it is not secure and you shouldn't leave your car here for an extended period – and particularly not for the time it takes to complete the trek.

The end of the Coast Path at Cromer is reached by following the A140 from Norwich or the A148 from King's Lynn. There are long-term car parks in Cromer. A transferable all-day parking pass will also allow you to park in Sheringham and Wells on any given day. The A149 links King's Lynn to Yarmouth and snakes along the coast connecting the small towns and villages rather than taking a more direct route inland.

LOCAL TRANSPORT

Local transport along the lengths of the Peddars Way and Norfolk Coast Path is of varied quality. The Peddars Way is very poorly served and a number of the smaller, more out-of-the-way villages are entirely unconnected to other towns or, at best, have one service a week. This is a problem if you are looking to do linear walks in the area or if you simply want to give your feet a rest and skip ahead. Once you arrive on the coast though the story improves, with a superb, dedicated service (see below) designed to help coastal walkers access the villages and towns along the route between Hunstanton and Cromer.

The public transport map on p46 shows the most useful bus and train routes and the box on pp47-8 gives details of the frequency of services and whom you should contact for timetable information.

The Brecks Bus

This community transport service, which operates on a dial-a-ride basis from Thetford, is the best way of reaching the start of the Peddars Way at Knettishall Heath (see box p47). The Brecks Bus was set up to help people get out into the countryside around Brandon and Thetford to access attractions and walking routes.

Coastal bus services

The excellent coastal bus service, the **Coasthopper** (💻 www.coasthopper.co.uk), is aimed directly at day-trippers and tired walkers. Run by the Norfolk Green bus company, it operates year-round along the North Norfolk coast and provides an invaluable service; see the public transport map and table, pp47-8, for more details. There is a summer and a winter timetable. During summer there are approximately two services an hour but in winter months the number of off-peak services is slightly reduced. Timetables are readily available from Norfolk Green's website but also at tourist information centres, hostels, cafés and other information outlets on and around the route.

The yellow, green and blue bus has a number of set pick-up and drop-off points but also operates on a hail-and-ride basis as long as it can stop in a safe place. Almost all buses are step free making them accessible to pushchairs and wheelchairs. Dogs are allowed on the buses but bicycles aren't. The buses are also low emission, minimising their impact on the local environment.

To get the best value buy a 1-, 3- or 7-day Coasthopper Rover ticket, which gives unlimited travel on Coasthopper buses from £6/15/30 (adult) respectively.

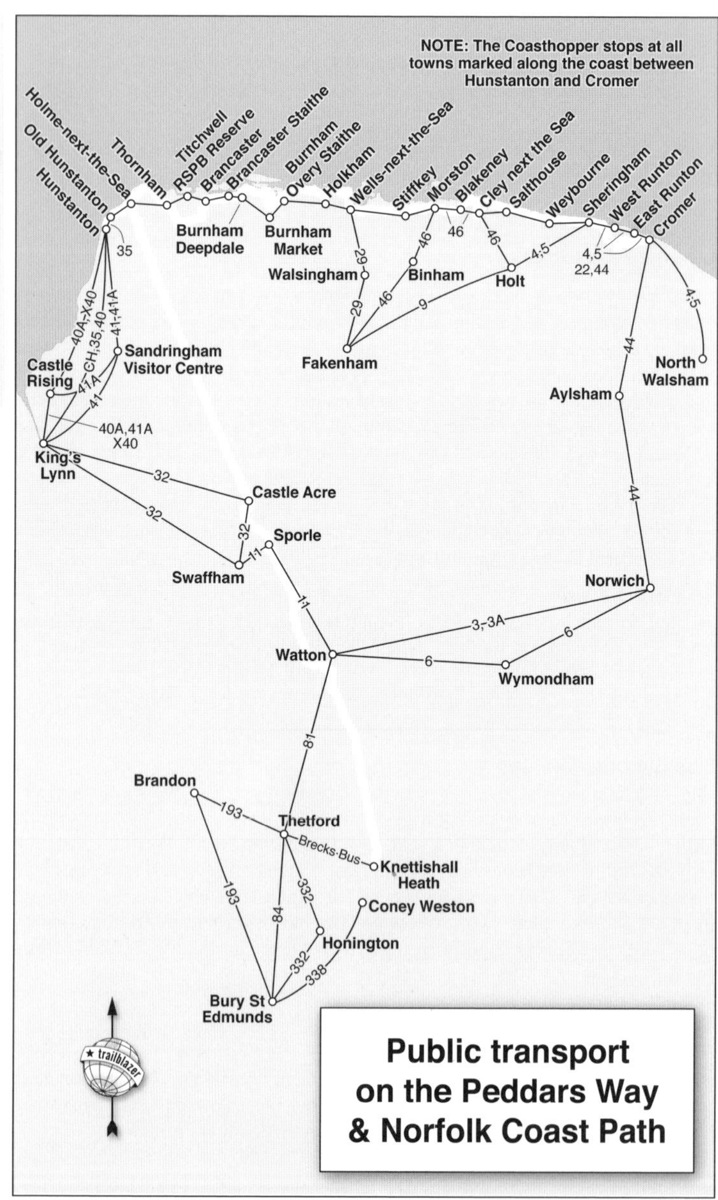

Public transport on the Peddars Way & Norfolk Coast Path

❑ Public transport services

The following list is not completely comprehensive but does cover the most important services. Unless specified otherwise services operate year-round, though services may be less frequent in winter. For full and up-to-date details of bus services and timetables contact the individual companies or visit their websites. Alternatively, for an overview of public transport in the region and to plan your journey call traveline ☎ 0871-200 2233 or visit their website (🖳 www.travelineeastanglia.co.uk).

Buses

Coach Services (☎ 01842-821509, 🖳 www.coachservicesltd.com)
81 Thetford to Watton, Mon-Fri 5/day
84 Bury St Edmunds to Thetford, Mon-Fri 9/day, Sat 6/day
332 Bury St Edmunds to Thetford via Honington, Mon-Sat 6-7/day
193 Bury St Edmunds to Thetford via Brandon, Mon-Sat 3/day

Brecks Bus (☎ 01638-608080, 🖳 www.brecks.org)
BB Thetford to Knettishall Heath; dial-a-ride service, operates Monday (except bank holidays) to Friday between 9am and 4pm but should be booked (call Mon to Fri between 9am and 1pm) at least two days in advance to secure seats. Since the bus is small (it seats five) dogs are not allowed, nor can bikes be taken. See also p45. The Flexibus (☎ 0845-600 2315) is a dial-and-ride service available Mon-Fri 7.30am-4pm; book by 5pm the day before

First Eastern Counties (🖳 www.firstgroup.com)
40 King's Lynn to Hunstanton, Mon-Fri 14/day, Sat 10/day
40A King's Lynn to Hunstanton via Castle Rising, Sun 3/day evenings only
41 King's Lynn to Hunstanton via Sandringham Visitor Centre, Mon-Fri 11/day, Sat 10/day, Sun 5/day
41A King's Lynn to Hunstanton via Castle Rising & Sandringham, Mon-Sat 5/day
X40 King's Lynn to Hunstanton via Castle Rising, Mon-Sat 8-10/day

Freestone Coaches (☎ 01362-860236; 🖳 freestonecoachesltd@tiscali.co.uk)
32 King's Lynn to Swaffham, Mon-Fri 3/day, Sat 1/day (via Castle Acre, Mon-Sat 1/day; see also Swaffham Community Transport)

Konectbus (☎ 01362-851210; 🖳 www.konectbus.co.uk)
3 Norwich to Watton, Mon-Sat 10-14/day
3A Norwich to Watton, Sun 4/day
6 Norwich to Watton via Wymondham, Mon-Sat hourly
11 Watton to Swaffham via Sporle, Mon-Fri 7/day, Sat 3/day

Norfolk Green (☎ 01553-776980, 🖳 www.norfolkgreen.co.uk)
CH Coasthopper (🖳 www.coasthopper.co.uk): services operate year-round but the frequencies below are for early April to end Oct; additional services, particularly on Sunday, operate between late May and early Sep; there are fewer services in winter (King's Lynn to Hunstanton is the No 35 bus service)
King's Lynn to Cromer via Hunstanton, Old Hunstanton, Holme-next-the-Sea, Thornham, Titchwell RSPB Reserve, Brancaster, Brancaster Staithe, Burnham Deepdale, Burnham Market, Burnham Overy Staithe, Holkham, Wells, Stiffkey, Morston, Blakeney, Cley, Salthouse, Weybourne, Sheringham, West Runton & East Runton, early Apr to end Oct daily 7/day plus Sat 1/day plus Mon-Sat 3/day to Sheringham plus Sun 1/day to Wells

(cont'd on p48)

❑ **Public transport services** *(cont'd from p47)*

Norfolk Green *(Coasthopper cont'd)*

Hunstanton to Cromer including the stops listed above, Mon-Sat 10/day, Sun 1/day

29 Fakenham to Wells-next-the-Sea via Walsingham, Mon-Sat 11/day, Sun 5/day

Sanders Coaches Limited (☎ 01263-712800, 🖳 www.sanderscoaches.com)

4 North Walsham to Holt via Cromer, East Runton, West Runton & Sheringham, Mon-Sat 1/hr

5 North Walsham to Holt via Cromer, East Runton, West Runton & Sheringham as well as many other villages between North Walsham & Cromer, daily 1/hr

9 Holt to Fakenham Mon-Sat 9/day (connects with No 4 at Holt)

22 Sheringham to Cromer via Beeston Campsite, West Runton & East Runton (an open-top double-decker service) daily Good Friday to end Sep, Oct Sat & Sun only 9/day

44 Norwich to Sheringham via Aylsham, Cromer, East Runton & West Runton, Mon-Sat 16/day, Sun 11/day

Simonds (☎ 01379-647300, 🖳 www.simonds.co.uk)

338 Bury St Edmunds to Coney Weston, Mon-Sat 7/day

Swaffham Community Transport (☎ 01760-720906)

32 Swaffham to Castle Acre, Mon-Fri 2/day

THE ENVIRONMENT & NATURE

2

To the uninitiated, the Peddars Way and Norfolk Coast Path don't seem all that distinctive. They lack many of the recognisable features of other national trails in England. Yet on closer examination it is possible to determine a wide variety of contrasting terrains and habitats from one end of the trail to the other: grasslands, heath, woodlands, forests, sand dunes, salt-marshes, wide beaches and vast stretches of coast. These varied environments are home to an equally diverse selection of flora and fauna. The following is not designed to be a comprehensive guide to all the animals, birds and plants you might encounter, but rather serves as an introduction to what you're likely to see.

By making an effort to look out for wildlife and plants as you walk the route you will garner a broader appreciation of the landscape and region you are passing through. You will begin to understand how the species you encounter interact with one another and will learn a little about the conservation issues that are so pertinent today.

LANDSCAPES

Norfolk has been moulded by a series of glaciations. The land has been shaped, smoothed and stripped by the passage of ice. The chalk ridge running through north-west Norfolk was rounded whilst wide swathes of clay and gravel were deposited on top of older rocks. Intriguing features such as the pingo ponds around Thompson Water (see box p90) remain as evidence of these successive ice ages. As the coast and cliffs have been subjected to erosion so they have given up a series of secrets. The bones and teeth of hippo, hyena and deer have been found whilst the 85%-complete fossil skeleton of a 15ft tall, 650,000-year-old elephant were unearthed in 1990 in the cliffs between East and West Runton, indicative of a time when the landscape looked very different indeed.

Within the Norfolk Coast AONB (see p52) there are eight distinguishable landscape types. The coastal region with its open, remote and wild panorama of wide skies and long views to the sea is the most typical of the area and the one that conjures the most ready images. Characteristic features include marshes, sand dunes and shingle ridges as well as small coastal settlements comprising flint

buildings, significant churches and windmills. In the east there are pollarded willows (heavily pruned each year to encourage a close, rounded head of branches) alongside long straight roads. In the west, rectilinear fields are defined by ditches, sparse hedges and occasional stands of trees.

Inland a varied, undulating landscape of rolling hills and large stretches of heathland dominates. Village estates are typified by buildings of attractive carrstone (coarse, grained, granular sandstone, usually yellowish brown).

In all, it is a region of wide and varied interest that is in a state of constant flux, being shaped and re-shaped by the elements and the tides.

Breckland Breckland is a fairly recent term for an internationally important landscape, coined to describe a much older setting identifiable from its surrounds by its terrain, land-use and distinctive wildlife. Broadly speaking, Breckland comprises a gently undulating, low plateau underlain by a bedrock of Cretaceous chalk, covered by thin deposits of sand and flint. What started as deciduous woodland was slowly razed by early Neolithic man in pursuit of flint (see box below), which was dug out of the ground here. The open heath was then grazed extensively by sheep and rabbits, removing the vegetation, exhausting the soil and turning it into a sea of loose, shifting sands, which meant that villages contracted and people moved out of the region or retreated to the river valleys. During the 18th and 19th centuries Scots pines were planted to try and bind the soil together and stabilise the land for cultivation, whilst in the 20th century land was given over to conifer plantations. The result is a modern landscape of open areas and flint-filled fields, dotted with stands of deliberately planted trees.

The greatest extent of remaining heathlands are centred on the Stanford Training Area and Brettenham Heath. The Brecks/Breckland are particularly cherished for this remaining heathland and the mosaics of grass-heath which support populations of invertebrates and ground-nesting birds. Traditionally they are areas of heather and grass although more recently they have been invaded by bracken and scrub. The area is significant for a wide range of flora and fauna dependent on open ground, arable margins and disturbed soil. Unique landforms such as pingo ponds are also important for insects. For more information see 💻 www.brecks.org.

Norfolk Coast The North Norfolk coast is one of the best examples of an unspoilt coastline in England. The coast is separated from adjacent areas by a

> **❑ Flint**
> Flint is a mineral found in bands within chalk and has played a big part in the history of the landscape across which the Peddars Way and Norfolk Coast Path travel. When man first found the ability to make tools, the people who lived in the region began to make arrowheads and knives from flakes of flint. It was also found to be useful in starting fires. Flint can still be seen in local village architecture as it is a very versatile building brick. The traditional fishermen's cottages all along the coast wouldn't look like they do today if it weren't for flint, and the atmosphere and the character of the area would be markedly different.

combination of light soils, climate, relief and land use. The area is drained by the rivers Wensum and Bure which flow south-eastwards into Broadland and by a number of smaller waterways such as the Glaven and Stiffkey that flow northwards, whilst the Nar drains westwards to the Wash. The gravels and sands left behind after the last Ice Age still determine the vegetation patterns. Habitats range from heaths and mires to woodlands and highly fertile soils that end in gently eroding sea cliffs. The coastal habitats themselves are constantly changing, with weather and waves responsible for shaping the shifting shingle ridges, sandflats, spits and dunes as well as filling the salt creeks and marshes that lie behind them. The result is that the coastline today is very different from the coastline in the past, and indeed the way it will look in the future; thriving ports are already landlocked or increasingly only accessible by small channels and rivulets as silt deposits choke access routes to the sea.

The significance and variety of habitats in the area means that it has been conserved as a series of connected nature reserves that run all the way from Holme to Weybourne. They are amongst the best examples of coastal environments in Britain and also feature biological and geomorphological sites of interest such as the barrier island at Scolt Head (see p142) and the shingle spit at Blakeney Point (see box p160).

CONSERVING THE PEDDARS WAY AND NORFOLK COAST PATH

As with much of the British Isles, the English countryside has had to cope with a great deal of pressure from the activities of an increasingly industrialised world. Even in Norfolk, which was largely by-passed by the industrial revolution and early developments, there are significant changes to land use and the way in which we live. Almost every acre of land has been altered in some way by man; the need to feed an increasingly large population led to the landscape being cleared of trees and ploughed for crops. Agricultural intensification and decades of chemical farming have drained swathes of the countryside of much of its wildlife. The result of this is the landscape we see today. Ironically the verdant green colour we associate most with the English landscape is the one that best conveys its decimation – green without relief or shading is unnatural. Mark Cocker notes in *Crow Country* (see p40) that '… in Norfolk the obduracy of water has been the saving grace for the wildly beautiful north coast…' Nonetheless, what remains today are fragments of semi-natural woodland and hedgerows stretched across farmland. The chopping and changing of this landscape has had a negative impact on its biodiversity and a number of species have been lost whilst others are severely depleted.

There is a positive note though. There are still pockets of enormous beauty and the resulting habitat is, in parts, a rare one that provides an essential niche for endangered species. What's more, in these increasingly enlightened times when environmental issues are correctly given greater prominence, both voluntary and government conservation bodies have begun to be heard as they campaign for the countryside to be preserved.

GOVERNMENT AGENCIES AND SCHEMES

Natural England

Primary responsibility for countryside affairs in England rests with Natural England; this organisation is responsible for enhancing biodiversity, landscape and wildlife in rural, urban, coastal and marine areas; promoting access, recreation and public well-being; and contributing to the way natural resources are managed. One of its roles is to designate national trails, national parks, areas of outstanding natural beauty, sites of special scientific interest, and national nature reserves, and to enforce regulations relating to all these sites.

The top level of protection is afforded to **National Parks**, a designation that recognises the national importance of an area in terms of landscape, biodiversity and as a recreational source. This title does not imply national ownership though and they are not necessarily uninhabited wildernesses, meaning that the conservation of these areas is a juggling act between protecting the environment and ensuring the rights and livelihoods of those living within the park. There are 15 National Parks in the UK, including the Norfolk and Suffolk Broads which was granted the status in 1989, but no part of the Peddars Way or Norfolk Coast Path falls inside the boundary.

The area the two paths pass through is afforded a degree of protection though, with much of the route designated an **Area of Outstanding Natural Beauty** (AONB), the second highest level of protection. The Norfolk Coast Path falls entirely within the **Norfolk Coast AONB**, an area of largely undeveloped coastal land accorded protection in 1968. The AONB comprises three separate areas of coast, including the inter-tidal area and hinterland that backs it – in places the boundary for the strip of land classified as an AONB extends up to 6km inland, and in total 450 square kilometres of land are protected. The bulk of the AONB is a long section of coast from Old Hunstanton in the west to Bacton in the east. Within this area, Sheringham and Cromer, as well as the stretch of coast between them, are excluded because development work was already underway when the regulations were established.

The majority of the AONB includes the wild and remote coastal marshes of the North Norfolk Heritage Coast, a mixture of sand and mud flats, dunes, shingle, salt-marsh, reed-beds and grazing marsh. It also includes the glacial sand and gravel cliffs east of Weybourne as well as the rolling farmland, estates and wood-

❑ The Norfolk Coast Partnership

The Norfolk Coast Partnership (NCP, 💻 www.norfolkcoastaonb.org.uk) was established in 1991, initially as the Norfolk Coast Project, to promote and co-ordinate policies amongst its member organisations. Established in response to the increased pressure put on the land by burgeoning visitor numbers and the perceived threat to the area's natural beauty that they represented, the partnership's objectives have broadly evolved in line with those of AONB designation, to bring about sustainable use of the Norfolk Coast whilst conserving and enhancing the natural features and ensuring that future generations can enjoy and benefit from the coast.

❑ Statutory bodies

• **Department for Environment, Food and Rural Affairs** (🖳 ww2.defra.gov.uk) Government ministry responsible for sustainable development in the countryside.

• **Natural England** (🖳 www.naturalengland.org.uk) Their relevant regional office is in Norwich (☎ 0300-060 3789).

• **English Heritage** (🖳 www.english-heritage.org.uk) Organisation whose central aim is to make sure that the historic environment of England is properly maintained. It is officially known as the Historic Buildings and Monuments Commission for England and manages Cluniac Priory (see p105), Castle Acre, and Seahenge (see box p132).

• **Norfolk County Council** (🖳 www.norfolk.gov.uk).

• **National Association for Areas of Outstanding Natural Beauty** (🖳 www.aonb.org.uk); **Norfolk Coast AONB** (see opposite)

land of the coastal hinterland and areas of heath that back the coast. In addition there are two small outlying designated areas: in the west an area north of King's Lynn that includes Sandringham Estate and the Wash mudflats, and in the east the sand dunes between Sea Palling and Winterton, where there is a small overlap with land designated part of the Norfolk and Suffolk Broads National Park.

Because the Norfolk Coast AONB is a large area and crosses a number of administrative boundaries, a wide number of groups and organisations are involved in managing it, and work in tandem with the **Norfolk Coast Partnership** (NCP; see box on p52) to ensure its preservation. The NCP is funded by Natural England, Norfolk County Council, North Norfolk District Council, the Borough Council of Kings Lynn and West Norfolk and Great Yarmouth Borough Council.

The National Trails Officer (see box p75) works closely with the above organisations and councils to keep the Peddars Way and Norfolk Coast Path in good condition, although work on the ground may sometimes by undertaken by local authorities.

The next level of protection includes National Nature Reserves and Sites of Scientific Interest. There are over 220 **National Nature Reserves (NNRs)** in England, where wildlife comes first. This doesn't mean that they are no-go areas for people, just that visitors have to be careful not to damage the fragile ecosystems and wildlife within these places. Those in Norfolk include Brettenham Heath (see p89) just before the A11 on leaving Knettishall Heath, Holme Dunes (see p122), Holkham (see p148), Scolt Head Island (see p142) off Burnham Overy Staithe, and Blakeney (see box p160). Thetford Heath, south west of Thetford, in Suffolk, is also a National Nature Reserve although the Peddars Way actually starts north-east of here.

There are over 4000 **Sites of Special Scientific Interest (SSSIs)** in England, covering some 7% of the country's land area. These range in size from little pockets protecting wild flower meadows, important nesting sites or special geological features, to vast swathes of upland, moorland and wetland. SSSIs are a particularly important designation as they have some legal standing; they are managed in accordance with the landowners and occupiers who must give notice before starting any work likely to damage the site, and they must not proceed without written consent from Natural England.

There are more than 160 SSSIs in Norfolk although they are not given a high profile and deliberately little attention is drawn to them. Those along the Peddars Way and Norfolk Coast Path include: Breckland Forest and Farmland, Thompson Water, the River Nar, Castle Acre Common, the Stanford Training Area, Ringstead Downs, Hunstanton Cliffs, the North Norfolk coast, Weybourne Cliffs, Sheringham and Beeston Regis Common, Beeston Cliffs, East and West Runton Cliffs and Felbrigg Woods.

Special Areas of Conservation (SACs) are designated by the European Union's Habitats Directive and provide an extra tier of protection to the areas they encompass and are a vital part of global efforts to conserve the world's biodiversity. Breckland and the North Norfolk coast both benefit from this increased protection.

For further information about all of these visit Natural England's website (see box p53).

The North Norfolk coast is also listed as a **Ramsar site** under the Convention on Wetlands of International Importance, particularly as a waterfowl habitat. It is also recognised internationally as a **UNESCO biosphere reserve**, a label that means that it serves as a 'living laboratory' for testing out and demonstrating integrated management of land, water and biodiversity.

These designations undoubtedly all play an important role in safeguarding the land they cover for future generations. However, the very fact that we require and rely on these labels for conserving small areas begs the question what are we doing to look after the vast majority of land that remains relatively unprotected? Surely we should be looking to conserve the natural environment outside protected areas just as much as within them.

CAMPAIGNING AND CONSERVATION ORGANISATIONS

The survival of so many important natural sites depends on the efforts of a great many. It was in fact on the North Norfolk coast that the Wildlife Trust movement (see box opposite) began through the efforts of the Norfolk and Norwich Naturalists Society; the first meeting took place in the George Inn in Cley in 1926 and the purchase of 400 acres of marsh at Cley to be held 'in perpetuity as a bird breeding sanctuary' provided a blueprint for nature conservation that has now been replicated across the UK. The importance of the coast had in fact already been recognised by Professor Oliver of London University, who had led the appeal that resulted in the purchase of Blakeney Point by the National Trust in 1912.

The tradition of caring continues today through a variety of diverse organisations, sympathetic landlords and volunteers. The idea of conservation has also gained momentum with an increase in public awareness and interest in environmental issues as a whole. There are now a large number of campaigning and conservation groups in the UK. Independent of the government, they are reliant on public support; they can concentrate their resources on acquiring land that

❑ Campaigning and conservation organisations – contact details

- **National Trust** (NT; 🖳 www.nationaltrust.org.uk).
- The umbrella organisation for the 47 wildlife trusts in the UK is **The Wildlife Trusts** (🖳 www.wildlifetrusts.org). **Norfolk Wildlife Trust**, the branch relevant to the Peddars Way and Norfolk Coast Path, is based in Norwich (☎ 01603-625540, 🖳 www.norfolkwildlifetrust.org.uk).
- **Royal Society for the Protection of Birds** (RSPB; 🖳 www.rspb.org.uk) The largest voluntary organisation body in Europe focusing on providing a healthy environment for birds and wildlife, with over 200 reserves in the UK. Their East of England regional office is based in Norwich.
- **Norfolk Ornithologists' Association** (🖳 www.noa.org.uk) Dedicated to the scientific study of birds; has six reserves in Norfolk in addition to its base at Holme.
- **Butterfly Conservation** (🖳 www.butterfly-conservation.org) The branch relevant to the Peddars Way and Norfolk Coast Path is Norfolk (🖳 www.norfolk-butterflies.org.uk).
- **Wildfowl & Wetlands Trust** (WWT; 🖳 www.wwt.org.uk) has a Norfolk branch in Welney (☎ 01353-860711, 🖳 www.wwt.org.uk/visit-us/welney) near Wisbech.

can then be managed for conservation purposes, or on influencing political decision makers by lobbying and campaigning.

The **National Trust** is a charity with some 3.6 million members, which aims to protect through ownership threatened coastline, countryside, historic houses, castles, gardens and archaeological remains for everybody to enjoy. In particular the NT cares for more than 600 miles of British coastline, 248,000 hectares of countryside and 300 historic buildings and monuments. It manages sections of Norfolk including Brancaster (see p136), Blakeney National Nature Reserve (see box p160) and Sheringham Park (see p171), but also owns properties including Felbrigg Hall (see p175).

The **Wildfowl and Wetlands Trust** (WWT) is the biggest conservation organisation for wetlands in the UK with over 400 acres of land under their management. Their regional visitor centre at Welney in Norfolk is well known and popular with visitors year-round.

The **Wildlife Trust** has a regional branch in Norwich. They undertake projects to improve conditions for wildlife and promote public awareness of it as well as acquiring land for nature reserves to protect particular species and habitats. The Norfolk Wildlife Trust manages nearly 10,000 acres of land right across the county, including nature reserves at Thompson Common, Wayland Wood close to Watton, Ringstead Downs, Holme Dunes, Cley Marshes and Salthouse Marshes set behind a shingle ridge on the way to Sheringham.

The **Royal Society for the Protection of Birds** (RSPB) was the pioneer of voluntary conservation bodies. It is responsible for maintaining 200 reserves across Britain including ones at Titchwell Marsh (see p136), on the Norfolk Coast Path, and Snettisham (see p60) to the south of Hunstanton on the Wash. **Norfolk Ornithologists' Association** is based at Holme Bird Observatory (see p134).

Butterfly Conservation was formed in 1968 by some naturalists determined to reverse the decline in the numbers of moths and butterflies in the UK.

They now have more than 30 branches including a Norfolk branch and operate a number of nature reserves and sites where butterflies are likely to be found.

BEYOND CONSERVATION

Pressures on the countryside continue to grow year on year. At the same time our awareness of environmental issues and the need for a sustainable approach to life means there is hope. That said, to maximise the chance of a bright future we all need to do our bit. The individual can readily play his or her part. Walkers in particular appreciate the value of wild areas and should ensure this attitude permeates other aspects of their lives. This is not just about recycling the odd bottle or newspaper, or walking to the shop rather than driving, but about adopting a sustainable and respectful approach to living, or even pushing for environmental policies to be heard in local and national government.

Walking is the most intimate way to explore a landscape, yet some people still find it difficult to shake off the chaos of modern life even when in the countryside. When you are out walking take time to slow down and immerse yourself in your surrounds. The rewards will be worth it.

Flora and fauna

BUTTERFLIES AND MOTHS

The best time to spot butterflies is from mid-July to mid-September. Many of their numbers have declined due to the large loss of inland habitats. Butterflies are also under threat from the large **harlequin ladybird** (*Harmonia axyridis*), an invasive non-native species of ladybird with orange, red or black spots, which feeds on the larvae of the native ladybirds as well as on butterfly and moth eggs. First spotted in Norfolk in 2004 its numbers have grown steadily as has its distribution.

The **cinnabar moth** (*Tyria jacobaeae*) is a night flier but can sometimes be seen during the day, when it is easily spotted due to its bright red spots and stripes on its upper charcoal grey forewings – the name derives from the bright red mineral cinnabar. The caterpillars are distinguished by their jet black and yellow-orange stripes and are often spotted decimating patches of ragwort. Found in open spaces, the moth is resident in heathland, well-drained grassland and sand dunes such as those at Holme. The **garden tiger** (*Arctia caja*) is a striking moth with brown forewings crossed with cream lines and red hind wings spotted with large blue dots, which it flashes when disturbed. The caterpillars are very hairy and known colloquially as 'woolly bears'. The large **ghost moth** (*Hepialus humuli*) is common across much of Norfolk. The name refers to its pale appearance and its tendency to hover over grassy areas at dusk, rising and falling slowly. **Hummingbird hawkmoths** (*Macroglossum stellatarum*) are day moths that can be seen on the wing from June to August, feeding on nectar from flowers in the same fashion as hummingbirds. The **lime hawkmoth** (*Mimas tiliae*) has attractive scalloped forewings that vary in colour from pink to olive green. The caterpillar, which is usually bright green with yellow stripes and a blue horn at the rear, feeds on limes. The **privet hawkmoth** (*Sphinx ligustri*) is the largest hawkmoth in the country and can be found on scrub. It has pink and black barring on the body and hind wings. The caterpillar is more striking, with lilac and white stripes down the length of its luminescent green body and a black horn at the rear.

The **comma** (*Polygonia c-album*) is bright orange with dark brown markings on its wings, on the underside of which is a distinctive white 'comma' shape. The ragged edges of the wings are actually easier to spot. Found in woodland clearings, hedgerows and gardens the comma has recolonised Norfolk over the last 70 years.

The **dingy skipper** (*Erynnis tages*), with its dull grey-brown, mottled appearance, looks like a moth but is in fact a small butterfly. It can be seen flitting quickly across open, sunny habitats such as heathland or stretches of chalk grassland found in Breckland. The **grizzled skipper** (*Pyrgus malvae*) has characteristic black and white patterned wings. Although not very common in Norfolk it can be seen on warm, sheltered spots with sparse vegetation.

The **grayling** (*Hipparchia semele*) is hard to spot as the brown and grey patterns are superb camouflage. It can be found in coastal areas such as dunes, especially around Burnham Overy Staithe, salt-marshes and cliffs as well as heathland and grasslands such as the Brecks.

The **orange tip** (*Anthocharis cardamines*) boasts bright orange tips to its white wings. Found on verges, in woodland glades and in damp meadows, unusually its numbers are on the increase and it is spreading. The **swallowtail** (*Papilio machaon britannicus*) is Britain's largest butterfly. It has stunning yellow and black markings and two long tail extensions that resemble a swallow's tail. Increasingly rare and restricted to the Broads you may just spot one if you are lucky.

The **white admiral** (*Limenitis camilla*) is also very striking with a bold white stripe across its wings. Common in woodland clearings and places with plenty of brambles, it is often seen in Norfolk, especially around Sheringham Park.

DRAGONFLIES

Norfolk is also an important breeding ground for dragonflies, which can be seen in areas of open water. There are some 34 species found here although new migrants swell the numbers. Look out for the **black-tailed skimmer** (*Orthetrum cancellatum*), which has a blue abdomen with a black tip and yellow arcs down each side. The **common darter** (*Sympetrum striolatum*) is widespread and often occurs in large numbers. They are red in colour and have a small patch of yellow at the base of their wings. **Migrant hawkers** (*Aeshna mixta*) are one of four species of hawker dragonfly to be found in Norfolk. They have mainly blue or yellow spots down their abdomen. The **Norfolk hawker** (*Aeshna isosceles*) is a rare dragonfly usually found only on the Broads, where it has its stronghold.

The **common pond skater** (*Gerris lacustris*) is a thin brownish-black bug often seen 'skating' across the surface of still patches of water, as a layer of water-repellent silvery hairs allows them to perch on top of the water. Thompson Water is particularly good for spotting them. You might also see green-black **great diving beetles** (*Dytiscus marginalis*) here. The **white clawed crayfish** (*Austropotamobius pallipes*) is the only native species of freshwater crustacean. Once widespread it is now seen in only a handful of rivers in the UK, amongst which is the River Wissey.

BIRDS

Few bird watchers, serious or amateur, will not have been to Norfolk or know of its reputation amongst twitchers. This is largely due to the county's strategic location facing Scandinavia, slap bang on a migration pathway, its long coast line and its extremely diverse range of coastal and inland habitats, many of which enjoy protected status as nature reserves (see box p60). The marshes and inter-tidal mudflats along the coast are important breeding grounds for a vast number of species as they offer feeding and safe roost sites.

The county has some of the best year-round birding sites in the country, with locations that consistently attract rare birds. The following lists give just a few of the more than 300 species that have been documented in Norfolk and ought to give you a flavour of what you should see whilst walking the Peddars Way and Norfolk Coast Path.

Scrubland, grassland and heaths

Lapwings (*Vanellus vanellus*) prefer the open country but can be seen on mudflats, marshes and in meadows; the reserve at Cley and the coast around Holkham are good spots to search them out. These medium-sized waders, which feed on insects and invertebrates close to the surface of ponds or puddles, are also known locally as peewits after their mournful cry. The seemingly black plumage is in fact green and purple, which contrasts with the bird's white underparts. Once killed for food, their eggs used to be collected and sold as delicacies, leading to a decline in numbers. Nowadays resident breeding pairs are less common but large flocks of immigrating birds gather briefly in Norfolk during autumn and winter.

Barn owls (*Tyto alba*) are distinctive, beautifully marked birds that appear totally white but actually have shades of grey, buff and brown on their backs and wings. Seen throughout the year they are most usually spotted hunting along roadsides or ghosting across farmland and coastal fields at dawn and dusk. Holme Dunes is a particularly good spot to look for these birds, which are known in Norfolk as Billywix or hushwing, due to their silent flight. **Short-eared owls** (*Asio flammeus*) are medium-sized owls with mottled brown bodies, paler underparts and yellow eyes. They commonly hunt during the day but are seen most widely during winter when they can be spotted on coastal marshes and wetlands.

❑ What to see when

There's plenty to see whatever the time of year; during **spring** there is an excellent diversity of species, and between April and May you'll enjoy the peak months for spring bird migration. Listen out for nightingales as well as the songs of recently arrived warblers, swifts and wheateaters. Watch the acrobatic displays of breeding marsh harriers and nesting avocets and keep an eye out for stone curlews nesting in the heaths. Passage waders in full plumage are particularly striking, especially the large flocks of Icelandic godwits. Rarer birds often spotted at this time include garganey, osprey, spoonbill, common crane, Mediterranean gull, black tern and wood sandpiper. Large colonies of black-headed gulls gather inland at traditional sites whilst common, sandwich and little terns collect on the coast.

In **summer** the heaths of the Breckland and Thetford Forest conceal nightjars, honey buzzards and hobbies. The coast is home to marsh harriers, bearded tits and avocets, who are at their best at this stage of the year. Terns and bitterns, one of the UK's rarest breeding birds, are also present now and the first Arctic skuas begin to appear. Look out too for raptors including kestrels, sparrowhawks and buzzards.

Autumn begins early and even by late July many of the wading birds have begun to return to the marshes, many still in their breeding plumage. By August the south-bound waders will certainly have arrived on the coast, featuring little stints and curlew sandpipers as well as large numbers of geese and ducks. You may also see rare red-backed shrikes or barred warblers, pied flycatchers, robins, goldcrests and impressive arrivals of starlings. Further inland you'll find woodpeckers, grey partridge, kingfishers, barn and tawny owls. With strong onshore winds come fulmars, gannets, arctic skuas, kittiwakes, sooty shearwaters and occasionally little auks.

Although coldest and with least daylight hours, **winter** offers the best spectacles of the year. The Wash is one of England's most important winter feeding areas for waders and wildfowl. In October, winter thrushes, wild geese and swans arrive; tens of thousands of raucous pink-footed geese, originally from Iceland, quit their night-time roosts to fly inland to feed, the dense flocks of birds forming spectacularly long lines and classic 'V' shapes in the sky. It is calculated that up to 100,000 pink-foots, around 40% of the UK winter population, can be seen on the Norfolk coast at this time. Thousands of wading birds are forced off the mudflats into the air in balletic style as high tide rolls in; this is also when vast wheeling flocks of knot form as they search for somewhere safe to land. Birds of prey also overwinter here; merlin, peregrine, hen harrier and short-eared owls can all be spotted most easily around dusk.

Winter is also a good time enjoy the area's woodland and farmland species, including Egyptian geese, common buzzards, woodcocks, barn owls, grey wagtails and flocks of thrushes, tits and finches.

Stone curlews (*Burhinus oedicnemus*) are easily identifiable by their wailing call, which contributes to its local nickname, the wailing heath chicken. They have brown, black and white plumage that provides perfect camouflage against the sandy heaths where they hide during the day before feeding at night. They have long yellow legs and large yellow eyes which are adapted for night-time foraging. Norfolk is a stronghold for the species, which can be particularly spotted in Breckland.

Yellowhammers (*Emberiza citronella*) are types of bunting that can be seen on commons, heaths and farmland, especially around Breckland. They are typically a vibrant golden colour and have an attractive song said to sound like 'a little bit of bread and no cheese'. **Reed bunting** (*Emberizza scheniclus*) are sparrow-sized, slim birds with long, deeply notched tails and a drooping moustache. They are largely seen on farmland or wetlands. **Snow buntings** (*Plectrophenax nivalis*) are large buntings with predominantly white underparts that contrast with a brown and mottled plumage. They breed all around the Arctic then migrate south in winter, arriving in coastal areas from late September, where they remain till February.

Skylarks (*Alauda arvensis*) are small birds with a streaky brown back and white underparts lined with dark brown. Often seen in open country such as grazing marshes, coastal dunes and heaths, they are often spotted and heard at Cley and Holme Dunes, when their melodic, seemingly endless song rings out from late winter to midsummer. In winter they form small flocks and descend on coastal salt-marshes.

Linnets (*Carduelis cannabina*) are reasonably common, slim finches with forked tails and red breasts. Their distinctive twittering call can be heard on heaths and commons, especially in Breckland and on the coast. They are seed-eaters and feed on grains, grass and wildflower seeds, often collecting in flocks to forage in fields or coastal marshes. **Twites** (*Carduelis flavirostris*) look similar to linnet but have brighter, yellowish bills that stand out in contrast to the dark feathers of their heads. They breed on moorland and stony areas near to the sea but over-winter on salt-marshes and shorelines, or continue across the North Sea to the Low Countries.

Grey partridges (*Perdix perdix*) often crop up on farmland or grasslands, especially in West Norfolk, when you can most easily spot them during autumn

❑ Reserves

- **Holme Bird Observatory and Reserve** (see p122) Managed by the Norfolk Ornithologists Association (see p55), this five-hectare patch of pine- and scrub-covered dunes is ideal for migrating thrushes, warblers and finches. Admission is £3 for non-members, under 16s are free.
- **Holkham National Nature Reserve** (see p148) Managed by Natural England (🖳 www.holkham.co.uk/naturereserve), this vast 4000-hectare (9580 acres) stretch between Burnham Norton and Blakeney offers fantastic diversity of habitat. Seasonal charges apply.
- **Blakeney National Nature Reserve** (see p160) Overseen by the National Trust, highlights include Stiffkey Marshes and Blakeney Point, where you can see vast numbers of birds congregating. There is an information centre at Morston Quay. Free entry.
- **Cley Marshes Reserve** (see p164) Founded in 1926 this is Wildlife Trust's oldest bird reserve in England, with boardwalks and hides close to the pools and roost sites. It is run by Norfolk Wildlife Trust and there is an excellent, modern information centre. Entry costs £3.75 for non members, children are free.
- **Snettisham RSPB Reserve** (see p118) Overlooking the Wash, there are bird hides with excellent views out over the islands, ideal for spotting waders and wildfowl. Free entry.

scavenging on ploughed or stubble fields. Plump with short legs and orangey-brown feathers, they spend the majority of their time on the ground. **Red-legged partridges** (*Alectoris ruta*) are larger than greys, have large white chin and throat patches bordered with black. They have greyish bodies and bold black flank stripes. Introduced to the UK from Europe they are now seen year-round in England especially in the east, usually in groups and open fields.

Nightjars (*Caprimulgas europaeus*) are summer visitors from Europe, which inhabit open heathland and moorland in close proximity to small stands of trees that provide roosting sites. They can sometimes be seen in Breckland. Largely nocturnal, they commence their feeding and courtship activities at dusk. This allied to their clever camouflage and tendency to hide in thick cover makes them difficult to see. Their song is very distinctive though and their strange churring song, like a chainsaw, can be heard ringing out over the copse at dusk.

Woodland

Buzzards (*Buteo buteo*) are the commonest bird of prey in the UK and can be seen soaring over farmland, moorland and more arable areas. They are quite large with broad rounded wings and a short neck and tail. Whilst gliding and soaring they hold their wings in a shallow 'V'. **Kestrel** (*Falco tinnunculus*) are another common sight, frequently seen hovering beside roadside verges or above heath and moorland. They have pointed wings and a long tail. Highly adaptable, they have adjusted to life in man-made environments and can be seen in a wide variety of habitats other than dense forests or treeless wetlands.

Hobbies (*falco subbuteo*) are about the same size as a kestrel with long pointed wings similar to a giant swift. The hobby has a similar dashing flight to a swift as well and will chase large insects and small birds, catching prey in its talons in flight. It arrives in the UK from April onwards and is most commonly seen hunting over woodland edges and heathlands until it departs again in September and October. **Sparrowhawks** (*Accipiter nisus*) have slate grey backs and white underparts, lined with orange. They are widespread and are identifiable from similar-sized raptors as they never hover like kestrels.

The **rook** (*Corvus frugilegus*) has all-black plumage and a bare, greyish face. They are sociable birds and are usually seen in flocks in open fields. Similar looking is the **crow** (*Corvus corone*), which is identifiable as it has a stockier beak and is more solitary, seen usually alone or in pairs.

As well as assorted **thrushes**, **tits** and **starlings** look out for **bullfinches** (*Pyrrhula pyrrhula*), which are easily identifiable by their red underparts and black cap. Often spotted in churchyards, tall hedgerows and woodlands including young forestry plantations, they establish territories in March and often pair for life.

Wetlands and marshes

The brilliantly camouflaged **bittern** (*Botaurus stellaris*) has warm brown plumage streaked with black markings, which make it difficult to spot in its favoured reed-bed habitat. Sightings of this elusive year-round resident are few and far between; you're more likely to hear the males' distinctive booming call, which carries for up to two kilometres, during the breeding season, March to June. Members of the heron family, they have long legs, a long neck, dagger-like beak and broad, rounded wings. Rarely seen far from reed-beds, they favour wetlands with extensive cover. For the best chance to spot one head to Cley or Titchwell Marshes, particularly in winter when their numbers are boosted by wintering bitterns from abroad. A one-time favourite with taxidermists and egg collectors, the bittern, known locally as a butterbump, was also persecuted and hunted for food.

Bearded tits (*Panurus biarmicus*) are bright, lively characters found in reed-beds. They have warm brown plumage and distinctive long, trailing tail feathers. The males also have blue-grey heads and black moustache-like markings. **Reed warblers** (*Acrocephalus scirpaceus*) are plain, unstreaked warblers with brown feathers and buff-coloured underparts. They are summer visitors to the UK with the largest concentrations descending on Norfolk in mid-April, where they concentrate in reed-beds. **Sedge warblers** (*Acrocephalus schoenobaenus*) are small, plump warblers with striking creamy stripes above each eye that arrive all across Norfolk in summer; the best spots to see them though are reed-beds or damp wetlands. They can be differentiated from reed warblers by their long, rambling warble as opposed to the more rhythmic call of the reed warbler.

There are significant breeding colonies of **common terns** (*Stirna hirundo*), which arrive in April and leave in August and September. These silvery-grey and white birds boast long tails that have led to them being nicknamed 'sea swallows'. They breed along the coast on shingle shores, where they collect in noisy groups and can be seen in graceful flight before plunging down into the water to fish. The breeding colony of **sandwich terns** (*Sterna sandvicensis*) at Scolt Head and Blakeney is also of international importance. They have black caps, short black legs and long, dark bills with a yellow tip. They arrive in late March and stay till September. **Little terns** (*Sterna albifrons*) are Britain's smallest tern. They are short-tailed and have a yellow bill with a black tip. They are fast and agile and have an acrobatic courtship display that involves the male carrying a fish and calling to a prospective mate who chases him high before he glides back down with his wings spread into a marked 'V'. The largest breeding colonies are found at Blakeney Point.

Dunlin (*Calidris alpine*) are the commonest small waders seen on the coast, when their flocks can sometimes number thousands. They roost in nearby fields and salt-marshes when the tide is high. They have dark underparts and a slightly down-curved bill. **Redshank** (*Tringa totanus*) are medium-sized waders with long red legs, grey feathers and white underparts, and a long straight bill. It is widespread and can be seen all along the coast, where its numbers are swelled by migrants from Iceland. Unfortunately the overgrazing of farmland and the draining of coastal marshes has reduced the number of suitable breeding habitats outside of nature reserves.

Oystercatchers (*Haematopus ostralegus*) are large, stocky waders with red-pink legs, black and white feathers and a long orange-red bill used for probing the ground. They are common on coastal stretches and around large estuaries, where they forage for mussels and cockles. In winter their numbers are swelled by migrants from Norway and their shrill calls become quite a cacophony. **Knot** (*Calidris canuta*) are dumpy, short-legged, stocky wading birds with grey feathers and white underparts. They form huge flocks in winter which wheel and turn in flight flashing their pale underwings as they twist and turn. They use UK estuaries as feeding grounds during the winter, with large numbers arriving on the Wash and coastal stretches around Holme from their Arctic breeding grounds in late August.

Woodcock (*Scolopax rusticola*) are large, bulky wading birds with short legs and a very long tapering bill. They are mostly nocturnal and spend daylight hours hidden in dense cover, making them difficult to see. **Bar-tailed godwits** (*Limosa lapponica*) are long-legged wading birds with long, pinkish bills usually seen in their winter plumage of grey-brown feathers when they visit the UK from Scandinavia and Siberia. Huge flocks arrive in the UK between November and February either to over-winter or as they pass through on the way south. **Sanderlings** (*Calidris Alba*) are small, plump waders with pale grey feathers, white underparts and a short straight bill. They don't breed in the UK either but visit during winter from the high Arctic to roost on the long sandy beaches.

Gannets (*Morus bassanus*) are large birds that have long pointed, white wings with black tips, a long neck and a pointed beak. They can be seen wheeling above the water before flying high and circling before plunging into the sea to grab a fish. **Fulmars** (*Fulmarus glacialis*) are grey and white, gull-like birds related to the albatross that are usually seen flying low over the sea. The medium-sized, dark-feathered **Arctic skua** (*Stercorarius parasiticus*) passes through the region in August and September. They are aggressive and will pursue terns to steal the food they have collected.

Wigeon (*Anas penelope*) are medium-sized ducks with round chestnut-coloured heads and small bills. Large numbers winter on the coast, when migrants from Iceland, Scandinavia and Russia add to the flock. **Teal** (*Anas crecca*) are attractive, small dabbling ducks with chestnut-coloured heads, dark green eye patches, spotted chests, grey flanks and black-edged tails. During the breeding months they congregate on northern moors before gathering on low-lying wetlands in winter, where they are joined by large numbers of continental birds from the Baltic and Siberia.

Garganey (*Anas querquedula*) are similar in size to teal but have more obvious pale eye stripes. They are also scarcer and more secretive. They migrate to Africa during the autumn but return to the reed-beds and shallow wetlands in March, where they flock to areas with plenty of flooded vegetation, making them difficult to see.

Goldeneye (*Bucephala clangula*) are medium-sized diving ducks. They have black and white feathers and either green or brown heads depending on their sex. They can be most readily be seen in winter along the coast. **Gadwalls** (*Anas strepera*) are grey-coloured dabbling ducks with a much darker rear.

They can be seen in coastal wetlands where there are small numbers of breeding birds making these nationally important populations.

The **common crane** (*Grus grus*) was once quite common in wetlands across East Anglia but it has suffered considerably due to habitat destruction and hunting. One of Europe's largest birds it has a grey body and black wing plumes making it appear to have a bushy tail. Its deep sonorous call can be heard several miles away.

Little egrets (*Egretta garzetta*) are a type of small heron with white feathers, long black legs and yellow feet. They feed by walking through water in search of small fish and crustaceans, but roost in trees, especially around Holkham and Titchwell, and are reasonably common along the north coast.

Kingfishers (*Alcedo atthis*) can be found on many of Norfolk's rivers. They can appear blue, green or almost black and have a very characteristic shape. Populations are restricted by the lack of suitable breeding sites, with the birds needing areas with plentiful supplies of fish and rivers with vertical sandy banks to nest in. Numbers in Norfolk have increased slightly over recent years as a result of the milder winters.

Marsh harriers (*Circus aeruginosus*), as the name implies, are usually found hunting above reed-beds and grazing marshes. Increasingly though they nest inland in arable land. They are the commonest, largest and broadest-winged harrier in Norfolk, with dark brown or rich rust feathers. They have a sharp yelping call and can be seen or heard at Cley or Titchwell Marshes year-round. At one time they were sufficiently widespread and common for ornithologists to dub them the Norfolk hawk, but following persecution and habitat loss their numbers dwindled. Since then successful conservation programmes have seen them re-establish themselves. **Hen harriers** (*Circus cyaneus*), which have pale grey feathers, visit Norfolk in small numbers during late autumn and winter but don't breed here and **Montagu's harriers** (*Circus pygargus*) are summer visitors, arriving in April and departing during early autumn. They are extremely rare breeding birds in the UK, which seem to increasingly frequent arable land rather than coastal marshes.

Pink-footed geese (*Anser brachyrhynchus*) are medium-sized geese that winter on freshwater and salt-marshes, arriving in vast flocks from their breeding grounds in Spitsbergen, Iceland and Greenland in October. They can also be seen feeding on stubble and crop fields, where they are identifiable by their short neck, small head and stubby bill. Don't rely on the pink feet as an identifier as **greylags** (*Anser anser*) also have pink legs and juvenile pink-footed geese have dull orange legs. Greylags are the largest and bulkiest of the wild geese native to the UK. They can be seen easily and often in large flocks in lowland areas.

Colour section (following pages)
(Opposite) The marshland beside Cley next the Sea (**top**, see p164) attracts many species of bird and part of this area now makes up the Cley Marshes Reserve (see p60). Some of the birds which may be seen here include (**clockwise from bottom left**) dunlin, avocet, marsh harrier, skylark, bearded tit (juvenile) and lapwing. (Bird photos © Derek Moore).

ABOVE (clockwise from bottom left): **knot**, **wood sandpiper**, **sandwich tern**, **oystercatcher**, **linnet**, **redshank** (all © Derek Moore), **common crane** (© Roderick Leslie).

ABOVE (clockwise from bottom left): **greylag goose**, **snow bunting**, **red-backed shrike**, **bullfinch**, **pink-footed geese**, **teal** (all photos © Derek Moore).

Gorse
Ulex europaeus

Meadow Buttercup
Ranunculis acris

Honeysuckle
Lonicera periclymemum

Tormentil
Potentilla erecta

Birdsfoot-trefoil
Lotus corniculatus

Scarlet Pimpernel
Anagallis arvensis

Common Ragwort
Senecio jacobaea

Primrose
Primula vulgaris

Cowslip
Primula veris

Ramsons (Wild Garlic)
Allium ursinum

Hogweed
Heracleum sphondylium

Yarrow
Achillea millefolium

Dog Rose
Rosa canina

Common Hawthorn
Crataegus monogyna

Germander Speedwell
Veronica chamaedrys

Self-heal
Prunella vulgaris

Silverweed
Potentilla anserina

Common Dog Violet
Viola riviniana

Sea Campion
Silene maritima

Sea Holly
Eringium maritimum

Thrift (Sea Pink)
Armeria maritima

Rowan (tree)
Sorbus aucuparia

Herb-Robert
Geranium robertianum

Red Campion
Silene dioica

Bluebell
Hyacinthoides non-scripta

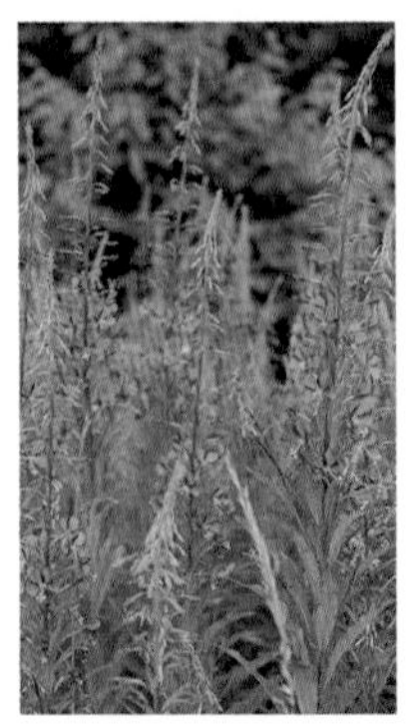

Rosebay Willowherb
Epilobium angustifolium

Foxglove
Digitalis purpurea

Egyptian geese (*Alopochen aegyptiacus*) are a similar size but have brown and pink-buff plumage and a distinctive black eye patch. They breed in open woodlands but winter on lakes and marshes. **Brent geese** (*Branta bernicla*) are small, dark geese with black heads, grey-brown backs and dark underparts. They fly in loose flocks and gather on salt-marshes in October, where they over winter until March. **White-fronted geese** (*Anser albifrons*) are actually grey, with a large white patch at the front of their head around the beak. They have orange legs and either pink or orange bills. They do not breed in the UK but migrate here during winter to escape the colder climate in Greenland and Siberia.

Avocets (*Recurvirostra avosetta*) have mostly white plumage, marked with thin black lines, blue legs and an upturned bill which they sweep from side to side through the water when feeding. They breed in shallow lagoons and often near estuaries. They are the symbol of the RSPB and representative of the bird-protection programme in Britain; their return to the UK in the 1940s and successful increase in numbers is indicative of what can be achieved.

FLOWERS

Many wildflowers have declined in parts of Norfolk as a result of habitat destruction. With grasslands and heaths ploughed up, flower-filled meadows have given way to arable crops. Elsewhere, the introduction of pesticides and toxins to kill weeds has reduced the successfulness with which plants pollinate.

The coast

Rock samphire (*Crithmum maritimum*) is a succulent plant found on beaches and growing in salt-marshes, which is more commonly known as sea asparagus. The term is thought to be a corruption of the plant's French name *herbe de Saint-Pierre*. Samphire is edible and usually steamed and then coated in butter (see box p17). Shakespeare referred to the dangerous practice of collecting rock samphire from the cliffs in the 17th century, writing in *King Lear*, 'Half-way down, Hangs one that gathers samphire; dreadful trade!' **Marsh samphire** (*Salicornia europaea*) is a different species, but is frequently confused with its namesake. Its jointed green stems, which turn red in autumn, are also edible.

Sea lavender (*Limonium vulgare*) is an attractive plant that thrives in salt-marshes and muddy saline pools. It is particularly prevalent at Titchwell and on Scolt Head Island. It has oval erect leaves and blue-purple flower clusters that give the plant its name; it is not related to true lavender though and does not have its distinctive smell. Nonetheless it is popular with insects, butterflies and bees in particular. **Sea aster** (*Aster tripolium*) is another native of salt -marshes. It has long fleshy leaves and loose flowerheads that resemble daisies in shades of blue, white or yellow.

Sea holly (*Eryngium maritimum*) is an attractive coastal plant found in dune systems and along shingle sections of the coast. It has blue-green spiky leaves and powder-blue flowers that bloom between June and September in cone-like clusters. Up to the end of the 19th century the roots were dug up and candied for use as a sweet treat and aphrodisiac, a practice that had a significant effect on the plant's distribution and from which it is only now recovering.

Sea campion (*Silene maritima*) is a clump-forming plant found on coastal cliffs and shingle, especially on Blakeney Point. In spring the young shoots form a compact cushion of leaves, from which emerge masses of white flowers with distinctive inflated calyces. **Thrift** (*Armeria maritima*) is a compact perennial that grows in low clumps and sends up long stems from which profusions of pink flowers blossom. It is common in marshes and along the coast.

Yellow horned-poppy (*Glaucium flavum*) grows on shingle banks and beaches and can most readily be seen between Blakeney and Weybourne or on Scolt Head Island, where its rosettes of grey-green, waxy leaves and bright yellow flowers, which bloom between June and September, stand out against the stones. Under threat due to declining habitat it is a protected species and must not be picked from the wild. **Bird's-foot-trefoil** (*Lotus corniculatus*) is an attractive trailing plant with yellow pea-like flowers that can be seen in grassy areas. It has easily recognisable seed pods, shaped like a bird's foot, which give it its name. **Alexanders** (*Smyrnium olusatrum*) is a tall plant (up to 1.5m high) with bright green, glossy leaves and yellow-green, umbrella-shaped flower heads, which appear from March to June. Introduced to Britain by the Romans as a food plant, Alexanders was once found only along the coast. With increasingly mild winters the plant has spread inland though and is now common in hedgerows and roadside verges.

Woodland and hedgerows

Bluebell (*Hyacinthoides non-scripta*) flowers are deep purple-blue and very attractive. Growing in light shade they are often found in patches of hundreds or thousands and, when in flower from mid-April to late May, form a carpet of colour. **Japanese knotweed** (*Fallopia japonica*) is a highly vigorous, invasive plant introduced to the UK from Japan. Growing up to 3m tall, it has fleshy red and green stems that look like bamboo, and small creamy white flowers and can be seen in hedgerows where there is a decent water supply. **Mistletoe** (*Viscum album*) forms rounded clumps often high in a tree canopy, where it can be identified by the white, semi-transparent berries visible between December and February. Although not common in Norfolk it can be seen in lime trees, but also appears in hawthorn and willow.

Other flowering plants to look for include **foxgloves** (*Digitalis purpurea*) with its trumpet-like flowers, **forget-me-not** (*Myosotis arvensis*) with tiny, delicate blue flowers and **cow parsley** (*Anthriscus sylvestris*), a tall plant with a large globe of white flowers.

Heathland and scrub

Bee orchids (*Ophrys apifera*) have a distinctive flower consisting of three pink 'wings' and a central hairy brown 'bee' body patterned with yellow spots and lines – the flowers look as if at the centre of the three petals a small bee is sucking nectar, an illusion designed to attract other bees. The flowers, which appear between May and July, project outwards from a spike that varies in height from just 5cm to more than 30cm. Notoriously unpredictable, bee orchids can be found on areas of grassland and coastal sand dunes or scrub.

The **common poppy** (*Papaver rhoeas*) is found throughout Norfolk on embankments, roadside verges, farmland and gardens. The translucent, papery-petalled scarlet flowers and pepper-pot seed capsules are highly distinctive, particularly when in bloom from June to August. The stretch of coast between Sheringham, Cromer and Overstrand is known as Poppyland, a name first given to the area by the writer Clement Scott in the 1880s. Today the common poppy has been voted the county flower for Norfolk. **Cowslip** (*Primula veris*), recognisable by its nodding yellow flowers hanging downwards in loose groups, grows in hedgerows, grassy verges and churchyards. Once picked for May Day celebrations and used to make cowslip wine and herbal infusions, the flower is in decline.

Giant hogweed (*Heracleum mantegazzianum*) can stand up to 5m tall. Introduced from Asia as an ornamental plant, it has run riot and out-competes native species. It has hollow, green stems with reddish blotches and jagged leaves arranged in a rosette around the stem. The stems, edges and undersides of the leaves have small hairs which contain poisonous sap that can cause skin irritation, blistering and sensitivity to the sun.

Another plant introduced as a garden ornamental but which has spread across the county is **Himalayan balsam** (*Impatiens glandulifera*), identifiable by its hollow, jointed pinkish-red stems and fragrant purple-pink slipper-shaped flowers. Growing in dense stands up to 3m in height, it suffocates competing plants.

Harebell (*Campanula rotundifolia*) is easily spotted due to its delicate, bell-shaped, blue flowers suspended from thin, wiry flower stems. Plants usually grow in clumps and are common in parts of Breckland (see p50) where they form blue splashes of colour whilst in bloom from late summer to early autumn. **Meadow saxifrage** (*Saxifraga granulata*) has white, five-petalled flowers that flower between April and June. Declining nationally, it is still prevalent in Eastern England and relatively widespread in Norfolk, where it is found in patches of well-drained soil.

Water mint (*Mentha aquatica*) grows in wet habitats such as wetland nature reserves. The flowers vary from mauve-purple to pink, lilac or blue although it is the distinctive minty aroma when crushed underfoot that often first draws attention to this species.

TREES

At one stage Norfolk used to be covered with forest. Sadly this is no longer the case. In the course of the trek, what forest there still is, is largely encountered along the Peddars Way, either as you start the trail on the wooded Suffolk–Norfolk border or progress north across a landscape dotted with plantations. The windswept northern coast is more barren but the beaches are also often backed by stands of trees.

None of the woodland can be described as completely natural and it has all been managed or altered in some way by man. In the past Neolithic communities stripped the countryside here to dig for flint; this left the countryside denuded. Heavy grazing exacerbated the deterioration of the soil, until the deliberate planting of trees again was the only way to bind the soil and prevent it from worsening further. This policy continues today and many of the clusters of woodland are in fact plantations.

Predominant tree species

Ash (*Fraxinus excelsior*) is widespread in Norfolk. The typical grey bark is smooth at first before developing ridges. The black buds in winter and early spring are also distinctive. The woods around Watton, allegedly the site of the *Babes in the Wood* legend, contain a number of impressive ash trees. Substantial, smooth-silvery-grey **beech** (*Fagus Sylvatica*) trees, which often develop strong domed canopies, can also be seen throughout the county. Some experts actually hold that Norfolk is the northern limit for native beech trees. Felbrigg Hall (see p175) has a particularly attractive beech woodland adjacent to it. The woodland there also boasts a number of magnificent, ancient **sweet chestnut** (*Castanea sativa*) trees, whose large oval leaves darken with age from pale green to a rich gold in autumn.

The **common oak** (*Quercus robura*) is widespread and easily identifiable by its distinctive leaves and acorns. Two species of willow, **white willow** (*Salix alba*) and **crack willow** (*Salix fragilis*), also appear throughout Norfolk, and thrive next to waterways. Catkins in March and April provide an early source of nectar for visiting birds and insects.

Hawthorn (*Crataegus monogyna*) is the most common small tree in Norfolk due in part to its use in roadside and farmland hedging. The trees are most apparent in spring when fragrant white blossom bursts forth during April and May. The red, oblong fruit, or haw, produced in autumn is popular with migrating birds, and trees on the coast can often seem alive with migrating thrushes and warblers during October as they feed on the fleshy fruit before moving south. Less widespread is the **common lime** (*Tilia vulgaris*) which can be distinguished by its red twigs and smooth, purplish grey bark. It is commonly found in parks and gardens, including those at Houghton Hall (see box p112).

REPTILES

Britain's two snake species are found in Norfolk. **Adders** (*Vipera berus*), Britain's only poisonous snake, can occasionally be seen on open heathland and the edges of woodland although their natural habitat is under threat. Identifiable by the bold dark zig-zag stripe down the back, adders come in a range of colours; the male is grey to white whilst the female is brown or copper coloured. During colder months they are inactive and hibernate but in spring they emerge to shed their skins and mate. The young are born in late August. More often than not adders move swiftly out of the way when disturbed but should you inadvertently step on one and get bitten, sit still and send someone else for help. The bite is unlikely to be fatal – it is designed to kill small mammals, not humans – but it does still warrant attention.

The **grass snake** (*Natrix natrix*) lives on open heathland, meadows and fens, often close to water. They are longer and slimmer than the adder, and are non-venomous although will emit a foul stench if you try to pick them up. Body colour varies from green to grey or brown although the most common characteristic is a yellow or orange collar immediately behind the head. Although it looks like a snake, the **slow worm** (*Anguis fragilis*) is actually a legless lizard and differs from snakes in that it has a cylindrical grey-brown body that does not taper at the neck. It can be found on dry grassy meadows, woodland margins and churchyards.

You may also hear or come across the **common frog** (*Rana temporaria*), which frequents woodlands, hedgerows and fields where there is plenty of water. Despite its name, numbers are declining due to the large number of predators including foxes, otters, herons and bitterns that hunt it. The **common toad** (*Bufo bufo*), identifiable from the frog by its warty skin and tendency to walk rather than jump, is relatively widespread whilst the **natterjack toad** (*Bufo calamita*), which has a bright yellow stripe running down its back, is restricted to a handful of coastal sand dune and salt-marsh sites such as the Norfolk Wildlife Trust reserve (see p134) at Holme.

MAMMALS

Badgers (*Meles meles*) are readily identifiable with their black-and-white-striped heads, short legs and broad, thickset bodies. Their distribution across Norfolk is unknown but there is plenty of evidence to indicate they are resident in reasonable numbers. Dawn and dusk are the best times to spot these elusive creatures, which live in family groups in underground 'setts'. The highly adaptable **red fox** (*Vulpus vulpus*) is the size of a small dog and has a warm reddish-brown coat and white underside as well as a white-tipped bushy tail. Opportunistic feeders, they tend to hunt at night but are not exclusively nocturnal, and eat a range of food and will scavenge from rubbish.

The seemingly ubiquitous **rabbit** (Oryctolagus cuniculus) can be seen on heaths and commons, where well-drained soils are ideal for their warrens. **Harvest mice** (*Micromys minutus*) are widespread in suitable tussocky grassland. Elusive and hard to see, they have orange-brown upperparts and white underparts, a blunt muzzle and a prehensile tail that can be twisted around plant stems to improve balance and help them climb.

Shy and elusive, **otters** (*Lutra lutra*) are mainly nocturnal so difficult to see. Often over a metre in length, they have a broad head and muzzle, small ears and a long tail. They prefer shallow water with plenty of fish and can be spotted in many of Norfolk's rivers including the Nar. **Stoats** (*Mustela erminea*) have long slim bodies with red-brown fur and creamy undersides, and short legs. Found throughout Norfolk they can be spotted year-round as they do not hibernate. Almost as common are **weasels** (*Mustela nivalis*) which are similarly coloured but slightly smaller. They are tunnel-hunters and mostly prey on rodents. Look out too for various species of **voles**, **mice** and **shrews**. The **common pipistrelle bat** (*Pipistrellus pipistrellus*) is Britain's smallest bat and its most common. Found feeding over open water, woodland and along hedgerows, they are often spotted on Thompson Common.

Roe deer (*Capreolus capreolus*) are small, native deer that tend to shelter in woodland. They can sometimes be seen alone or in pairs on the edges of fields or clearings in the forest, but you are more likely to hear the sharp dog-like bark they use as an alarm call upon detecting your presence.

The diminutive **Chinese water deer** (*Hydropotes inermis*) stands little taller than a medium-sized dog. They have large rounded ears that stand proud above the head. The males are identifiable by the tusks they grow instead of antlers. These are in fact modified teeth and are used for fighting during territorial disputes. They are common in the Broads and make the most of tall, wet vegetation to remain concealed. Beyond this there are sightings along the coast and in river valleys. **Muntjac** (*Muntiacus reevesi*), which also originate in China, are the smallest deer in Britain, standing only 45cm high at the shoulder and can be seen in coniferous woodland and scrub throughout Norfolk. Generally brown, they are slightly hunched as the hind limbs are longer than the fore. Males have short, straight horns as well as large protruding canine teeth. They are nicknamed the barking deer because of their loud, barking call.

The coast is also home to several marine mammals. **Harbour porpoises** (*Phocoena phocoena*) are the smallest cetaceans found in the UK and rarely reach 2m in length. Preferring shallow coastal waters, the porpoises are hardly ever seen from shore but can be spotted when out on the water, when their small triangular dorsal fin and short rounded head with no beak make them identifiable. **Common seals** (*Phoca vitulina*) can be seen on Blakeney Point (see box p160), where there is a permanent breeding colony, which you can visit on foot or on a boat trip from Morston or Blakeney. The seals haul out on the exposed sands at low tide and then move westwards onto the shingle as the tide comes in to ensure they always have access to deep water. There is another population living in The Wash. The seals are brown, tan or grey, with identifiably 'v' shaped nostrils. They also have a proportionally large, rounded head. An adult can grow up to 6ft long and live for 20-30 years. They are gregarious and form good-sized groups, returning to favoured breeding sites. Pups are born during June and July. The largest numbers are seen in August and early September whilst the seals are moulting. **Grey Seals** (*Halichoerus grypus*) share the shingle at Blakeney Point. They are medium-sized seals and are distinguishable from their common counterparts by their straight head profile and wide-spaced nostrils. They also have fewer spots on their bodies. They give birth in November and December, and the adults moult in spring.

MINIMUM IMPACT & OUTDOOR SAFETY

3

Minimum impact walking

In this chaotic world in which people live their lives at an increasingly frenetic pace, many of us living in overcrowded cities and working in jobs that offer little free time, the great outdoors is becoming an essential means of escape. Walking in the countryside is a wonderful means of relaxation and gives people the time to think and rediscover themselves.

Of course as the popularity of the countryside increases so do the problems that this pressure brings. The Peddars Way and Norfolk Coast Path are situated within easy reach of one of the most populated areas of Britain so are particularly vulnerable. Their relative accessibility further adds to their appeal and places more pressure on the land. It is important for visitors to remember that the countryside is the home and workplace of many others. Walkers in particular should be aware of their responsibilities. Indeed a walker who respects and understands the countryside will get far more enjoyment from their trip.

Minimum impact walking is all about a common-sense approach to exploring the countryside, being mindful and respectful of the wildlife and of those who live and work on the land. By following a few simple guidelines while walking the Peddars Way and Norfolk Coast Path, you can have a positive impact not just on your own well-being but also on local communities and the environment, thereby becoming part of the solution. Simple measures such as not dropping litter, keeping dogs on leads and leaving gates as you find them ought to be second nature to anyone who regularly uses the countryside. However, some things are not as well known and thus are worth consideration.

ECONOMIC IMPACT

Support local businesses

Rural businesses and communities in Britain have been hit hard in recent years by a seemingly endless series of crises. In light of the economic pressures that many businesses are under there is something else you can do: buy local.

Look and ask for local produce (see box p17) to buy and eat; Norfolk has a fantastic reputation for home-grown produce and the seafood available on the doorstep is of the highest quality. Not only does this cut down on the amount of pollution and congestion that the transportation of food creates (the so-called 'food miles'), but also ensures that you are supporting local farmers and producers; the very people who have moulded the countryside you have come to see and who are in the best position to protect it. If you can find local food which is also organic so much the better.

It's a fact of life that money spent at local level – perhaps in a market, or at the greengrocer, or in an independent pub – has a far greater impact for good on that community than the equivalent spent in a branch of a national chain store or restaurant. While no-one would advocate that walkers should boycott the larger supermarkets, which after all do provide local employment, it's worth remembering that businesses in rural communities rely heavily on visitors for their very existence. If we want to keep these shops and post offices, we need to use them.

Encourage local cultural traditions and skills

No part of the countryside looks the same. Buildings, food, skills and language evolve out of the landscape and are moulded over hundreds of years to suit the locality. Discovering these cultural differences is part of the pleasure of walking in new places. Visitors' enthusiasm for local traditions and skills brings awareness and pride, nurturing a sense of place; an increasingly important role in a world where economic globalisation continues to undermine the very things that provide security and a feeling of belonging.

ENVIRONMENTAL IMPACT

A walking holiday in itself is an environmentally friendly approach to tourism. The following are some ideas on how you can go a few steps further in helping to minimise your impact on the natural environment while walking the Peddars Way and Norfolk Coast Path.

Use public transport whenever possible

Although there is minimal public transport along the Peddars Way, public transport on the Norfolk coast is good and in the case of the Coasthopper Bus (see p45) specifically geared towards the coast-path walker. By using the local bus you will help to keep the standard of public transport high. Public transport is always preferable to using private cars as it benefits everyone: visitors, locals and the environment.

Never leave litter

Leaving litter shows a total disrespect for the natural world and others coming after you. As well as being unsightly litter kills wildlife, pollutes the environment and can be dangerous to farm animals. Please carry a degradable plastic bag so you can dispose of your rubbish in a bin in the next village. It would be very helpful if you could pick up litter left by other people too.

• **Is it OK if it's biodegradable?** Not really. Apple cores, banana skins, orange peel and the like attract insects and ruin a picnic spot for others. Using the excuse that they are natural and biodegradable just doesn't cut any ice.
• **The lasting impact of litter** A piece of orange peel left on the ground takes six months to decompose; silver foil 18 months; a plastic bag 10 years; clothes 15 years; and an aluminium can 85 years.

Erosion

• **Stay on the main trail** The effect of your footsteps may seem minuscule but when they are multiplied by several thousand walkers each year they become rather more significant. Avoid taking shortcuts, widening the trail or taking more than one path; your boots will be followed by many others.
• **Consider walking out of season** The maximum disturbance by walkers coincides with the time of year when nature wants to do most of its growth and repair. In high-use areas, like that along much of the coast path, the trail never recovers. Walking at less busy times eases this pressure while also generating year-round income for the local economy. Not only that, but it may make the walk a more relaxing experience with fewer people on the path and less competition for accommodation.

Respect all wildlife

Care for all wildlife you come across along the path; it has as much right to be there as you. Tempting as it is to pick wild flowers leave them so the next people who pass can enjoy them too. Don't break branches off or damage trees in any way.

If you come across wildlife keep your distance and don't watch for too long. Your presence can cause considerable stress, particularly if the adults are with young, or in winter when the weather is harsh and food is scarce. Young animals are rarely abandoned. If you come across young birds keep away so that their mother can return. Anyone considering a spot of climbing on the sea cliffs should bear in mind that there are restrictions in certain areas due to the presence of nesting birds. Check with the local tourist information office.

The code of the outdoor loo

'Going' in the outdoors is a lost art worth re-learning, for your sake and everyone else's. As more and more people discover the joys of the outdoors this is becoming an important issue.

In some parts of the world where visitor pressure is higher than in Britain walkers and climbers are required to pack out their excrement. This could soon be necessary here. Human excrement is not only offensive to our senses but, more importantly, can infect water sources.

• **Where to go** Wherever possible **use a toilet**. Public toilets are marked on the trail maps in this guide and you will also find facilities in pubs, cafés and campsites along the coast path.

If you do have to go outdoors choose a site at least **30 metres away from running water**. Carry a small trowel and **dig a small hole** about 15cm (6 inches) deep to bury your excrement in. It decomposes quicker when in contact with the top layer of soil or leaf mould. Use a stick to stir loose soil into your deposit as well as this speeds up decomposition even more. Do not squash it under rocks as this slows down the composting process. If you have to use rocks to cover it make sure they are not in contact with your faeces.

Make sure you do not dig any holes on ground that is, or could be, of historic or archaeological interest.

• **Toilet paper and tampons** Toilet paper takes a long time to decompose whether buried or not. It is easily dug up by animals and may then blow into water sources or onto the path. The best method for dealing with it is to **pack it out**. Put the used paper inside a paper bag which you then place inside a plastic bag (or two). Then simply empty the contents of the paper bag at the next toilet you come across and throw the bag away.

You should also pack out **tampons** and **sanitary towels** in a similar way; they take years to decompose and may also be dug up and scattered about by animals.

Wild camping

Unfortunately, wild camping is not encouraged along either the Peddars Way or Norfolk Coast Path. In any case there are few places where it is a viable option. This is a shame since wild camping is an altogether more fulfilling experience than camping on a designated site. Living in the outdoors without any facilities provides a valuable lesson in simple, sustainable living where the results of all your actions, from going to the loo to washing your plates, can be seen.

If you do insist on wild camping **always** ask the landowner for permission. Anyone contemplating camping on a beach should be very aware of the times and heights of the tide. Follow these suggestions for minimising your impact and encourage others to do likewise.

• **Be discreet** Camp alone or in small groups, spend only one night in each place and pitch your tent late and move off early.

• **Never light a fire** The deep burn caused by camp fires, no matter how small, damages the turf which can take years to recover. Cook on a camp stove instead.

• **Don't use soap or detergent** There is no need to use soap; even biodegradable soaps and detergents pollute streams. You won't be away from a shower for more than a day or so. Wash up without detergent; use a plastic or metal scourer or, failing that, a handful of fine pebbles from the beach or some bracken or grass.

• **Leave no trace** Learn the skill of moving on without leaving any sign of having been there: no moved boulders, ripped up vegetation or drainage ditches. Make a final check of your campsite before departing; pick up litter that you or anyone else has left, thus leaving the place in a better state than you found it.

ACCESS

Britain is a crowded cluster of islands with few places where you can wander as you please; the south-east corner of the country is the most populated area with some of the busiest roads in the country. Most of the land is a patchwork of fields and agricultural land, and the countryside the Peddars Way cuts across is no different. However, there are countless public rights of way, in addition to both this and the coast path, that criss-cross the land. This is fine, but what happens if you feel a little more adventurous and want to explore the beaches, dunes, moorland, woodland and hills that can also be found within the national park boundaries? Most of the land the Peddars Way and Norfolk Coast Path pass through is private land or nature reserve and, unless you are on a right of way, is off limits. However, the 'Right to Roam' legislation (see below) has opened up some previously restricted land to walkers.

Rights of way

As a designated National Trail (see box below) the Peddars Way and Norfolk Coast Path is a public right of way – this is either a footpath, a bridleway or a byway; the route is in fact made up of all three.

Rights of way are theoretically established because the landowner has dedicated them to public use. However, very few rights of way are formally dedicated in this way. If people have been using a path without interference for 20 years or more the law assumes the owner has intended to dedicate it as a right of way. If a path has been unused for 20 years it does not cease to exist; the guiding principle is 'once a highway, always a highway'.

Farmers and land managers must ensure that paths are not blocked by crops or other vegetation, or otherwise obstructed, and the route is identifiable and the surface restored soon after cultivation. If crops are growing over the path you have the right to walk through them, following the line of the right of way as closely as possible. If you find a path or right of way is blocked you should report it to the appropriate authority, Norfolk County Council (see box p53) or the National Trail officer (💻 nationaltrail@norfolk.gov.uk).

Right to roam

In October 2005 the Countryside & Rights of Way Act (CRoW) 2000, or 'Right to Roam' as dubbed by walkers, came into effect after a long campaign to allow

❑ National Trails

The Peddars Way and Norfolk Coast Path is one of 15 National Trails (💻 www.nationaltrail.co.uk) in England and Wales. These are Britain's flagship long-distance paths which grew out of the post-war desire to protect the country's special places, a movement which also gave birth to national parks and AONBs.

National Trails are funded by the government through Natural England with additional contributions from local highway authorities and other partners. The trails are managed on the ground by a National Trail Officer. They co-ordinate the maintenance work undertaken by the local highway authority and landowners to ensure that the trail is kept to nationally agreed standards.

Maintenance of the paths is carried out by the National Trail Officer. Teams of rangers, wardens and volunteers undertake various tasks throughout the year.

Where erosion of the path becomes a problem wooden causeways or steps are constructed and particularly boggy areas are drained by digging ditches. Occasionally the authorities will re-route the path where erosion has become so severe as to be a danger to the walker. During the winter some sections of the path can be swamped by storms, requiring the shingle or sand to be cleared.

greater public access to areas of countryside in England and Wales deemed to be uncultivated open country. This essentially means moorland, heathland, downland and upland areas. It does not mean free access to wander over farmland, woodland or private gardens.

Some land is covered by restrictions (ie high-impact activities such as driving a vehicle, cycling, horse-riding are not permitted) and some land is excluded (such as gardens, parks and cultivated land). Full details are given on the Countryside visitors page on 💻 www.naturalengland.org.uk.

With more freedom in the countryside comes a need for more responsibility from the walker. Remember that wild open country is still the workplace of farmers and home to all sorts of wildlife. Have respect for both and avoid disturbing domestic and wild animals.

The Countryside Code

This all seems like common sense but sadly some people still seem to have no understanding of how to treat the countryside they walk in. The Countryside Code (see box) was revised and relaunched in 2004, partly because of the changes brought about by the CRoW Act (see p75). Below is an expanded version of the new Code launched under the logo 'Respect, Protect, Enjoy'.

> **❑ The Countryside Code**
> - Be safe – plan ahead and follow any signs
> - Leave gates and property as you find them
> - Protect plants and animals and take your litter home
> - Keep dogs under close control
> - Consider other people

- **Be safe** You're responsible for your own safety so follow the simple guidelines outlined on pp77-80.
- **Take your litter home** 'Pack it in, pack it out'. Litter is not only ugly but can be harmful to wildlife; small mammals often become trapped in discarded cans and bottles. Many walkers think that orange peel and banana skins don't count as litter. Even biodegradable foodstuffs attract common scavenging species such as crows and gulls to the detriment of less-dominant species. Carry a plastic bag to put yours and other people's litter and food scraps in and take it home or find a bin. See p72.
- **Keep your dog under close control** The only place you can safely allow your dog off the lead is along the beaches but there are restrictions in the summer (see p22). Across farmland dogs should be kept on a short lead at all times but this is essential between 1 March and 31 July on most areas of open country and common land. If a farm animal starts to chase you/your dog let your dog off the lead. Also take care that your dog does not disturb birds nesting on the ground, or other wildlife. During lambing time (mid March to mid May) they should not be taken with you at all.
- **Enjoy the countryside and respect its life and work** Access to the countryside depends on being sensitive to the needs and wishes of those who live and work there. Being courteous and friendly to those you meet will ensure a healthy future for all based on partnership and co-operation.
- **Guard against all risk of fire** Accidental fire is a great fear of farmers and

foresters. Never make a camp fire and take matches and cigarette butts out with you to dispose of safely.

- **Keep to paths across farmland** Stick to the official path across arable or pasture land. Minimise erosion by not cutting corners or widening the path.
- **Leave all gates as you find them** Normally a farmer leaves gates closed to keep livestock in but may sometimes leave them open to allow livestock access to food or water.
- **Leave livestock, crops and machinery alone** Help farmers by not interfering with their means of livelihood.
- **Help keep all water clean** Leaving litter and going to the toilet near a water source can pollute people's water supplies. For information on going to the toilet in the outdoors see p73-4.
- **Protect wildlife, plants and trees** Respect all wildlife you come across. Don't pick plants, break trees or scare wild animals. If you come across young birds that appear to have been abandoned leave them alone. If you visit any of the islands always stick to the designated paths to avoid disturbing nesting seabirds.
- **Take special care on country roads** Cars travel dangerously fast on narrow winding lanes. To be safe walk facing the oncoming traffic and carry a torch or wear highly visible clothing when it's getting dark.
- **Make no unnecessary noise** Enjoy the peace and solitude of the outdoors by staying in small groups and acting unobtrusively.

Outdoor safety

AVOIDANCE OF HAZARDS

With good planning and preparation most hazards can be avoided. This information is just as important for those out on a day walk as for those walking the entire coast path.

Ensure you have suitable **clothes** (see pp37-8) to keep you warm and dry whatever the conditions and a spare change of inner clothes. A compass, whistle, torch and first-aid kit should be carried and are discussed on p38. The **emergency signal** is six blasts on the whistle or six flashes with a torch. A **mobile phone** may also be useful.

Take plenty of **food** with you for the day and at least one litre of **water** although more would be better, especially on the long northern stretches of the Peddars Way. It is a good idea to fill up your bottle whenever you pass through a village since stream water cannot be relied upon. You will eat far more walking than you do normally so make sure you have enough food for the day, as well as some high-energy snacks (chocolate, dried fruit, biscuits) in the bottom of your pack for an emergency.

Stay alert and know exactly where you are throughout the day. The easiest way to do this is to **check your position regularly** on the map. If visibility suddenly decreases with mist and cloud, or there is an accident, you will be able to make a sensible decision about what action to take based on your location.

If you choose to walk alone you must appreciate and be prepared for the increased risk. It's a good idea to leave word with someone about where you are going and remember to contact them when you have arrived safely.

Safety on the Peddars Way and Norfolk Coast Path

Although the Peddars Way and Norfolk Coast Path are both ostensibly fairly easy routes, through gentle terrain, there is always the potential for an accident to happen. Do not become complacent or underestimate the route and the terrain just because it seems straightforward.

Always err on the side of over-caution and think twice about walking if you are tired or feeling ill. This is when most accidents happen. To ensure you have a safe trip it is well worth following this advice:

- Keep to the path – avoid walking on the marshes or muddy inlets at low tide
- Avoid walking in windy weather – the coast can be very exposed
- Wear strong sturdy boots with good ankle support and a good grip rather than trainers or sandals
- Be extra vigilant with children
- Keep dogs under close control
- Wear or carry warm and waterproof clothing
- In an emergency dial ☎ 999 and ask for the police, ambulance or coastguard.

Safety on the beach

Norfolk's beaches are spectacular in any weather but it's when the sun is shining that the sweaty walker gets the urge to take a dip. The sea can be a dangerous environment and care should be taken if you do go for a swim and even if you're just walking along the beach. Follow this common-sense advice:

- If tempted to take a shortcut across a beach be aware of the tides to avoid being cut off or stranded
- Do not sit directly below cliffs and do not climb them unless you are an experienced climber with the right equipment, or with someone who has experience
- Don't swim immediately after eating, or after drinking alcohol; swimming in itself can be dangerous
- Be aware of local tides and currents – don't assume it is safe just because other people are swimming there; if in doubt consult the tide tables (see opposite) or check with the nearest tourist information centre
- Be extra vigilant with children
- In an emergency dial ☎ 999 and ask for the coastguard.

DEALING WITH AN ACCIDENT

- Use basic first aid to treat the injury to the best of your ability.
- Work out exactly where you are. If possible leave someone with the casualty while others go to get help. If there are only two people, you have a dilemma. If you decide to get help leave all spare clothing and food with the casualty.

- Telephone ☎ 999 and ask for the police, ambulance or coastguard. They will assist in both offshore and onshore incidents.

TIDE TABLES

Tide tables are available from newsagents in the area. You can also get them from tourist information centres along the coast.

WEATHER FORECASTS

The Norfolk coast is exposed to whatever the North Sea can throw at it. Even when it's sunny, sea breezes usually develop during the course of the day so it's worth taking weather forecasts with a pinch of salt. A warm day can feel bitterly cold when you stop for lunch on a cliff top being battered by the wind. Try to get the local weather forecast from the newspaper, TV or radio, or one of the internet/telephone forecasts before you set off. Alter your plans for the day accordingly.

Internet/telephone forecasts

Weather call (💻 www.weathercall.co.uk; ☎ 09068-500408 for Norfolk and Suffolk) provides frequently updated and generally reliable weather forecasts. However, calls are charged at the expensive premium rate. For detailed online weather forecasts, including local five-day forecasts, check out 💻 www.bbc.co.uk/weather or 💻 www.metoffice.gov.uk.

BLISTERS

It is important to break in new boots before embarking on a long walk. Make sure the boots are comfortable and try to avoid getting them wet on the inside. Air your feet at lunchtime, keep them clean and change your socks regularly. If you feel any hot spots stop immediately and apply a few strips of zinc oxide tape and leave them on until it is pain-free or the tape starts to come off.

If you have left it too late and a blister has developed you should surround it with 'moleskin' or any other blister kit to protect it from abrasion. Popping it can lead to infection. If the skin is broken keep the area clean with antiseptic and cover with a non-adhesive dressing material held in place with tape.

HYPOTHERMIA

Also known as exposure, this occurs when the body can't generate enough heat to maintain its normal temperature, usually as a result of being wet, cold, unprotected from the wind, tired and hungry. It is usually more of a problem in upland areas. However, even on the Norfolk coast in bad weather the body can be exposed to strong winds and driving rain making the risk a real one. The northern stretches of the Peddars Way path are particularly exposed and there are fewer villages making it difficult to get help should it be needed.

Hypothermia is easily avoided by wearing suitable clothing, carrying and eating enough food and drink, being aware of the weather conditions and checking the morale of your companions. Early signs to watch for are feeling cold and tired with involuntary shivering. Find some shelter as soon as possible and warm the victim up with a hot drink and some chocolate or other high-energy food. If possible give them another warm layer of clothing and allow them to rest until feeling better.

If allowed to worsen, strange behaviour, slurring of speech and poor co-ordination will become apparent and the victim can quickly progress into unconsciousness, followed by coma and death. Quickly get the victim out of wind and rain, improvising a shelter if necessary. Rapid restoration of bodily warmth is essential and best achieved by bare-skin contact: someone should get into the same sleeping bag as the patient, both having stripped to their underwear, any spare clothing under or over them to build up heat. Send urgently for help.

HYPERTHERMIA

Heat exhaustion is often caused by water depletion and is a serious condition that could eventually lead to death. Symptoms include thirst, fatigue, giddiness, a rapid pulse, raised body temperature, low urine output and later on, delirium and coma. The only remedy is to re-establish water balance. If the victim is suffering severe muscle cramps it may be due to salt depletion.

Heat stroke is caused by failure of the body's temperature-regulating system and is extremely serious. It is associated with a very high body temperature and an absence of sweating. Early symptoms can be similar to those of hypothermia, such as aggressive behaviour, lack of co-ordination and so on. Later the victim goes into a coma or convulsions and death will follow if effective treatment is not given. To treat heat stroke sponge the victim down or cover with wet towels and fan them vigorously. Get help immediately.

SUNBURN

Even on overcast days the sun still has the power to burn. Sunburn can be avoided by regularly applying sunscreen. Don't forget your lips and those areas affected by reflected light off the ground; under the nose, ears and chin. You may find that you quickly sweat sunscreen off, so consider wearing a sun hat. If you have particularly fair skin, wear a light, long-sleeved top and trousers.

(Colour section (following pages)

- **C1 (Opposite) Castle Acre** (see p105) lies about halfway along the Peddars Way and is said to have some of the finest village earthworks (**top**) in England. Also interesting are the ruins of the Cluniac Priory here (**right and bottom**), founded in 1089.
- **C2** The vast skies and wide sands of **Holkham Beach** (see p146).
- **C3 Holkham Hall** (**top**, see p146) was built in the Palladian style for Thomas Coke, 1st Earl of Leicester, inspired by the buildings he'd seen on his Grand Tour of Europe in the early 18th century. (**Bottom left**): Colourful beach huts on the sands at Wells-next-the-Sea (see p148). (**Bottom right**): Finger post showing the way along Holme Dunes.
- **C4 (Top):** Low tide at Burnham Overy Staithe. (**Middle**): Sea cliffs beyond Weybourne where the Norfolk Coast Path climbs and falls more frequently. (**Bottom**): Grassy path across Harpley Common, typical landscape of the gently undulating Peddars Way.

CASTLE ACRE

ROUTE GUIDE & MAPS 4

Using this guide

The trail guide and accompanying maps have not been divided up into rigid daily stages since people walk at different speeds and have different interests. The route summaries below describe the trail between significant places and are written as if walking north towards the coast and then east along it since this is by far the most popular direction for people tackling the trail. To enable you to plan your own itinerary, practical information is shown clearly on the trail maps. This includes walking times for both directions, places to stay, camp and eat, as well as shops where you can stock up on supplies. Further service details are given in the text under the entry for each place. For an overview of this information see Itineraries, pp28-30.

TRAIL MAPS [for map key see p189]

Scale and walking times

The trail maps are drawn at a scale of 1:20,000 (1cm = 200m; 3¹/₈ inches = 1 mile). Walking times are given along the side of each map and the arrow indicates the direction to which that time refers. Black triangles show the points between which the times have been taken. See **note on walking times**, below.

The time-bars are there as a guide and are not to judge your walking ability. Any number of variables will affect the speed at which you actually walk, from the weather conditions to the number of beers you drank the previous evening. After the first few hours' walking you should be able to gauge how your speed relates to the timings on the maps.

Up or down?

The trail on the maps is marked as a broken line. An arrow across the trail indicates an incline: it always points to the higher ground. Two arrows show that the slope is steep. If, for example, you are walking

❑ **Important note – walking times**
Unless otherwise specified, **all times in this book refer only to the time spent walking**. You will need to add 20-30% to allow for rests, photography, checking the map, drinking water etc. When planning the day's hike count on 5-7 hours' actual walking.

from A (at 80m) to B (at 200m) and the trail between the two is short and steep it would be shown thus: A– – – > > – – –B. If the arrow heads were reversed they would indicate the trail was downhill.

Accommodation

Apart from in the larger towns along the coast where some selection of places to stay has been necessary, almost every accommodation option within easy reach of the trail is marked. Details of each place are given in the accompanying text. Rates are summer high-season prices either per room, assuming there are two people sharing a room, or per person (pp). The number and type of rooms are given after each entry: S = single room, T = twin room, D = double room, F = family room (sleeps at least three people). Where possible, places where facilities include a bath are specified and also places that accept dogs.

Note that many places only accept bookings for a minimum of two nights, particularly in the summer months. However, to help walkers they may offer a pick-up, drop-off service. At the time of research many places had not decided whether they would change their tariffs bearing in mind the 2.5% VAT rate increase in January 2011. Thus rates may differ from those quoted here.

Other features

Other features are marked on the maps when pertinent to navigation. To avoid cluttering the maps and making them unusable not all features have been marked each time they occur.

Peddars Way and Norfolk Coast Path

THETFORD **[see map opposite]**

If you are arriving by train or bus, Thetford is the closest stop to the start of the trail at Knettishall Heath some 15 miles away. Thetford was once the capital of Saxon East Anglia. An important medieval religious centre, its fortunes changed when the Dissolution of the Monasteries meant the religious buildings were destroyed, removing much of Thetford's wealth and prestige.

Nowadays it is pleasant enough and boasts a number of significant historic buildings including the **Cluniac Priory** (see box p84) dating from 1107. The extensive remains (free admission), although little more than outlines of structures, are all that's left of one of the most important East Anglian monasteries; see also p105. Other sites include **St Peter's Church** from the 1300s as well as older Iceni-fortified ramparts at **Gallows Hill** dating from AD40, Saxon defences, and a Norman castle built on a massive man-made mound, **Castle Hill**, dating from the 1070s. The earth works, the tallest in England, stand 81ft high and measure 1000ft around the base. The largest area of lowland pine forest left in Britain, **Thetford Forest**, also stands on the edge of the town.

On King St there is a gilded, bronze **statue of Thomas Paine** who was born in Thetford in 1737. He worked as an excise man here before going to America, where his pamphlets *Rights of Man* and *Age of Reason* made him famous in the late 1700s. He played an active part in both the American and the French revolutions.

Snetterton Circuit (see p27), 12 miles/20km north-east of Thetford on the A11, is a motor-racing track that hosts British touring cars, Formula Three and superbike events.

Services

Everything of importance, including shops, a **supermarket** and **banks** can be found by turning left out of the station and walking into the centre of town. There is a **tourist information centre** (☎ 01842-751975; Mon-Fri 9am-5pm, Sat to 4pm) in New Horizons travel agency on Market Place. They can provide information about accommodation but do not do any bookings.

Transport

[See also pp46-8] There are regular **train** services between Thetford, with changes at Cambridge or Ely, and London Kings Cross. National Express **coach** NX490 (see p44) from London Victoria to Great Yarmouth stops here. Coach Services' Nos 84, 193 and 332 **bus** services run to/from Bury St Edmunds; their No 81 runs to Watton.

The best way to get to the start of the Peddars Way at Knettishall Heath is by booking the **Brecks Bus** (see p45) to take you from Thetford to the car park nearest to where the Peddars Way begins. Unfortunately there are currently no scheduled bus services from Thetford to the trailhead.

Alternatively, you can take a **taxi** from the train station. There are usually cars waiting but, if not, try: A1 Cars (☎ 01842-755555), C&S Taxis (☎ 01842-760322), Daley's Taxis (☎ 01842-750777), Kes Kabs (☎ 01842-766900), or Fairway Taxis (☎ 01842-763865). The journey will take 10-15 minutes and cost around £15 one way.

Although there is a car park at the start of the Peddars Way, it is not secure and you shouldn't leave your vehicle there for any length of time, especially the time it takes to trek the whole trail.

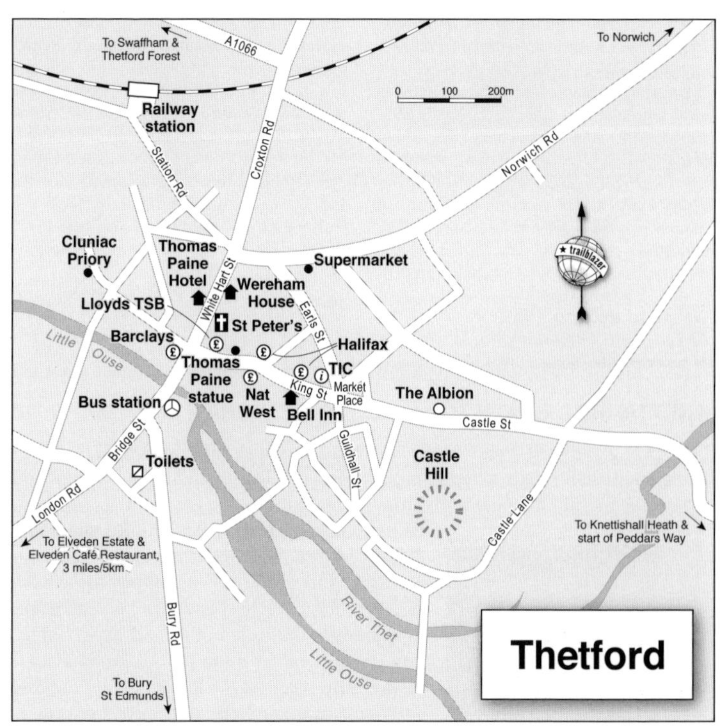

❑ **Cluniac Order**
The Cluniac Order was a medieval organisation of Benedictines centred on the abbey at Cluny in France. Founded in 910, the order became the furthest reaching religious reform movement of the Middle Ages and at its height was second only to the papacy as the chief religious force in Europe. Gradually superseded by the Cistercians and finally suppressed by the French Revolution.

There is also a 15-mile **path** from Thetford to Knettishall Heath that forms part of the Iceni Way (see p31) should you want to walk to the trailhead.

Where to stay

If you choose to overnight in Thetford, try the large ***Bell Inn*** (☎ 01842-754455, 💻 www.bellinn-thetford.co.uk; 6S/22D/15T, all en suite with bath and shower; dogs welcome), on King St, which has B&B from £59 for a single and from £69 for two sharing; or the historical ***Thomas Paine Hotel*** (☎ 01842-750372, 💻 www.thethomaspainehotel.co.uk; 7D/1T, all en suite, bath available), on White Hart St, named after the eponymous local alumnus (see p82); B&B costs £95-105 (£75-85 single occupancy). ***Wereham House*** (☎ 01842-761956, 💻 www.werehamhouse.co.uk; 1S/4D/2T/1F, all en suite), on White Hart St, has comfortably furnished rooms with B&B for £55/74/88 (sgl/dbl or twin/fml) – sole occupancy of a double room is £64 – and a large secluded garden.

Where to eat and drink

Elveden Café Restaurant (☎ 01842-898068, 💻 www.elveden.com; daily 9.30am-5pm) is a good-quality café located within the stylishly converted farm buildings on the Elveden Estate; the buildings also house a series of upmarket shops. The café's eclectic menu includes generous sandwiches (from £4.95) and good cakes (from £1.95), as well as daily specials such as mushroom and blue cheese risotto (£9.25) and Elveden hotpot (£9.25).

The restaurant in ***The Thomas Paine Hotel*** (see Where to stay; daily noon-2.30pm & 6-9pm) has a range of bar meals (£4.95-10.95) as well as daily specials and a fine dining restaurant alongside locally brewed real ale.

If you're after a sharpener before you start, ***The Albion*** (☎ 01842-752796; Mon-Wed & Sun noon-11pm, Thur till 11.30pm, Fri-Sat 11am-12.30am), on Castle St, is a small pub in a row of flint cottages close to the centre of town. The patio overlooks the earthworks of Castle Hill and Castle Park. Food is not served but you are allowed to eat takeaways in the pub.

There are **fast-food restaurants** on Market Place and Guildhall St.

KNETTISHALL HEATH TO LITTLE CRESSINGHAM MAPS 1-8

Easy-going and well-maintained paths make this first **14½ miles (23km, 5hrs)** from Knettishall Heath, actually in Suffolk, a gentle introduction to the trail and the route ahead. Meandering through tranquil woods the path, formerly a Bronze Age trading route and Roman road, quickly crosses into Norfolk and breaks out across farmland before beginning to cross a series of attractive heaths where you can begin to appreciate the scale of the landscape. Before you begin, bear in mind that accommodation on the early stages of the Peddars Way is scarce and make sure you have something booked.

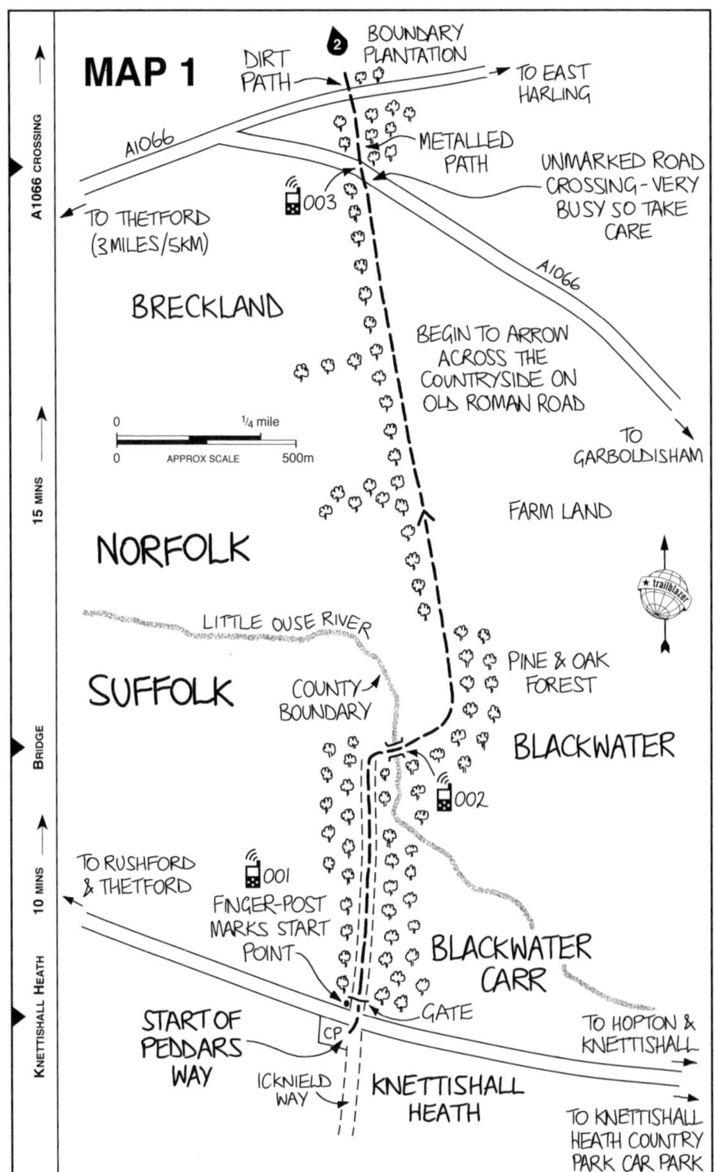
MAP 1
A1066 CROSSING
15 MINS
BRIDGE
10 MINS
KNETTISHALL HEATH
BOUNDARY PLANTATION
DIRT PATH
TO EAST HARLING
A1066
METALLED PATH
UNMARKED ROAD CROSSING - VERY BUSY SO TAKE CARE
003
TO THETFORD (3 MILES/5KM)
A1066
BRECKLAND
BEGIN TO ARROW ACROSS THE COUNTRYSIDE ON OLD ROMAN ROAD
0
1/4 mile
0
APPROX SCALE
500m
TO GARBOLDISHAM
FARM LAND
NORFOLK
trailblazer
LITTLE OUSE RIVER
PINE & OAK FOREST
SUFFOLK
COUNTY BOUNDARY
BLACKWATER
002
TO RUSHFORD & THETFORD
001
FINGER-POST MARKS START POINT
BLACKWATER CARR
GATE
START OF PEDDARS WAY
CP
TO HOPTON & KNETTISHALL
ICKNIELD WAY
KNETTISHALL HEATH
TO KNETTISHALL HEATH COUNTRY PARK CAR PARK

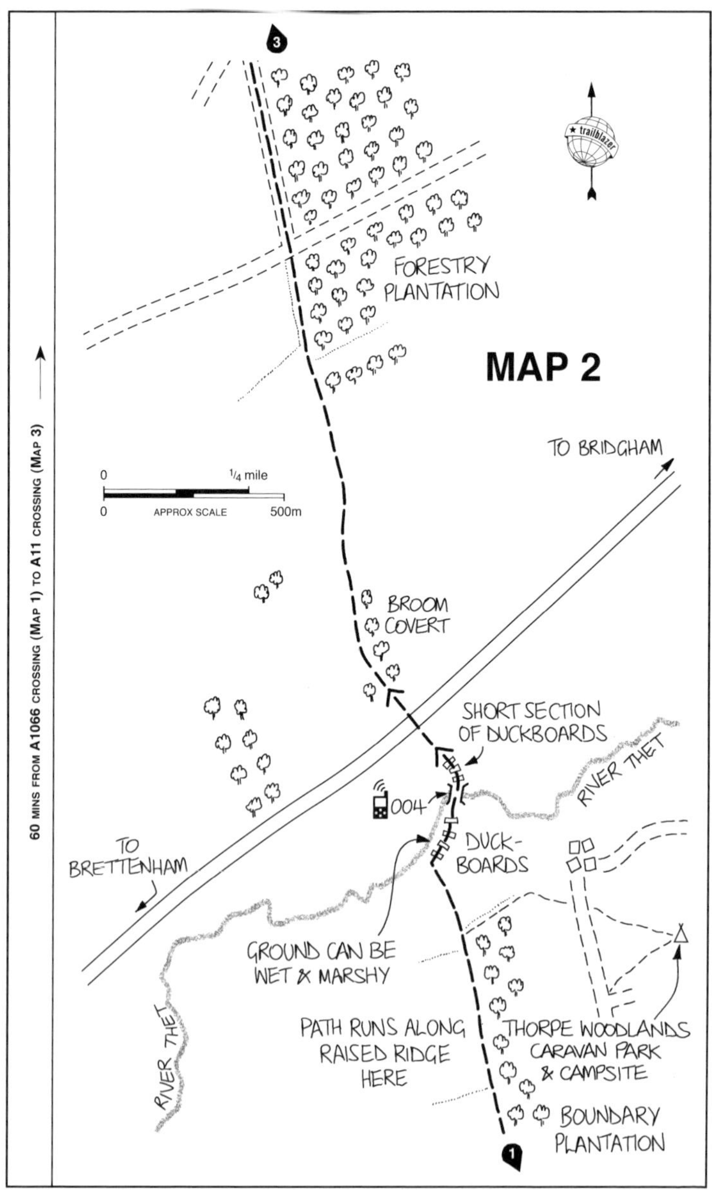

MAP 2
60 MINS FROM A1066 CROSSING (MAP 1) TO A11 CROSSING (MAP 3)
FORESTRY PLANTATION
TO BRIDGHAM
0
1/4 mile
0
APPROX SCALE
500m
BROOM COVERT
SHORT SECTION OF DUCKBOARDS
RIVER THET
004
DUCK-BOARDS
TO BRETTENHAM
GROUND CAN BE WET & MARSHY
PATH RUNS ALONG RAISED RIDGE HERE
THORPE WOODLANDS CARAVAN PARK & CAMPSITE
RIVER THET
BOUNDARY PLANTATION
trailblazer

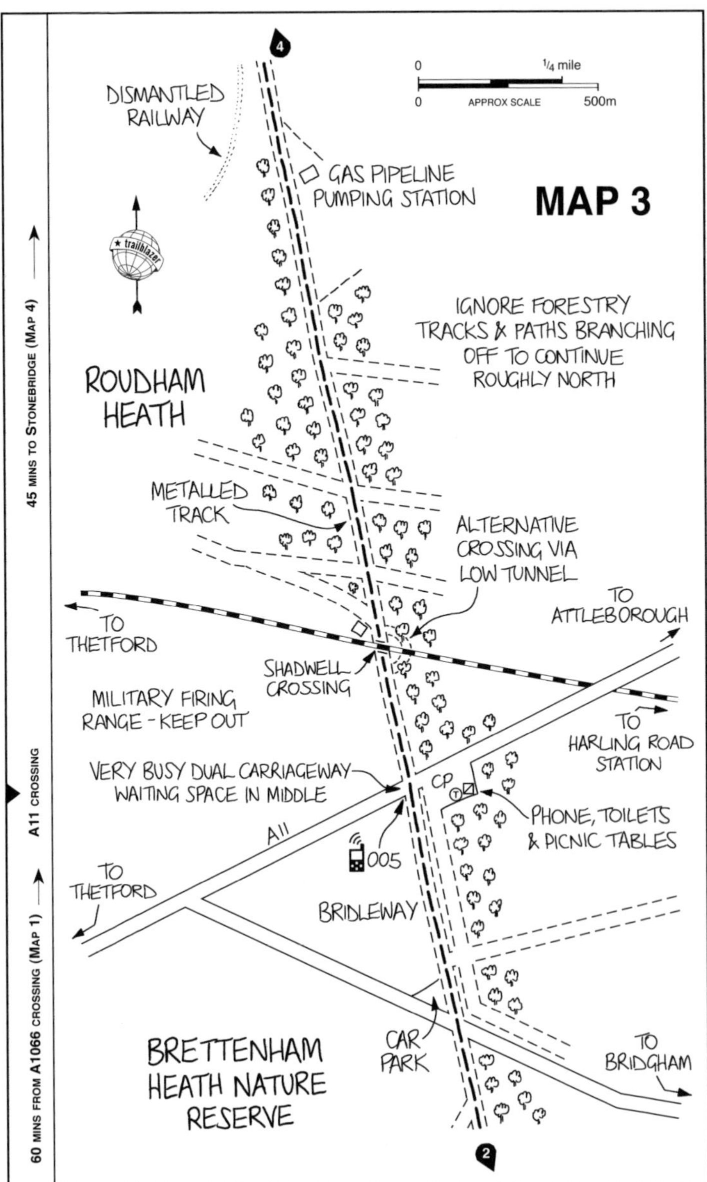
MAP 3
0 1/4 mile
0 APPROX SCALE 500m
DISMANTLED RAILWAY
GAS PIPELINE PUMPING STATION
trailblazer
IGNORE FORESTRY TRACKS & PATHS BRANCHING OFF TO CONTINUE ROUGHLY NORTH
ROUDHAM HEATH
METALLED TRACK
ALTERNATIVE CROSSING VIA LOW TUNNEL
TO ATTLEBOROUGH
TO THETFORD
SHADWELL CROSSING
MILITARY FIRING RANGE - KEEP OUT
TO HARLING ROAD STATION
VERY BUSY DUAL CARRIAGEWAY WAITING SPACE IN MIDDLE
CP
PHONE, TOILETS & PICNIC TABLES
A11
005
TO THETFORD
BRIDLEWAY
CAR PARK
BRETTENHAM HEATH NATURE RESERVE
TO BRIDGHAM
45 MINS TO STONEBRIDGE (MAP 4)
A11 CROSSING
60 MINS FROM A1066 CROSSING (MAP 1)

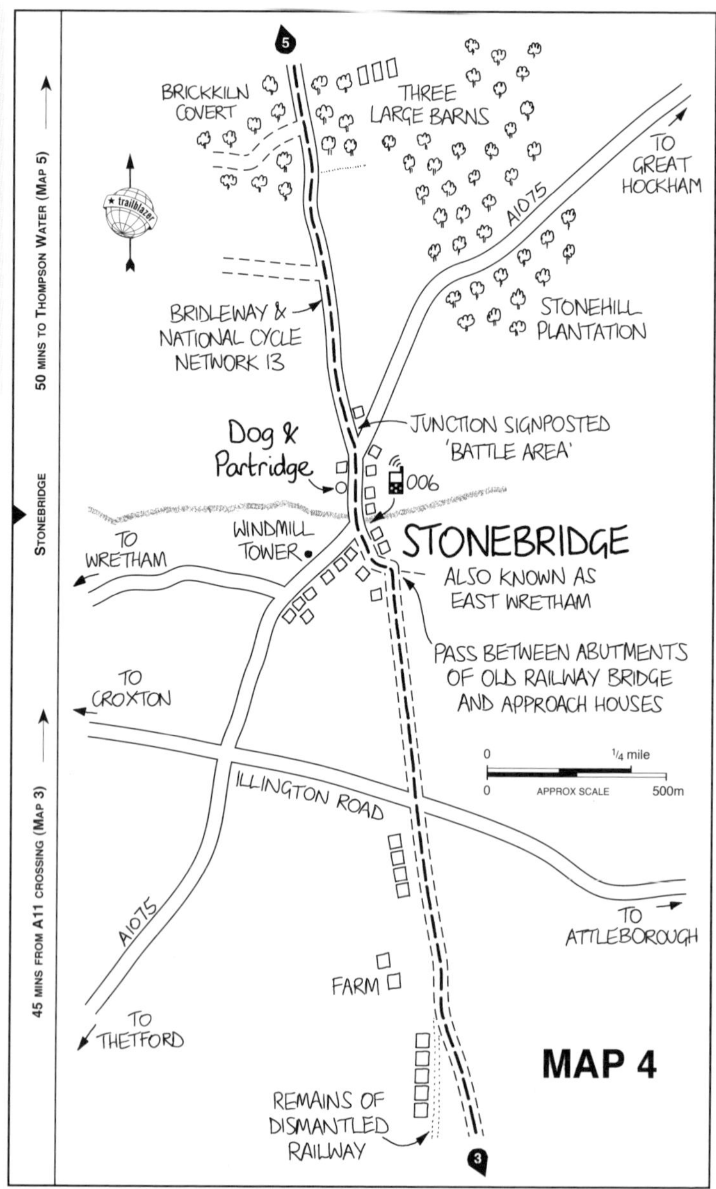
5
BRICKKILN COVERT
THREE LARGE BARNS
TO GREAT HOCKHAM
A1075
STONEHILL PLANTATION
BRIDLEWAY & NATIONAL CYCLE NETWORK 13
JUNCTION SIGNPOSTED 'BATTLE AREA'
Dog & Partridge
006
WINDMILL TOWER
STONEBRIDGE
ALSO KNOWN AS EAST WRETHAM
TO WRETHAM
PASS BETWEEN ABUTMENTS OF OLD RAILWAY BRIDGE AND APPROACH HOUSES
TO CROXTON
0
1/4 mile
0
APPROX SCALE
500m
ILLINGTON ROAD
TO ATTLEBOROUGH
A1075
FARM
TO THETFORD
MAP 4
REMAINS OF DISMANTLED RAILWAY
3
50 MINS TO THOMPSON WATER (MAP 5)
STONEBRIDGE
45 MINS FROM A11 CROSSING (MAP 3)

Alternatively, be prepared to detour from the path and try your luck in one of the larger villages close by.

To get to the start of the Peddars Way from Coney Weston, head west on Thetford Rd. Turn right at a crossroads and head north on Norwich Lane until you reach a T-junction where you turn right to Knettishall Heath.

The Peddars Way in fact begins rather quietly from a finger-post adjacent to a B road, next to Blackwater Carr – a surprisingly low-key and easy-to-miss way of signalling the start of a National Trail. Opposite is a car park with no facilities but this is where the Brecks Bus (see p45) stops; it is also where the Icknield Way (see p31) ends. At the nearby Knettishall Heath Country Park, however, there is a pay and display car park with public toilets.

Pass through the gate beyond the finger-post and head roughly straight on into a light wood. After 700m bend right and cross the Little Ouse, leaving Suffolk and entering Norfolk, where you pass through **Breckland** (see p50), a landscape of light, dry, sandy soils bound together by Scots pine and conifer plantations.

Passing through attractive woods, the path climbs gently to a pair of main roads and then meanders alongside a forest on a raised Roman causeway (or *agger*) almost 5m wide, until it arrives at the River Thet. To the east of here is Thorpe Woodlands Caravan Park and Campsite. However, campers can stay here only if they have a chemical toilet since there are no facilities on site.

Just before the River Thet there is a section of **duckboards** which continue once you have crossed the river on a small humpback bridge, useful as the ground can be marshy and wet here, and then cross a minor road. Following the road there are excellent views of Brettenham Heath to the west, one of the largest areas of heathland in Norfolk and a haven for birdwatchers. Cross the A11, a dual carriageway connecting London and Norwich, and the Ely–Norwich railway line at a level crossing, to re-enter the woods.

Beyond a **gas pipeline pump station** the path climbs gently alongside farmland and piggeries. Having crossed another minor road it ambles alongside the disused Thetford–Watton railway line and past a farm to pass eventually between the abutments of an old railway bridge and arrive at Stonebridge.

STONEBRIDGE [see Map 4]

Named after the stone bridge that used to cross the railway line, the village, which is sometimes referred to as **East Wretham** depending on which side of the road you're standing, is little more than a straggle of houses along a single road but it is home to ***The Dog and Partridge*** pub (☎ 01953-497014, 🖳 www.dog-and-partridge.org.uk; daily noon-11pm, Sun till 10.30pm, food served Tue-Sat noon-9pm, Sun till 7pm; Oct-Easter Mon-Fri from 3pm). Pause at this homely, traditional pub for a pint and a chance to refuel – a Stilton and vegetable crumble costs £8.45, a rump steak is £11.95, and the 12-inch pizzas are filling; a basic pizza costs £6.95, additional toppings are 70p each. They also offer a **cashback** service if you have spent £10 on food or drink. Motorhomes can park in the car park for £5 per night; however, the pub will give motorhome drivers a £5 voucher to spend in the pub.

Turn right when you reach the road and walk past the pub before branching off left at a junction signposted 'Battle Area'. This is also a bridleway and

National Cycle Network 13 so expect to see horses and cyclists. The metalled path dwindles to a broad forest track as it strikes off across The Brecks, past the **Stanford Military Training Zone**, a large, closed military training area that is still used today; when you see red flags hanging at the gated entrances to the zone it means the army are on exercise.

On this section you pass the first of a series of modern stone sculptures inscribed with verse. These are part of the **Norfolk Songline** (see box below).

To the north and east lies **Thompson Common** (see box below).

❑ A Norfolk Songline

...as they hunted and gathered over thousands of years
those first people pressed patterns into the ground with their feet...
track-ways and paths.'

'...the eastern-most strand of the final stretch of that tangle of tracks,
between Knettishall Heath and Holme,
between Blackwater Carr and Sea-Gate,
has come to be called the Peddars Way.

A Norfolk Songline (🖳 www.norfolksongline.co.uk) was an arts project inspired by the Peddars Way. A Songline is originally an Australian Aboriginal concept that explores the connection between a track and the landscape it passes though. In the form of a song, the history of the path and the formations around it are told. The Norfolk Songline was created by Hugh Lupton, who wove poetry, imagery and song together to bring the landscape of the Peddars Way to life. A series of temporary sculptures, including arranged stones, reed vanes, earth rings and flint mounds, first accompanied the story, but subsequently five stone sculptures inspired by the project have been created and set along the trail, providing a reminder of the past and history of the countryside whilst acting as waymarkers. A music CD and book connected with the project are available from Hugh Lupton, the co-creator (🖳 www.angelfire.com/folk/hughlupton/index.html). The sculptures appear on maps 5, 6, 11, 16 and 23.

❑ Pingo ponds on Thompson Common

This area is an important patchwork of grasslands, ponds, woods and scrub covering 346 acres. **Thompson Water**, a shallow lake artificially created in 1845 by draining a tributary of the River Wissey, covers 40 acres.

Unusual landscape features include *pingo* ponds. Pingos were low hillocks formed 20,000 years ago during the last Ice Age when spring water below the surface froze to form lenses of ice that pushed the earth upwards. In warmer months, when the ice melted, the surface soil would slough off and gather around the rim of the hillocks. Once all the ice had melted the remnants of the hillocks collapsed to leave shallow craters which have filled with water to become ponds. The name comes from the Eskimo word for hill; pingos are currently found only in areas of permafrost, such as the Arctic tundra

Most pingo ponds in England have been ploughed up or lost, but a number remain in the Brecks, the best examples of which can be seen on **Thompson Common**. The ponds are home to a unique range of wildlife and are excellent breeding grounds for amphibians, dragonflies and damselflies.

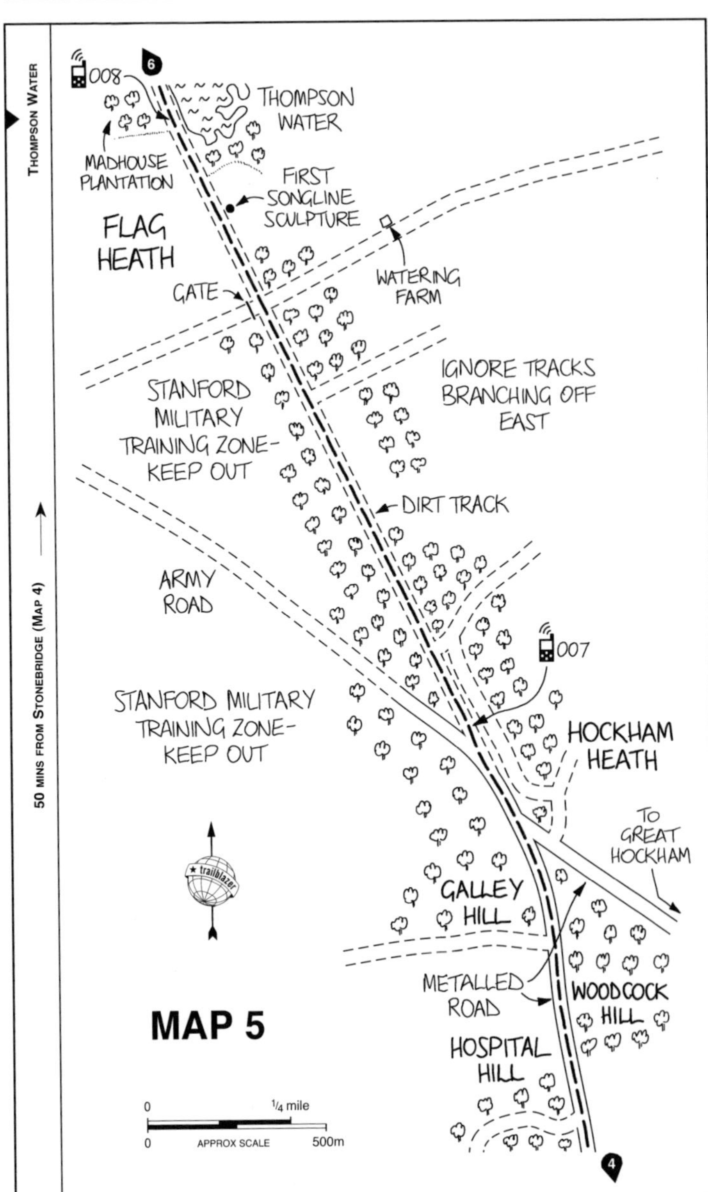
THOMPSON WATER
50 MINS FROM STONEBRIDGE (MAP 4)
008
6
THOMPSON WATER
MADHOUSE PLANTATION
FIRST SONGLINE SCULPTURE
FLAG HEATH
WATERING FARM
GATE
IGNORE TRACKS BRANCHING OFF EAST
STANFORD MILITARY TRAINING ZONE - KEEP OUT
DIRT TRACK
ARMY ROAD
007
STANFORD MILITARY TRAINING ZONE - KEEP OUT
HOCKHAM HEATH
TO GREAT HOCKHAM
trailblazer
GALLEY HILL
METALLED ROAD
WOODCOCK HILL
MAP 5
HOSPITAL HILL
0
1/4 mile
0
APPROX SCALE
500m
4

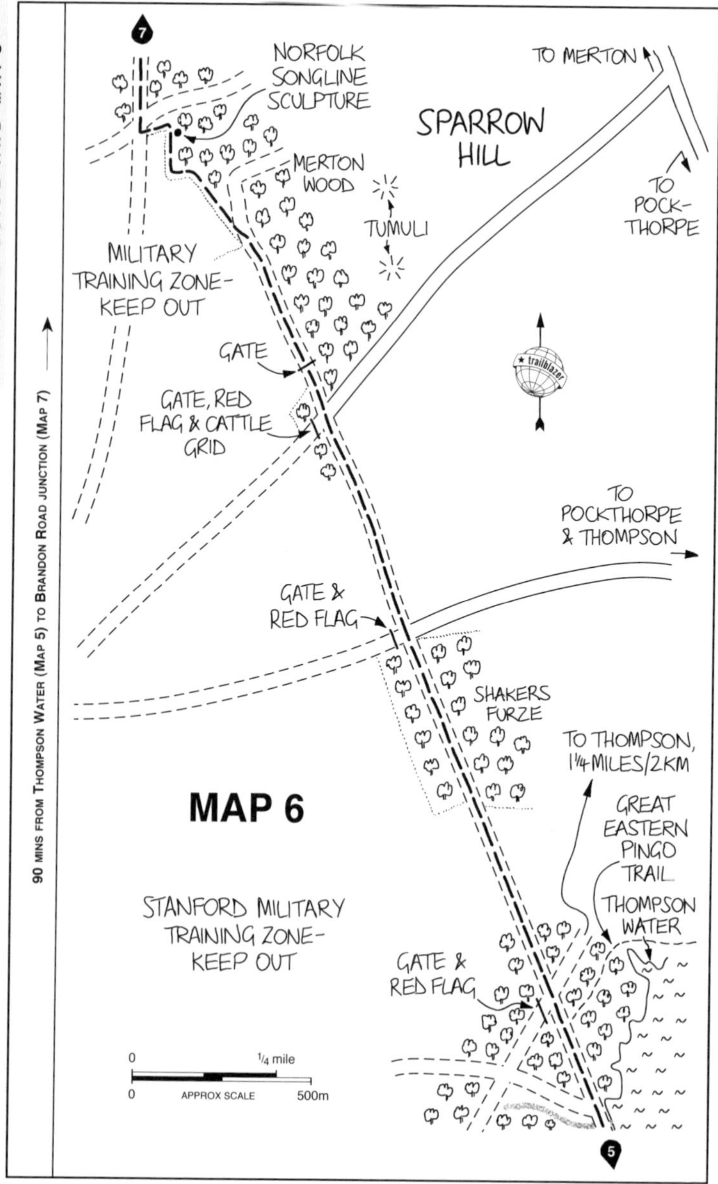

90 MINS FROM THOMPSON WATER (MAP 5) TO BRANDON ROAD JUNCTION (MAP 7)
7
NORFOLK SONGLINE SCULPTURE
TO MERTON
SPARROW HILL
MERTON WOOD
TUMULI
TO POCK-THORPE
MILITARY TRAINING ZONE-KEEP OUT
GATE
GATE, RED FLAG & CATTLE GRID
TO POCKTHORPE & THOMPSON
GATE & RED FLAG
SHAKERS FURZE
TO THOMPSON, 1¼ MILES/2KM
MAP 6
GREAT EASTERN PINGO TRAIL
THOMPSON WATER
STANFORD MILITARY TRAINING ZONE-KEEP OUT
GATE & RED FLAG
0
¼ mile
0
APPROX SCALE
500m
5

Beyond Thompson Water is a path that leads east to **Thompson** village, just over a mile away. The **Great Eastern Pingo Trail** is an eight-mile circular walk that takes in Thompson Water, Thompson Common and the village itself; it passes through wooded countryside and wetlands as it completes the circuit.

THOMPSON

This small historic village is thought to have Danish origins and appears in the *Domesday Book* as Tomesteda.

The village is centred on the 14th-century flint church, **St Martin's**. There are few facilities but it does have a **post office** (Mon-Tue and Thur-Fri 9am-1pm) containing a **cash machine** (ATM).

It is also home to ***The Thompson Chequers*** (☎ 01953-483360, 💻 www.thompsonchequers.co.uk; 3D, all en suite; Mon-Fri 11.30am-2.30pm & 6.30-11pm, Sat & Sun 11.30am-10.30pm, food served daily noon-2pm & 6.30-9pm). This 16th-century inn, which has a low-slung thatched roof, serves up renowned hearty food such as deep-fried breaded scampi (£7.95), homemade vegetable curry (£7.95) and a substantial mixed grill (£16.95) – booking is recommended. The inn also offers free wi-fi and has a beer garden; dogs are welcome if booked in advance. The rooms boast modern amenities and B&B costs £65 (£45 for single occupancy).

There are several other accommodation options in the village; B&B at the 600-year-old ***College Farm*** (☎ 01953-483318; 💻 rwolstenholme@aol.com; 2D/1T, all with private facilities with a bath) costs from £35pp. ***Lands End*** (☎ 01953-488070, 💻 Jean@jmorton34.freeserve.co.uk; 2D/ 1D or F; shared bathroom with bath and shower), on Butters Hall Lane, charges £25pp. They will also stable horses and feed them if you are riding. The charming 16th-century ***Thatched House*** (☎ 01953-483577, 💻 www.thatchedhouse.co.uk; 1D/ 2T, two of the rooms have private facilities, bath available), on Mill Rd, charges £70 (£40 for single occupancy). If booked in advance the owners will prepare you a packed lunch.

The main Peddars Way path pushes straight on, past Sparrow Hill, to arrive at **Merton Estate**, home to the de Grey family since the late 1330s. The current owner, Lord Walsingham, was responsible for allowing a path to be opened along this stretch of the Peddars Way.

Beyond Merton Estate the path passes **Home Farm**, which offers accommodation: ***Peddars Way B&B*** (☎ 01953-880180, 💻 www.farmholidaysnorfolk.co.uk; 2D/2T, all with private facilities with bath) is perfectly placed on the trail and has a smart double for £80 and twin rooms for £70. Single occupancy of a twin costs £50. If booked by at least the day before, the owners will either rustle up a locally sourced supper (£18 for two courses, £20 for three) or run you to and from one of the local pubs; they can also prepare you a packed lunch (from £6). They also do luggage transfer; contact them for details.

Beyond the farm the metalled road reaches a crossroads where you can go straight over for Watton. Instead, join a green lane that bears left then right to reach the B1108, Brandon Rd. The Peddars Way continues left from here. About 1½ miles to the right though is the vibrant market town of Watton.

WATTON

An historic market town, these days Watton is still a bustling place. The parish church, **St Mary's**, dates from the 12th century and has a Norman tower and octagonal belfry. In the heart of the village stands an unusual **bell tower** dating from 1679, which was erected after a fire destroyed most of the town in 1674, reputedly so the bells could warn townsfolk of any future disaster. On the town sign are the two 'babes' from the popular fairy tale *Babes in the Woods*; it is rumoured that nearby **Wayland Wood** is where the two unfortunate children met their fate. A hare ('wat' in the local dialect) and barrel ('tun') also feature on the sign and account for the town's name. The town also hosts an annual craft fair (see p26) showcasing locally made products.

Services

There is an **information centre** (☎ 01953-880212, 🖳 www.wayland-tourism.org.uk; Easter to Oct Mon-Fri 10am-4pm & Sat 10am-1pm) in Wayland House, which is on the corner of the High St and George Trollope Rd; staff can provide you with leaflets and directions. General information is available year-round but staff may not always be available. The town also has a **library**, **post office** (☎ 01953-881201; Mon-Fri 9am-5.30pm, Sat 9am-12.30pm) and several **banks**, all along the High St. The **market** takes place along the High St on Wednesdays and there is a farmer's market on the first Saturday of every month.

Transport

[See also pp46-8] Konectbus's No 11 service links Watton to Sporle and Swaffham and their 3/3A operates daily between Watton and Norwich. Coach Services' No 81 runs to Thetford.

Where to stay

Half a mile before the village on Brandon Rd is a traditional family pub, ***The Hare & Barrel*** (☎ 01953-882752, 🖳 www.hare-and-barrel-hotel-norfolk.co.uk; Mon-Sat 11.30am-11.30pm, Sun noon-5pm, food Mon-Sat noon-2pm & 6.30-9pm, Sun noon-5pm; 4S/2D/4D or F/4T/1F sleeping four, all en suite), which serves standard pub grub and which charges £45-55/£65/£75-90 (sgl/dbl and twin/family) for B&B. The pub is closed on bank holidays.

Close by, on Richmond Rd, is ***Broom Hall Country Hotel*** (☎ 01953-882125, 🖳 www.broomhallhotel.co.uk; 9D/4T/2F, all en suite, bath available), a rather grand Victorian country house set in two acres of gardens, which has B&B for £100-174; single occupancy costs £75-100. There is an indoor pool and massage treatments are available (if booked in advance; separate charge) for aching limbs. Dogs are welcome (£5 for one night) if prebooked.

Watton itself has a couple of accommodation options, handy if the only place to stay in Little Cressingham (see p96) is fully booked. ***The Crown Hotel*** (☎ 01953-882375; 1D/4T, all en suite), dating from the 1760s, stands on the High St. It has clean, comfy rooms for £50 (single occupancy £35); the rate includes breakfast. ***The Willow House*** (☎ 01953-881181, 🖳 www.thewillowhouse.co.uk; 3S/2D or T/2T, D or F, all en suite), also on the High St, is a Grade II listed thatched building dating from the 16th century. Converted into a period hostelry full of low beams, it has chalet-style rooms for £65 and single rooms for £50-55; rates include a full breakfast. Dogs (£5) are welcome.

Where to eat and drink

Food is available in the ***Ivy Room Bar*** (Tue-Sun noon-2pm & Mon-Sat 6.30-8.30pm) and ***Swallowtails Restaurant*** (Mon-Sat 6.30-8.30pm, Sun noon-2pm & 6.30-7.15pm), at Broom Hall Country Hotel (see Where to stay); the later offers more formal dining – a three-course meal will set you back £20. Light lunches and cream teas are served (daily 10am-4.15pm) in the Conservatory or on the Terrace.

The Willow House (see Where to stay) is open daily (food served Mon-Sat noon-2pm & 7-9pm, Sun noon-3pm) and has bar meals as well as more elaborate à la carte dishes including a honey-coated neck fillet of lamb (£14.95), or fillets of sea bass (£15.50). If you're after a snack, ***Express Fish Bar*** (Mon-Thur 11am-2pm & 4-11pm, Fri-Sat 11am-11pm, Sun 4-11pm) sells fish and chips, and fried chicken and salad boxes – walkers get a free bottle of water with every meal.

The bars in ***The Crown Hotel*** (see Where to stay) offer a wide range of locally brewed ales but they do not serve food.

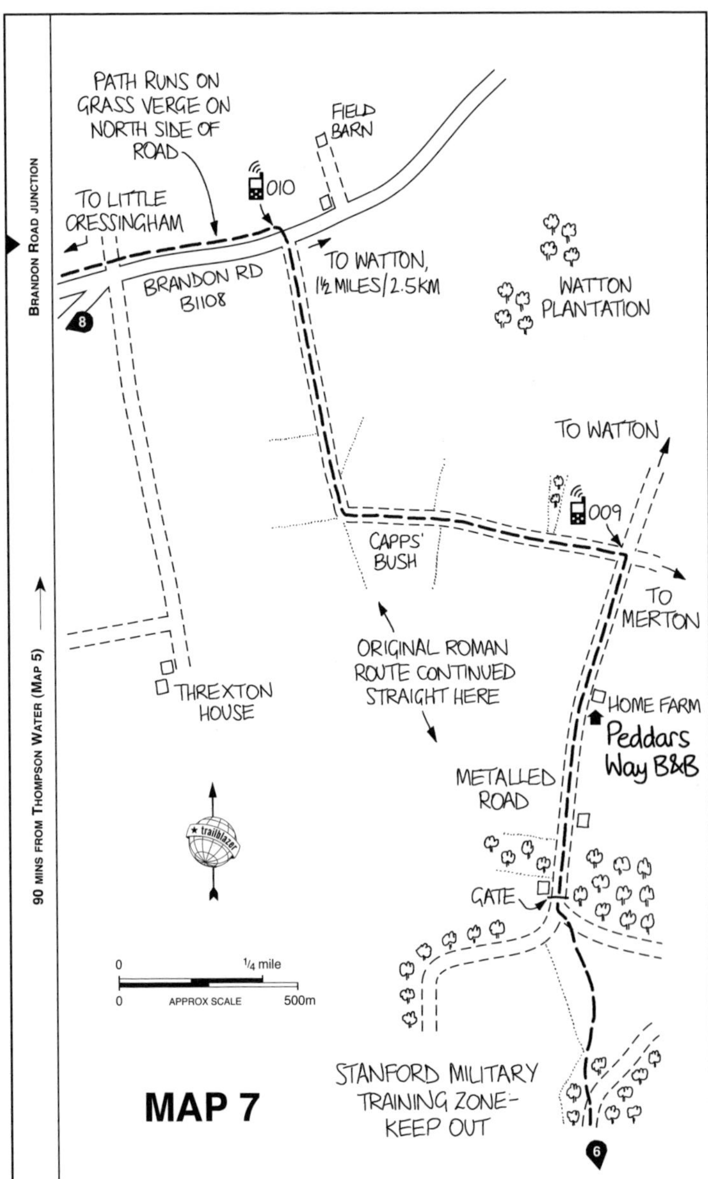
PATH RUNS ON GRASS VERGE ON NORTH SIDE OF ROAD
FIELD BARN
010
TO LITTLE CRESSINGHAM
TO WATTON, 1½ MILES/2.5KM
BRANDON RD B1108
WATTON PLANTATION
8
BRANDON ROAD JUNCTION
TO WATTON
009
CAPPS' BUSH
TO MERTON
ORIGINAL ROMAN ROUTE CONTINUED STRAIGHT HERE
THREXTON HOUSE
HOME FARM
Peddars Way B&B
METALLED ROAD
90 MINS FROM THOMPSON WATER (MAP 5)
trailblazer
GATE
0
¼ mile
0
APPROX SCALE
500m
STANFORD MILITARY TRAINING ZONE - KEEP OUT
MAP 7
6

Once on the B1108 pick up a grassy path running alternately along the verge or following the edges of adjoining fields. At a crossroads look right and you'll see **All Saints Church**, seemingly stranded amidst fields to the north, and at a fork bear left to stroll downhill into Little Cressingham.

LITTLE CRESSINGHAM

[see Map 8]

Another small hamlet, centred on a crossroads just off the main road, Little Cressingham is a sleepy place with no services and just the one accommodation option.

Over the crossroads and just down the hill stands a partially collapsed church, **St Andrews**, whose ruined tower makes for a striking silhouette whilst the nave is still in use for services.

A little further on is a striking **water and wind mill** built around 1821; this mill boasts an unusual double action where two pairs of stones at the base of the tower were driven by power from the waterwheel and two in the upper half of the tower were powered by the sails. The mill ceased using wind power in 1916 and water power in 1952 but has been well maintained and restored since.

Where to stay and eat

There is a distinct lack of accommodation actually on the early stage of the Peddars Way, and the only place to stay here is ***Sycamore House*** (☎ 01953-881887, 🖳 j.wittridge@btinternet.com; 1S/2D/1T, one double is en suite, the others share bathroom facilities), which offers B&B in a very welcoming, chintzy house. The single costs £35 and the rate for two sharing is £60-65. The shared bathroom has a Jacuzzi. Evening meals are not available but the owner will kindly run you to and from The Olde Windmill Inn in Great Cressingham (see below) for supper. In the morning he will prepare a packed lunch for £5, which is very handy as there are no food stops on the first part of the following day's walk. Dogs are welcome if booked in advance.

LITTLE CRESSINGHAM TO CASTLE ACRE — MAPS 8-13

These **11½ miles (18.5km, 4hrs 10 mins-4½hrs)** again form an almost arrow-straight track, much of it metalled, which continues to push across the broad farmland and lightly wooded countryside. The landscape of rolling hills, cultivated, chequered fields and the occasional stand of trees is subtle rather than dramatic, but nonetheless charming.

Leave Little Cressingham from the crossroads in the middle of the hamlet, on a road called Pilgrims Way, and follow the Peddars Way as it undulates gently north. Cross the road to **Great Cressingham** and continue northwards towards **South Pickenham**.

GREAT CRESSINGHAM

Almost two miles from the Peddars Way, Great Cressingham is a picturesque village with a fine church, **St Michaels**. There is also a **priory**, set inside the moat of an earlier manor house that dates from the 16th century. In addition the village boasts a good pub with accommodation and a B&B.

The Olde Windmill Inn (☎ 01760-756232, 🖳 www.oldewindmillinn.co.uk; 5D, 3D or T, en suite, bath available; open daily 11am-11pm, food served daily 11.30am-2pm & 5.30-10pm, Sun till 9.30pm), at Water End, has been operating since the mid-17th century. It is a rambling, rustic building supported by oak beams, with three bars, separate dining areas, a modern extension and a beer garden.

The extensive menu includes steak and kidney pudding (£9.95), steaks from

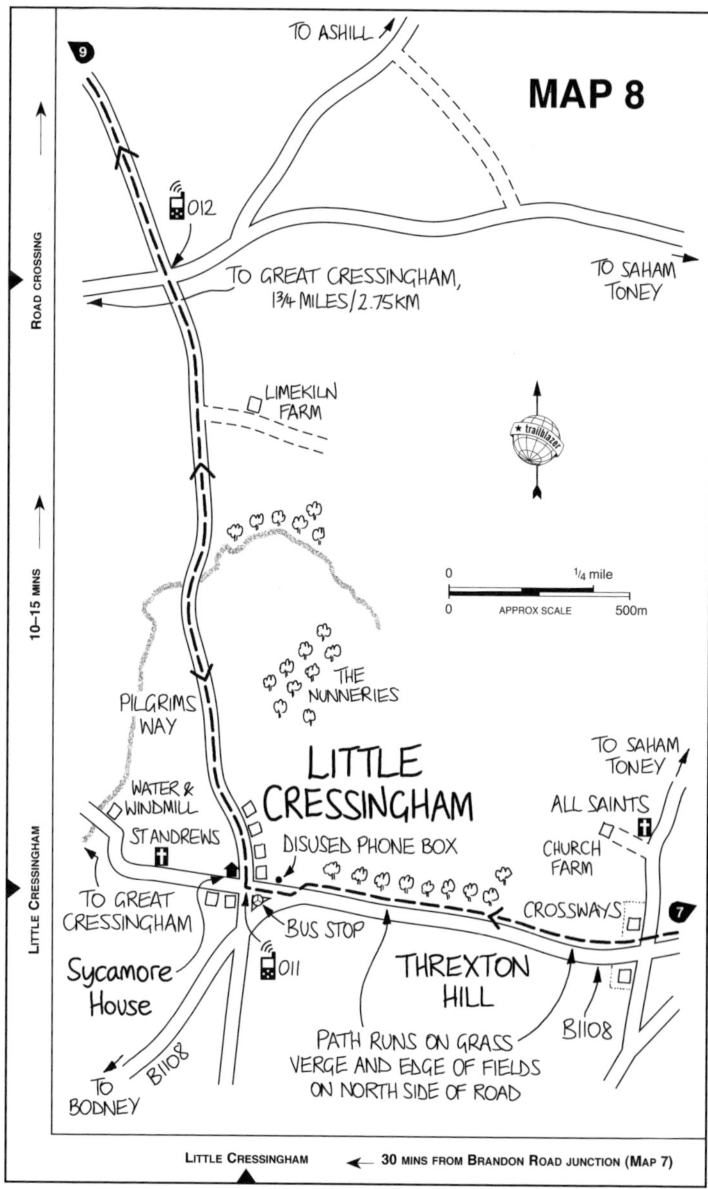
MAP 8
TO ASHILL
9
012
TO GREAT CRESSINGHAM,
1¾ MILES/2.75KM
TO SAHAM
TONEY
LIMEKILN
FARM
trailblazer
0
¼ mile
0
APPROX SCALE
500m
THE
NUNNERIES
PILGRIMS
WAY
LITTLE
CRESSINGHAM
TO SAHAM
TONEY
ALL SAINTS
WATER &
WINDMILL
ST ANDREWS
DISUSED PHONE BOX
CHURCH
FARM
CROSSWAYS
7
TO GREAT
CRESSINGHAM
BUS STOP
Sycamore
House
011
THREXTON
HILL
B1108
PATH RUNS ON GRASS
VERGE AND EDGE OF FIELDS
ON NORTH SIDE OF ROAD
TO
BODNEY
B1108
ROAD CROSSING
10–15 MINS
LITTLE CRESSINGHAM
LITTLE CRESSINGHAM
30 MINS FROM BRANDON ROAD JUNCTION (MAP 7)

£15.25, and vegetarian dishes such as Indian-style vegetable masala (£8.25). Their signature sandwich, a bacon and cheese hoagie prepared 'Windmill style', costs £5.35. Wash the meal down with a pint of the house beer, Windy Miller, or one of the 30 malt whiskies stocked behind the bar. The smart rooms are traditional in style but have modern amenities. Rooms cost £55-60 per night, single occupancy £52.75. Breakfast is served 7.30-9.30am and a full English costs £8.95; non-residents are welcome if they book in advance. Dogs are welcome; £5 per night per dog.

The Vines (☎ 01760-756303, 💻 www.thevinesbedandbreakfast.co.uk; 3D/1T, all en suite, bath available), on The Street, is a Grade II listed, timber-framed 15th-century cottage in a peaceful location, offering high-quality rooms for £59-75; single occupancy costs £40. Dogs are welcome (£5 per dog per night or £8 for two dogs).

As you ease gently northwards past **Caudle Common** and approach Hall Farm, keep an eye out for the chimneys of **Pickenham Hall** to the west, looming over the trees. It is owned by the Packiri family, who are still landlords for many of the properties in the village of South Pickenham. There has been a hall at Pickenham since Tudor times, but the present red-brick building was enlarged and rebuilt in the style of the Arts and Crafts movement in the first few years of the 20th century. Surrounded by parkland, the hall is relatively modest, built for comfort rather than to impress, a factor which has ensured its survival as it is easy to maintain.

There is a crossroads immediately after Hall Farm; to the left is **South Pickenham**. There are no facilities in the village but just beyond Pickenham Hall is an historic church, **All Saints**; it has a distinctive Norman round tower and medieval crown and flint walls dating from 1075. Inside are some well-preserved historic memorials, a 15th-century wall painting of St Christopher, an elegant piscine and 14th-century font as well as an impressive organ with winged doors, considered to be one of the great East Anglian art treasures of the 19th century. The wings open out to show images of the Nativity and the Adoration of the Magi, and the keys still produce a fine sound.

One mile to the east of Hall Farm crossroads is ***Brick Kiln Farm and Spauls Caravan & Camping Park*** (☎ 01760-441300, 💻 brickkiln@onetel.com; open year-round), which has tent pitches for £6 plus £1 per person per night and decent shower and washroom facilities. Advance booking is preferred.

North of the crossroads the path leaves the road and runs parallel to it behind a hedge before dropping into the River Wissey valley to cross the river. Before descending though there is a side track that climbs to **St Mary's Church** (☎ 01760-440470 , 💻 www.hoh.org.uk), set on the summit of a small hill to the east. The rather pretty 11th-century church, all that remains of the hamlet of Houghton, has been restored; during the restoration Romanesque wall paintings were uncovered. The church is open daily from 2pm and stays open as long as people are there. The round-trip diversion takes 15-20 minutes.

Having skirted around a series of fields to descend to the river, the path crosses it and climbs away alongside a further series of fields before edging around a school and joining a road opposite a **war memorial** commemorating

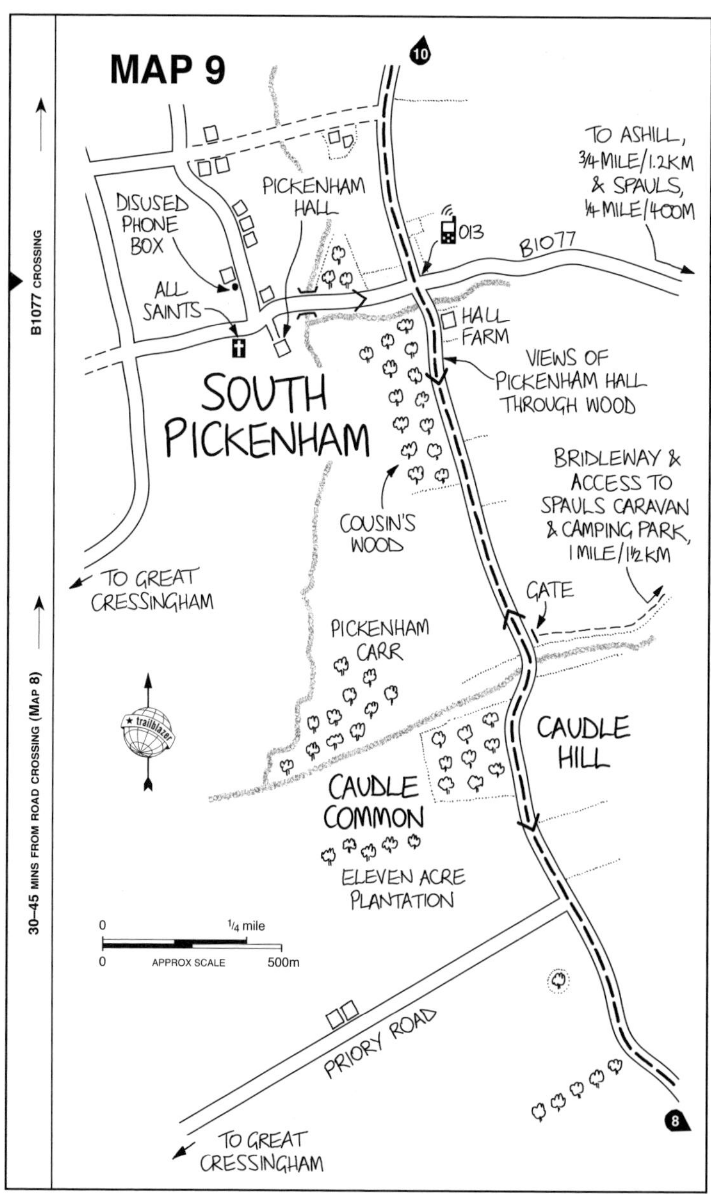
MAP 9
B1077 CROSSING
30–45 MINS FROM ROAD CROSSING (MAP 8)
10
TO ASHILL,
3/4 MILE/1.2KM
& SPAULS,
1/4 MILE/400M
DISUSED
PHONE
BOX
PICKENHAM
HALL
013
B1077
ALL
SAINTS
HALL
FARM
VIEWS OF
PICKENHAM HALL
THROUGH WOOD
SOUTH
PICKENHAM
BRIDLEWAY &
ACCESS TO
SPAULS CARAVAN
& CAMPING PARK,
1 MILE/1½KM
COUSIN'S
WOOD
TO GREAT
CRESSINGHAM
GATE
PICKENHAM
CARR
trailblazer
CAUDLE
HILL
CAUDLE
COMMON
ELEVEN ACRE
PLANTATION
0
1/4 mile
0
APPROX SCALE
500m
PRIORY ROAD
TO GREAT
CRESSINGHAM
8

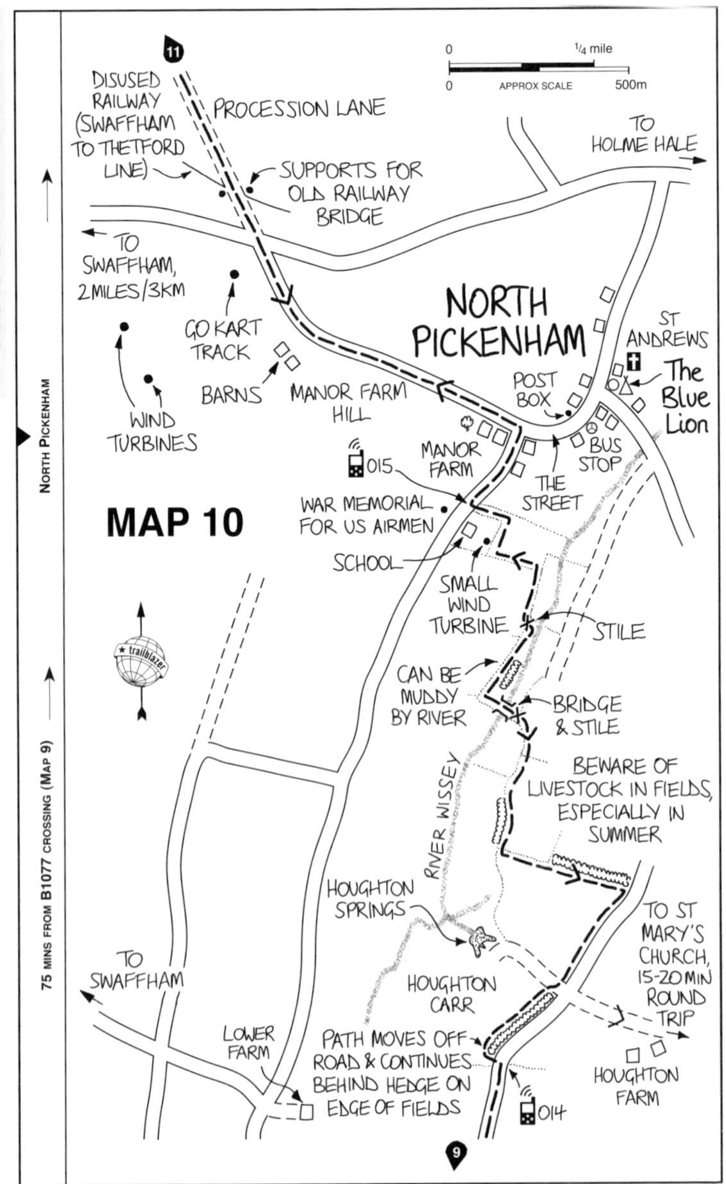
ROUTE GUIDE AND MAPS
MAP 10
75 MINS FROM B1077 CROSSING (MAP 9)
NORTH PICKENHAM
11
9
0 1/4 mile
0 APPROX SCALE 500m
DISUSED RAILWAY (SWAFFHAM TO THETFORD LINE)
PROCESSION LANE
SUPPORTS FOR OLD RAILWAY BRIDGE
TO HOLME HALE
TO SWAFFHAM, 2 MILES/3KM
GO KART TRACK
NORTH PICKENHAM
ST ANDREWS
The Blue Lion
POST BOX
BARNS
MANOR FARM HILL
WIND TURBINES
MANOR FARM
BUS STOP
THE STREET
015
WAR MEMORIAL FOR US AIRMEN
SCHOOL
SMALL WIND TURBINE
STILE
trailblazer
CAN BE MUDDY BY RIVER
BRIDGE & STILE
BEWARE OF LIVESTOCK IN FIELDS, ESPECIALLY IN SUMMER
RIVER WISSEY
HOUGHTON SPRINGS
TO ST MARY'S CHURCH, 15-20 MIN ROUND TRIP
HOUGHTON CARR
TO SWAFFHAM
LOWER FARM
PATH MOVES OFF ROAD & CONTINUES BEHIND HEDGE ON EDGE OF FIELDS
HOUGHTON FARM
014

the American airmen stationed here during World War II. More than 500 members of 42nd Bomb Group lost their lives in 64 missions flown over three months in 1944. The airfield has been converted and is now home to eight wind turbines, visible on the skyline. Turn right and walk to a T-junction. The Peddars Way continues left, whilst right takes you into North Pickenham.

There's little in **North Pickenham** to keep you here, although there is a **church**, St Andrew's, that's part medieval and part 19th century, and an unpretentious pub, ***The Blue Lion*** (☎ 01760-440289; Mon-Fri 4-11pm, Sat noon-midnight, Sun noon-4pm & 7-10.30pm), which will quench your thirst. They will also allow you to **camp** in the pub garden for free, although there are no facilities. However, the pub was on the market at the time of writing so these details may have changed.

From the T-junction turn left onto Manor Farm Hill Rd and continue along the tarmac road. Cross over the next road to Swaffham, and join Procession Lane, a wide dirt track that begins by the remains of two supports for an old railway line bridge that used to cross the path here. Undulate north passing another Norfolk Songline Sculpture (see box p90) until you reach the A47, connecting King's Lynn to Norwich. Just to the left, before a roundabout, is a petrol station where you can pick up snacks and cold drinks, and a McDonald's fast food restaurant. There are also public **toilets** and a card **phone** here. Beyond the roundabout the road left continues to **Swaffham** which is two miles from the Peddars Way.

SWAFFHAM

Swaffham is a small market town that developed during Norfolk's wealthy medieval agricultural past, and was once a bustling social centre with a theatre, racecourse and dance hall. Although the Market Place still has Georgian buildings and a domed rotunda the other features and entertainments are now gone.

Set on a slight rise the town's two wind turbines are easily identifiable against the skyline whilst the Georgian and Victorian façades hide mostly medieval houses. The tall, slender church of **St Peter and St Paul** is particularly impressive, with 88 flying angels set in its roof and medieval carving still evident in the Victorian benches and choir stalls. Once home to Howard Carter who famously discovered Tutankhamen's tomb, the town has various useful services for the walker.

The Carter connection is explored at **Swaffham Museum** (☎ 01760-721230, 🖳 www.swaffhammuseum.co.uk; Easter to Christmas Tue-Sat 10am-4pm; £2.50), housed in a Grade II listed town house at 4 London St, which has local historical information as well as material on ancient Egypt. There is a **tourist information centre** (☎ 01760-722255, 🖳 tic@swaffhammuseum.co.uk; Easter to Christmas Tue-Sat 10am-4pm) in the museum. They have information on accommodation but don't do bookings.

Eco Tech (☎ 01760-726100, 🖳 www.ecotech.org.uk; Mon-Fri 10am-4pm, free), an award-winning sustainable environmental education centre that offers turbine tours (3/day; adults £6, children £4) during which you are guided to the top of the E66 wind turbine. The two wind turbines power the centre and provide the majority of Swaffham's energy requirements.

Transport

[See also pp46-8] There is a daily National Express **coach** service (NX496) to and from London Victoria. National Express's NX308 stops here en route between Birmingham and Great Yarmouth; see p44.

Freestones' No 32 **bus** runs to and from King's Lynn; one of the three services a day (Mon-Sat) goes via Castle Acre. West Norfolk Community Transport's bus No 32 connects Swaffham to Castle Acre twice a day on weekdays. Konectbus No 11 runs to and from Sporle and Watton.

Where to stay

If you're camping head to ***Breckland Meadows*** (☎ 01760-721246, 💻 www.breck landmeadows.co.uk; open all year) to the west of Swaffham on Lynn Rd, a caravan touring park that has a small number of tent pitches (£8 for a one-man tent and £11.50 for a tent with two people), washrooms, laundry facilities and a small shop which is open daily. Booking is recommended in the summer months.

Several places offer B&B. Try ***Purbeck House*** (☎ 01760-721805, 💻 pur beckhouse@yahoo.com; 1S/3D/2T, all en suite, bath available), at 46 Whitsands Rd, where the rate for two sharing is £50; the single is £30 but single occupancy of a double/twin is £35.

Lydney House Hotel (☎ 01760-723355, 💻 www.lydney-house.demon.co .uk; 1S/6D/1T, all en suite, bath available) located next to the town's medieval church has good-quality rooms and charges £75 for B&B; the single is £65.

Strattons Hotel (☎ 01760-723845, 💻 www.strattonshotel.com; 14D, all en suite, bath available), at 4 Ash Close, is a more upmarket boutique hotel with excellent green credentials, and it charges accordingly. The rooms are individual and funky; doubles start at £150 and suites cost upwards of £200. Single occupancy costs £120-130 inclusive of bed and breakfast. Dogs are accepted in some of the rooms.

Where to eat and drink

For fish and chips pop into ***Mother Hubbard's*** (☎ 01760-721933; Mon 11.30am-2pm & 4.30-9pm, Tue-Thur 11.30am-2pm & 4.30-10pm, Fri 11.30am-10pm, Sat 10.30am-10pm, Sun 4-9pm), at 91 Market Place, where good-sized portions of award-winning grub cost from £5.50.

Market Cross Café (☎ 01760-336671; Mon-Wed 10am-6pm, Thur-Sat 10am-11pm, Sun 10am-4pm, Dec-Easter closed Sun), in Market Place, serves good coffee as well as light lunches and evening meals, and is licensed.

If you're after a pint the bar in ***Lydney House Hotel*** (see Where to stay; daily 11am-10.30pm) is a relaxing place to unwind with a pint of Woodforde's Wherry or other good quality real ale; you can also try playing one of their traditional pub games.

The award-winning restaurant at ***Strattons Hotel*** (see Where to stay; daily 6.30-9pm) serves locally sourced produce such as monkfish cheek pie with smoked dapple mash and Swiss chard (£15), or grilled mackerel with German potato and runner bean salad and creamed horseradish (£12). They also have a coffee shop and deli (Tue-Sat 8am-6pm) which serves morning coffee, light lunches, afternoon teas and the ingredients for a packed lunch.

For something less local there's good Chinese food at ***East Garden Chinese Restaurant*** (☎ 01760-725722; Tue-Sun noon-2pm & 5-11pm), on London St.

Beyond the A47 a metalled road continues, passing over a disused railway line (the old King's Lynn to Dereham line) before zigzagging abruptly and branching off the road that leads to the pretty village of Sporle, to join Palgrave Rd to Palgrave Hall.

In **Sporle**, just over a mile to the east, accommodation is available at ***Corfield House*** (☎ 01760-723636, 💻 www.corfieldhouse.co.uk; 2D/2T, all en suite, bath available), on The Street; B&B is good value at £60 for two sharing and £40 for single occupancy. There is a pub, ***The Squirrels Drey*** (☎ 01760-724842, 💻 www.thesquirrelsdrey.co.uk; open daily, food served Tue-Sun noon-2pm & 6-9.30pm) where you can eat (the menu includes both meat and fish dishes; most mains cost £12-15), and a small shop, **Threeways General**

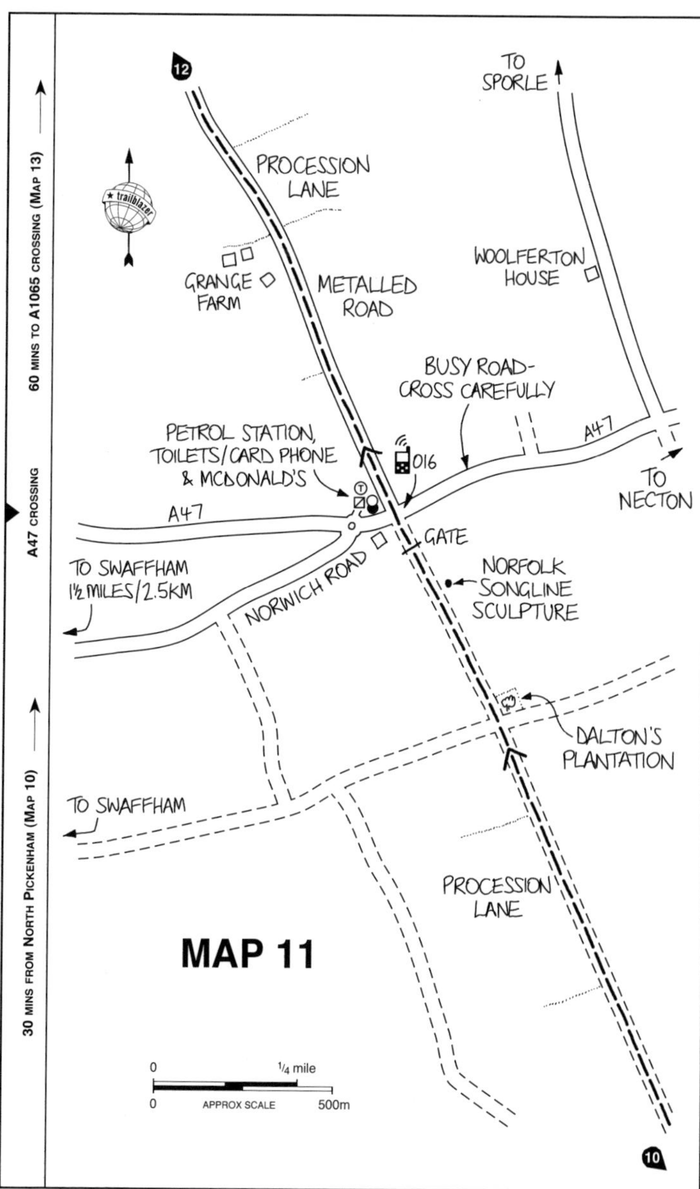
60 MINS TO A1065 CROSSING (MAP 13)
A47 CROSSING
30 MINS FROM NORTH PICKENHAM (MAP 10)
12
TO SPORLE
PROCESSION LANE
GRANGE FARM
METALLED ROAD
WOOLFERTON HOUSE
BUSY ROAD-CROSS CAREFULLY
PETROL STATION, TOILETS/CARD PHONE & MCDONALD'S
016
A47
A47
TO NECTON
GATE
TO SWAFFHAM 1½ MILES/2.5KM
NORWICH ROAD
NORFOLK SONGLINE SCULPTURE
DALTON'S PLANTATION
TO SWAFFHAM
PROCESSION LANE
MAP 11
0 ¼ mile
0 APPROX SCALE 500m
10

Store (☎ 01760-724300; Mon-Sat 6am-7pm, Sun 7.30am-7pm), where you can buy basic supplies. **Konectbus** No 11 stops outside the stores.

Pass Palgrave Hall before turning left at a T-junction and following the minor road that skirts Hungry Hill and descends to cross the A1065 Swaffham to Fakenham Rd at Bartholomew's Hills. A metalled track then descends

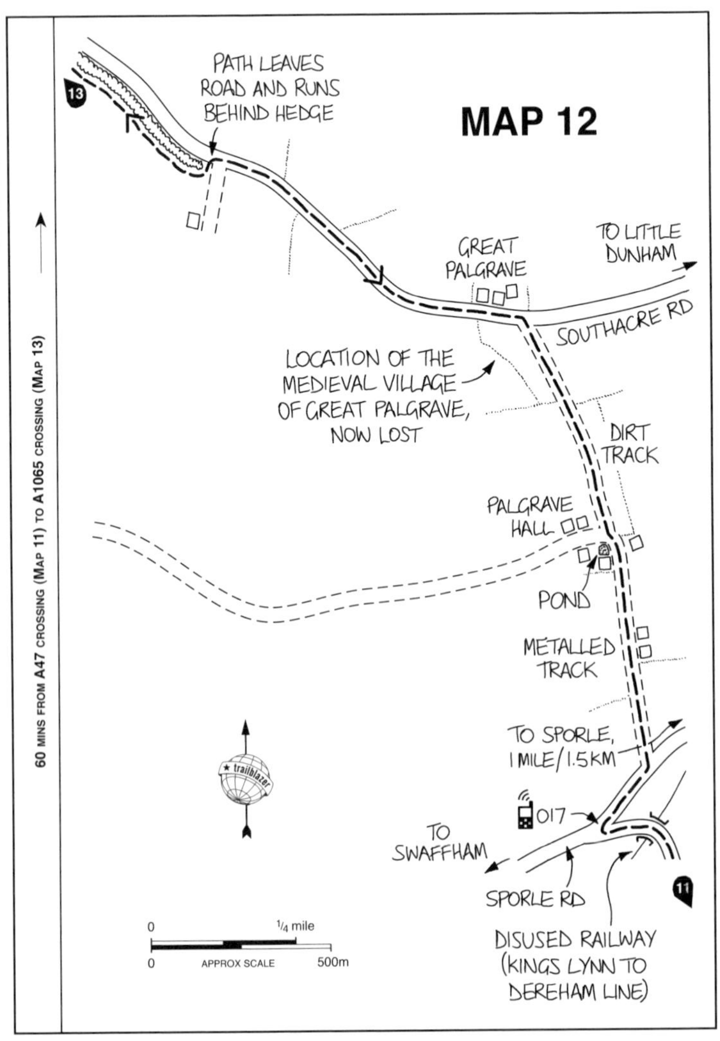

towards South Acre and another crossroads. Cross straight over and take the road signed 'Ford, unsuitable for motors' and descend to the **River Nar** on a narrow road, with glimpses through the trees and hedgerow of Castle Acre and its ruined priory in the distance. There is a footbridge over the river or you can splash through the shallow ford to emerge opposite the Cluniac priory ruins (see below). There is a short path beyond a stile that curves round to the ruins and provides access to the site. Turn right along the river briefly and ascend into Castle Acre, entering the centre of the village by passing beneath a bailey gate.

CASTLE ACRE [see map p107]

The medieval village occupies a strategic location overlooking the River Nar and controlling traffic on the Peddars Way. Roughly halfway along the Peddars Way it makes for a good base. The village itself lies within the outer bailey of an 11th-century castle and the road into the village still passes under the **Bailey Gate**, the former north gateway to the planned walled town. The village takes its name from the Norman castle, built soon after the Conquest by William de Warrene, first Earl of Surrey, which lies off Bailey St. Initially a stone country house it was converted into a keep defended by stone walls and a system of ditched earthworks. Although now only its walls and ramparts remain, it still provides an impressive indication as to what the castle must once have looked like, and some consider these the finest village earthworks in England. Access is from Bailey St, adjacent to the Old Red Lion (see Where to stay) and is free. Interpretative panels dotted about the site provide information and reveal just how extensive the planned village and fortifications were in their prime.

The **Cluniac Priory** (Apr-Sep daily 10am-5 or 6pm, Oct-Mar Thur-Mon 10am-4pm; adult £5.30, child £2.70, English Heritage members free) is thought to have been founded in 1089 and was inspired by the monastery at Cluny in France. Originally built within the walls of the castle it was too small for the monks, so was moved to its current location by the River Nar. Although tumbledown, the ruins, which are in the care of English Heritage, are still in good condition. It's possible to see the great west front of the building, complete with tiered ranks of intersecting round arches, and much of its core structure including a 15th-century gate house and porch. The substantial prior's lodgings are also well preserved and boast traces of wall paintings and two fine oriel windows. At its height 25 monks resided here in fine style, but all of this was wiped away with the Dissolution in 1536. Next to the priory is a recreated herb garden. There is also a visitor centre with a display of artefacts, a site model and exhibition as well as a small shop selling snacks and public toilets.

Centred on Stocks Green, Castle Acre itself is an attractive place with plenty of pretty houses. The church of **St James the Great** stands at one end of the Green and enjoys sweeping views out over the countryside. The interior of the substantial church is bright and lofty. An unusual font and pulpit make popping in worthwhile.

Services

The good-sized Costcutter **supermarket** (Mon-Sat 6am-7.30pm, Sun 8am-6pm) in the village sells groceries and newspapers and also offers **cashback** when you spend £5 or more. There is also a **post office** (Mon-Fri 9am-5pm, Sat 9am-noon) in the shop.

Transport

[See also pp46-8] Freestones' No 32 **bus** service calls here once a day (Mon-Sat) en route between King's Lynn and Swaffham. West Norfolk Community bus No 32 service to Swaffham calls here (Mon-Fri 2/day).

Where to stay

Good-value accommodation can be had at the ***Old Red Lion*** (☎ 01760-755557, 💻 www.oldredlion.org.uk; 2 dorms/3D/2T, one double is en suite, the other rooms

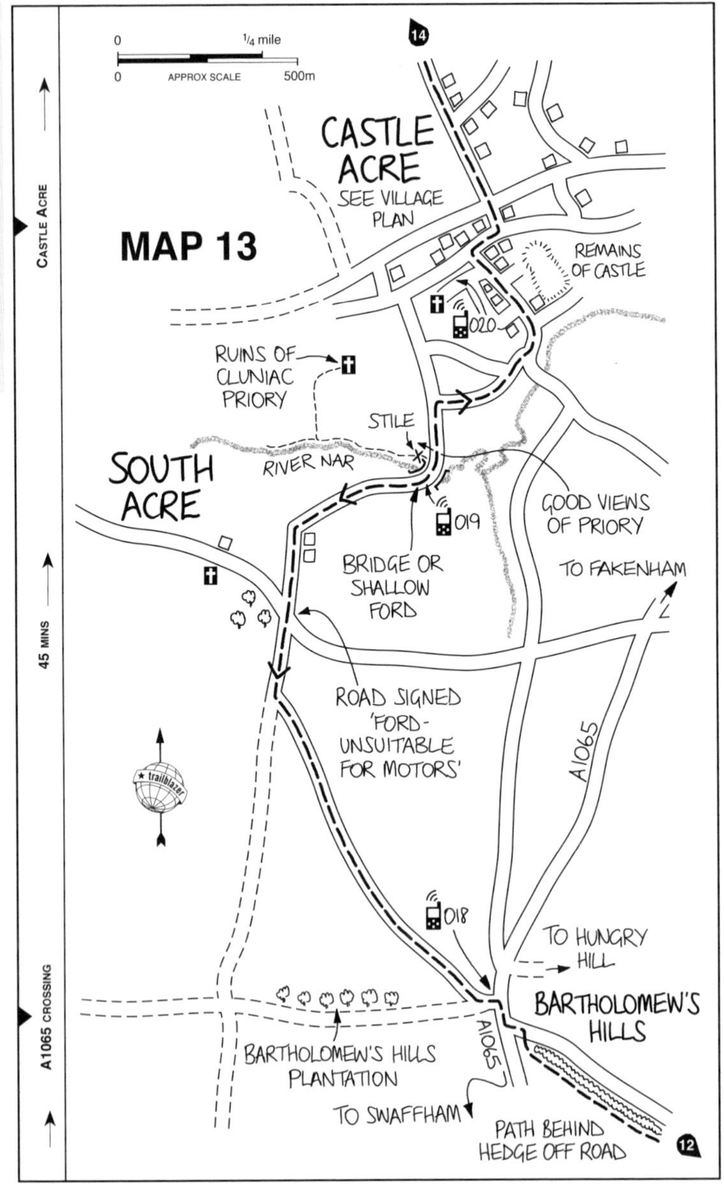

MAP 13
0 1/4 mile
0 APPROX SCALE 500m
CASTLE ACRE
45 MINS
A1065 CROSSING
14
CASTLE ACRE
SEE VILLAGE PLAN
REMAINS OF CASTLE
020
RUINS OF CLUNIAC PRIORY
STILE
RIVER NAR
SOUTH ACRE
GOOD VIEWS OF PRIORY
019
BRIDGE OR SHALLOW FORD
TO FAKENHAM
ROAD SIGNED 'FORD-UNSUITABLE FOR MOTORS'
A1065
trailblazer
018
TO HUNGRY HILL
BARTHOLOMEW'S HILLS
BARTHOLOMEW'S HILLS PLANTATION
A1065
TO SWAFFHAM
PATH BEHIND HEDGE OFF ROAD
12

share bathroom facilities), on Bailey St (main entrance round the back), just before the Bailey Gate. This former 17th-century pub has been lovingly converted into a hostel-cum-B&B with dorm beds for £22.50/pp and private rooms for £25-35/pp (£30-45 for single occupancy). There is a small but fully equipped kitchen as well as a very cosy snug where you can meet fellow guests. All rates include bedding, a towel and a vegetarian wholefood self-service breakfast with homemade breads; the kindly owner will lead you in a couple of yoga stretches before you head on if you're feeling the aches and pains of the previous day – she gives classes for locals on Monday, Tuesday and Friday. Dogs accepted by arrangement.

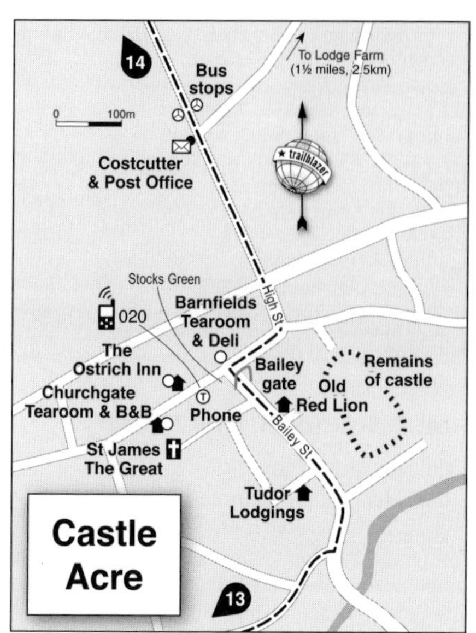

Churchgate Tea Room and Bed and Breakfast (☎ 01760-755551, 🖳 www.churchgatecastleacre.co.uk; 3D/1T, all en suite), close to the church on Stocks Green, is a family-run business set in a house dating from the mid-1700s. The smart, tasteful rooms cost £65 (£45 single occupancy). They have drying facilities and also offer a luggage-transfer service; contact them for details. If you prefer a bath to a shower ask if their holiday cottage (1D/1T, both en suite) is available as the bathroom for the double has a bath; price on application.

Also on Stocks Green, ***The Ostrich Inn*** (☎ 01760-755398, 🖳 www.ostrichcastleacre.com; 2D/2T/1F, all en suite, bath available) is an impressive 16th-century coaching inn with bright, generous rooms, most of which look out over the Green. Rates are £80 per night and include breakfast. Single occupancy costs £65.

Tudor Lodgings (☎ 01760-755334, 🖳 www.tudorlodgings.co.uk; 2T, both en suite), on Pales Green, has B&B in The Old Cottage for £65 (single occupancy £45). They also provide stabling and grazing if you are riding in the area.

Lodge Farm (☎ 01760-755506, 🖳 www.lodgefarmcastleacre.co.uk; 1D/1T, both en suite with bath/1F with private bathroom), 1½ miles from the Peddars Way to the north of Castle Acre on Rougham Rd, charges £30-35pp but the rate for the family room is negotiable. **Camping** is available if booked in advance; pitches cost £10 and include access to toilet and shower facilities. Breakfast is available for £7.50pp; horses can either be stabled (£10 per horse) or given grass to graze (£5 per horse). Dogs are welcome if prebooked.

Where to eat and drink

For homemade cakes (such as Granny's fruitcake and Victoria sponge), or light lunches with a changing selection of specials, visit the homely ***Churchgate Tea Room*** (see Where to stay; Tue-Sun 10.30am-5pm); the tea room has an original inglenook fireplace and dark wood beams giving it plenty of character. Cream teas are £3.40 whilst sandwiches cost from £3.20 and jacket potatoes from £3.40 (with a filling from £4).

Alternatively, ***Barnfields Tea Room*** (☎ 01760-755577; Fri-Mon 10am-4pm), also on Stocks Green, serves breakfast till 11.15am and lunch till 2.30pm. The full English (£6.25) is generous and will set you up well for what's ahead, as will the Welsh rarebit (£5.25) and their sandwiches (from £3.95). The small **shop** next door sells local produce and local ice-cream.

The Ostrich Inn (see Where to stay; daily 10am-11pm, food daily noon-3pm & 6-9pm except Sun when the kitchen is closed in the evening) is comfy and warm, with striking décor and a good atmosphere. It wears its 400 years well although the walls aren't all straight and the ceiling is slightly skew-whiff. The beer garden is well-maintained and tranquil. The menu changes regularly (see the website for the latest) but for lunch may include the Houghton Hall venison stew and dumplings (£11.95), or a substantial panini (£7.95). In the evening the menu may include fish stew (£17.95) or a grilled rack of lamb (£10.95). If you've space, puddings are old school and substantial, or there is a great cheese-board that includes Binham Blue and Norfolk Dapple (£7.95).

CASTLE ACRE TO RINGSTEAD — MAPS 13-22

The path from Castle Acre to Ringstead doesn't look all that appealing on a map. Much of the **17-mile (27km, 6-6¼hrs) route** appears to be along minor roads. However, the route usually follows a grassy path parallel to the metalled surface alongside rolling, cultivated fields, meaning you can take in the wide, expansive views that lend the section a particularly remote feel. There are no food options actually on this section of the path, so bring a packed lunch or be prepared to deviate from the route to find a pub.

The path begins shadowing the road north from the village on a grassy verge behind a hedge. Beyond a **stile** immediately before a crossroads and the Old Wicken Cottages it rejoins the road to descend into a hollow. If you go west at the crossroads you will come to ***Wicken View*** (☎ 01760-755652, 💻 www.wickenview.co.uk; 2D shared bathroom), a former farmhouse dating from the mid 1800s with views of the rolling countryside that offers bed and breakfast for £50 (£40 for single occupancy) with an attractive Victorian-style private bathroom. Dogs are welcome by arrangement.

At the bottom of the slight depression following the crossroads the path once again takes to the grass verge and climbs to another crossroads, where it switches from left to right.

At a pronounced bend in the road, **Shepherd's Bush**, a broad grass track continues straight on, past an old **triangulation pillar**. At 92m (302ft), this signifies the high point on the Peddars Way. The grass track descends alongside Massingham Heath, an expanse of land littered with evidence of Stone Age man, where axes, arrowheads and other implements are frequently unearthed. The path continues towards the B1145, following which a metalled road continues straight ahead, past Betts Field Barn. Continuing over two roads that lead to Great Massingham it climbs to yet another crossroads, to the right of which two **radio masts** can be seen.

The broad grass track which heads east here goes to **Great Massingham**, ¾-mile away. There is a village **shop** (daily 8am-5.30pm except half days on Wed and Sun) here in addition to the well-known traditional country pub, ***The***

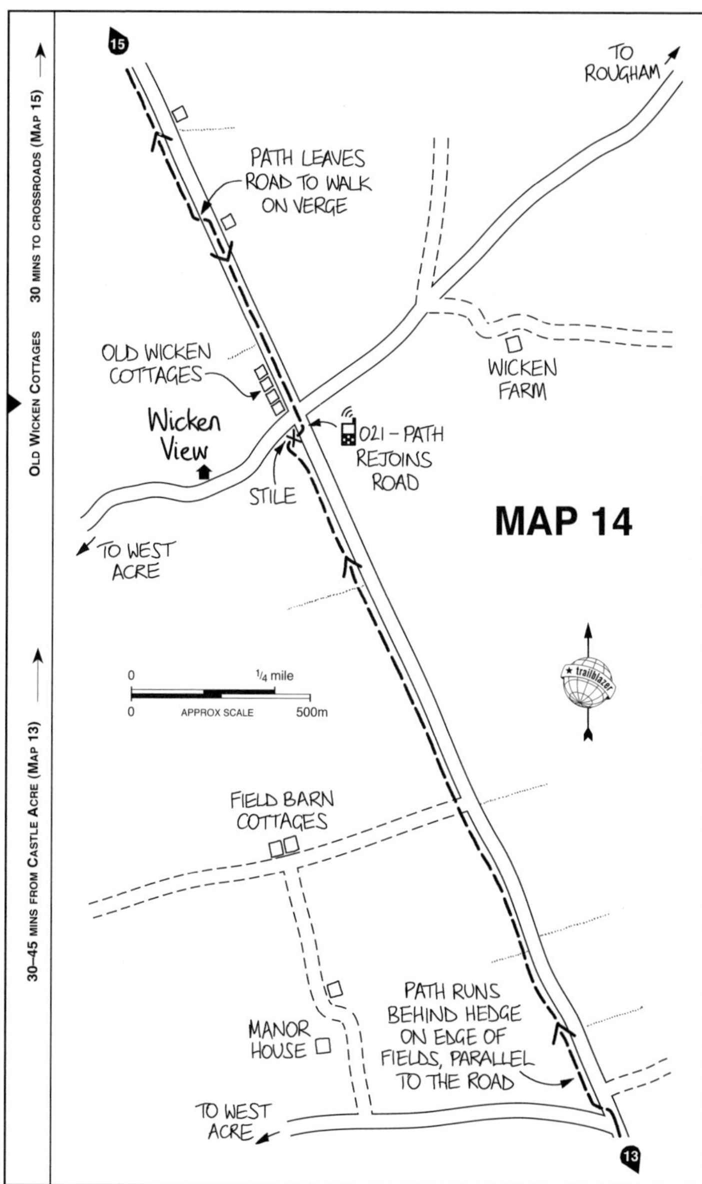

OLD WICKEN COTTAGES
30 MINS TO CROSSROADS (MAP 15) →
30–45 MINS FROM CASTLE ACRE (MAP 13) →
TO ROUGHAM
PATH LEAVES ROAD TO WALK ON VERGE
OLD WICKEN COTTAGES
Wicken View
WICKEN FARM
021 – PATH REJOINS ROAD
STILE
MAP 14
TO WEST ACRE
0
1/4 mile
0
APPROX SCALE
500m
trailblazer
FIELD BARN COTTAGES
PATH RUNS BEHIND HEDGE ON EDGE OF FIELDS, PARALLEL TO THE ROAD
MANOR HOUSE
TO WEST ACRE
15
13

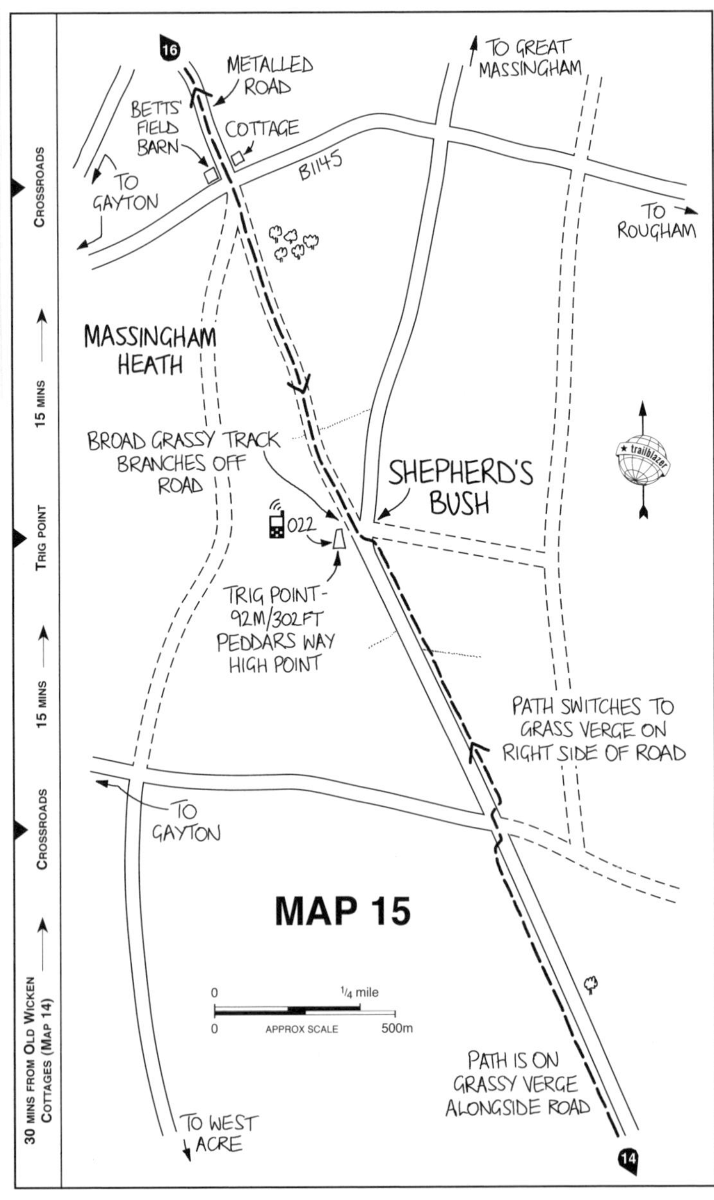

30 mins from Old Wicken Cottages (Map 14)
Crossroads
15 mins
Trig point
15 mins
Crossroads
16
METALLED ROAD
BETTS' FIELD BARN
COTTAGE
B1145
TO GAYTON
TO GREAT MASSINGHAM
TO ROUGHAM
MASSINGHAM HEATH
BROAD GRASSY TRACK BRANCHES OFF ROAD
SHEPHERD'S BUSH
022
TRIG POINT- 92M/302FT PEDDARS WAY HIGH POINT
PATH SWITCHES TO GRASS VERGE ON RIGHT SIDE OF ROAD
TO GAYTON
MAP 15
0
1/4 mile
0
APPROX SCALE
500m
PATH IS ON GRASSY VERGE ALONGSIDE ROAD
TO WEST ACRE
14
trailblazer

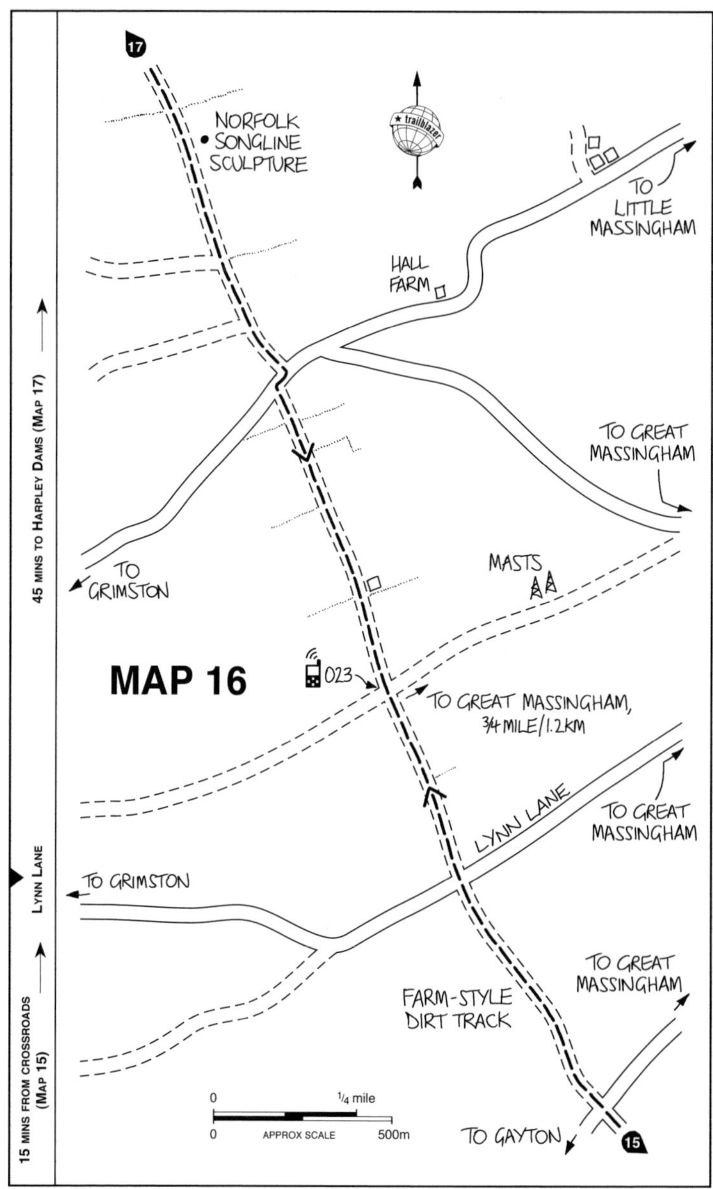
17
NORFOLK
SONGLINE
SCULPTURE
trailblazer
TO
LITTLE
MASSINGHAM
HALL
FARM
TO GREAT
MASSINGHAM
TO
GRIMSTON
MASTS
MAP 16
023
TO GREAT MASSINGHAM,
3/4 MILE/1.2KM
LYNN LANE
TO GREAT
MASSINGHAM
TO GRIMSTON
TO GREAT
MASSINGHAM
FARM-STYLE
DIRT TRACK
0
1/4 mile
0
APPROX SCALE
500m
TO GAYTON
15
45 MINS TO HARPLEY DAMS (MAP 17)
LYNN LANE
15 MINS FROM CROSSROADS
(MAP 15)

Dabbling Duck (☎ 01485-520827, 💻 www.thedabblingduck.co.uk; 5D/1T, all en suite, bath available; Mon-Sat noon-11pm, Sun noon-10.30pm), at 11 Abbey Rd. The pub is set between two ponds that have their origins as fish ponds and is connected to an 11th-century Augustinian Abbey. The pub lets its tastefully decorated rooms for £80 for B&B (single occupancy £55). The changing menu in the bar (food served daily noon-2.30pm & 6.30-9pm) showcases seasonal local produce and there's always a good selection of local ales on handpump at the bar, which is shaped from a giant slab of tree trunk. Well-behaved dogs are welcome.

The Peddars Way passes a striking Norfolk Songline sculpture (see box p90) and then descends gently past Clarke's Farm and then a fuel pipe installation to arrive at a disused railway line running parallel to the busy A148 Hillington to Fakenham road. Cross both of these (cross the A148 carefully) and push on over the minor road beyond that which is the most pleasant way of walking to **Harpley**, 1½ miles away, where B&B is available at ***Meadow House*** (☎ 01485-520240; 2D or T, en suite, bath available) from £40pp; packed lunches on request. At the time of writing the ***Rose and Crown*** pub was closed but it is possible it will reopen.

❑ Houghton Hall

The 18th-century politician Robert Walpole, generally considered to be Great Britain's first Prime Minister, was educated in Great Massingham. He also built Houghton Hall (💻 www.houghtonhall.com; Easter to end Sep, Wed, Thur, Sun and Bank Holiday Mondays 11.30am-5.30pm, with access to the house itself available 1.30-5pm; adult £8.80, child £3.50) nearby.

The Hall, set in 350 acres of parkland that are home to a herd of white fallow deer, is one of the finest surviving Palladian mansions in England. Designed for entertaining on a grand scale, the hall was meant to symbolise the great power of its owner. In fact, plans for the Hall were so grand that it was feared the village of Houghton wouldn't be in keeping with the house so it had to be destroyed and rebuilt a mile further away. During Walpole's heyday the Hall was filled with magnificent treasures including china, tapestries, sculptures and a collection of Old Masters. Sadly in 1779 the paintings were sold by Walpole's grandson to Catherine the Great of Russia and now form part of the collection in the Hermitage in St Petersburg. The Hall does still boast an impressive collection of more than 20,000 model soldiers gathered together by the 6th Marquess, who was fascinated by the campaigns of the Napoleonic period. Complex battle scenes are depicted from the battle of Waterloo to the Second World War.

The walled garden was renovated at the start of the 1990s and now features a series of ornamental gardens in various styles. The rose garden is planted with around 150 varieties, whilst the box-edged parterre is based on the ceiling design in the Hall's White Drawing Room.

Stables Restaurant (days/hours as for the hall) on the premises serves light lunches and homemade cakes and pastries as well as hot drinks. Horse trials (see p26) and the Brancaster Midsummer Music (see pp26-7) are also held here.

To reach the Hall follow the path north-east as shown on Map 17 and head to New Houghton around three miles away; from there you head north a further mile to the Hall.

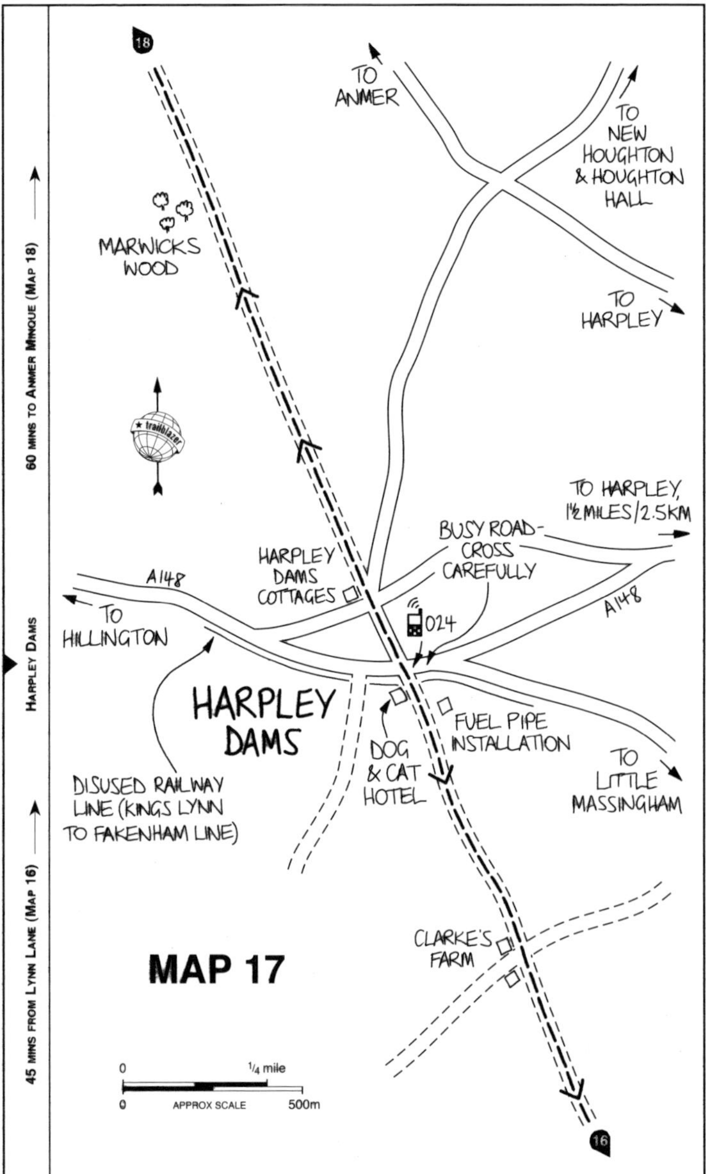
60 mins to Anmer Minque (Map 18)
Harpley Dams
45 mins from Lynn Lane (Map 16)
18
TO ANMER
TO NEW HOUGHTON & HOUGHTON HALL
MARWICKS WOOD
TO HARPLEY
trailblazer
TO HARPLEY, 1½ MILES/2.5KM
BUSY ROAD - CROSS CAREFULLY
HARPLEY DAMS COTTAGES
A148
TO HILLINGTON
024
A148
HARPLEY DAMS
FUEL PIPE INSTALLATION
DOG & CAT HOTEL
TO LITTLE MASSINGHAM
DISUSED RAILWAY LINE (KINGS LYNN TO FAKENHAM LINE)
CLARKE'S FARM
MAP 17
0
1/4 mile
0
APPROX SCALE
500m
16

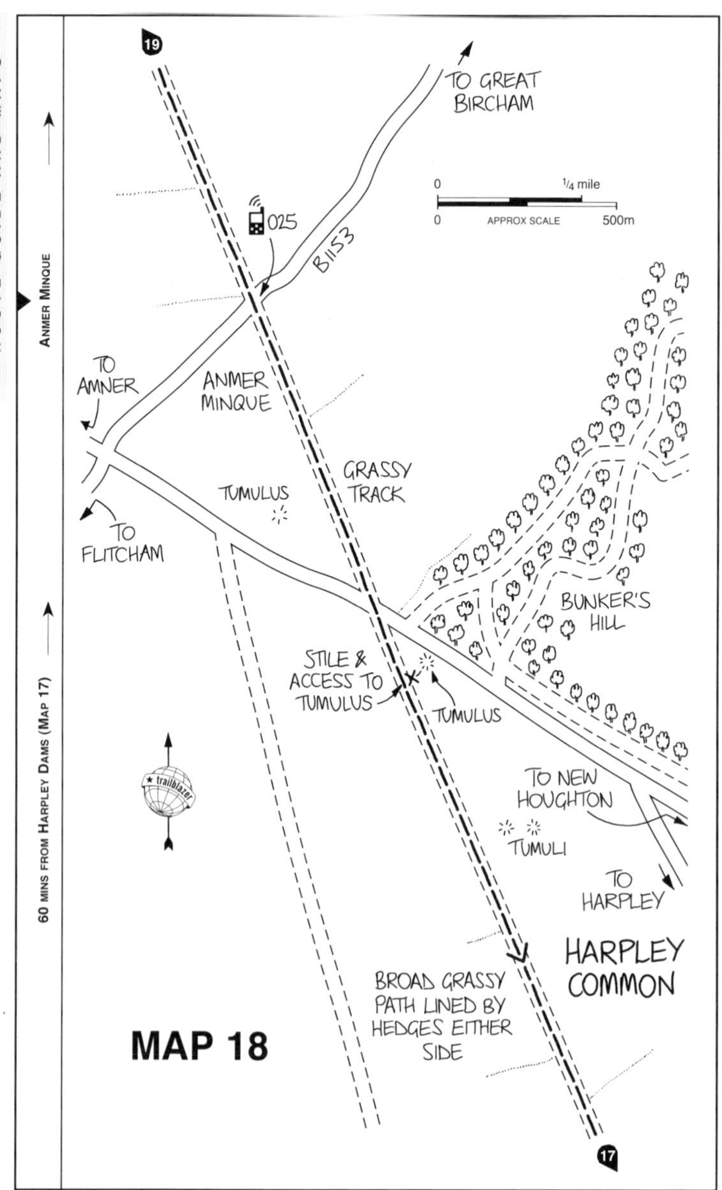

19
TO GREAT BIRCHAM
0
1/4 mile
0
APPROX SCALE
500m
025
B1153
ANMER MINQUE
TO AMNER
ANMER MINQUE
GRASSY TRACK
TUMULUS
TO FLITCHAM
BUNKER'S HILL
STILE & ACCESS TO TUMULUS
TUMULUS
TO NEW HOUGHTON
TUMULI
TO HARPLEY
HARPLEY COMMON
BROAD GRASSY PATH LINED BY HEDGES EITHER SIDE
MAP 18
60 MINS FROM HARPLEY DAMS (MAP 17)
trailblazer
17

Ascend slowly past Harpley Dams Cottages and then Marwicks Wood. A broad grass path makes its way imperiously across the unspoilt countryside of crop fields, with a number of **tumuli** visible to both east and west. There is access to one of these Bronze Age burial mounds, dating from 1500-1300BC via a stile just before a tarmac road.

Beyond the tarmac road a grassy track ambles past a triangular field, **Amner Minque**, crosses the B1153 to Great Bircham and continues to head straight across the countryside. Eventually, to the east amidst undulating fields are views of the white-capped **Bircham Windmill** and a number of giant cranes at a construction-industry training site. The best way to Great Bircham from the Peddars Way is via Fieldbarn Farm (see Map 19).

GREAT BIRCHAM

Easily identifiable courtesy of the restored Bircham Windmill, one of the few remaining working mills in the region, Great Bircham is a sleepy place 1½ miles from the Peddars Way. Visitors to the village can explore the **windmill** (Apr/Easter-Sep daily 10am-5pm; £3.75/2; see also Where to stay and Where to eat), built in 1846, and climb five floors to the fan stage; on windy days it's still possible to see the sails turn and the machinery in action.

Services

There is a small village **store** (☎ 01485-576006; Mon-Sat 8am-6pm, Sun 9am-noon) that sells hot snacks, homemade soup (in the winter months) and sandwiches to take away as well as groceries and other provisions. For **cycle hire**, see box p35.

Where to stay

Bircham Windmill (☎ 01485-578393, 💻 www.birchamwindmill.co.uk) allows **camping** in the months when the windmill is open; for this reason you may not be able to set up camp before 5pm and you may need to vacate the pitches by 10am. They cost £10 per night. There is access to toilets, wash basins and an outdoor tap.

The King's Head Hotel (☎ 01485-578265, 💻 www.the-kings-head-bircham.co.uk; 11D or T all en suite with bath/1D en suite) is a Grade II listed coachhouse that has been tastefully made over into a stylish modern hotel with contemporary rooms. B&B costs from £110 to £130 (single occupancy £75). Dinner costs an additional £30pp. There's also a drawing room to relax in.

Where to eat and drink

There's a small tearoom and bakery at ***Bircham Windmill*** (see Where to stay; daily 10am-5pm) that still uses its original coal-fired oven. Cream teas are a speciality but you can also buy bread and the flour milled on the premises.

The restaurant of ***The King's Head Hotel*** (see Where to stay; Mon-Sat noon-2pm, Sun noon-3pm & daily 7-9pm) overlooks a sheltered courtyard. Food is carefully prepared and sourced locally. The menu changes regularly and, depending on the season, may include salad of local asparagus (£5.50), pan-seared scallops and local samphire with caper and saffron sauce (£9.75), whilst mains might include pan-fried fillet of black bream with chorizo and home-made gnocchi (£12.25), or roast rump of English lamb (£13.95). During the summer they also host BBQs, and there are events such as jazz evenings that cement the pub's place in the local community.

At a couple of points the path crosses minor roads heading east to the hamlet of **Fring** hidden amidst the trees and west to the larger village of **Snettisham** 2½ miles away. **St Mary's church** in Snettisham has what is reputed to be one of the finest windows in England, containing a complex tracery pattern all the more remarkable given that it dates from the late Middle Ages.

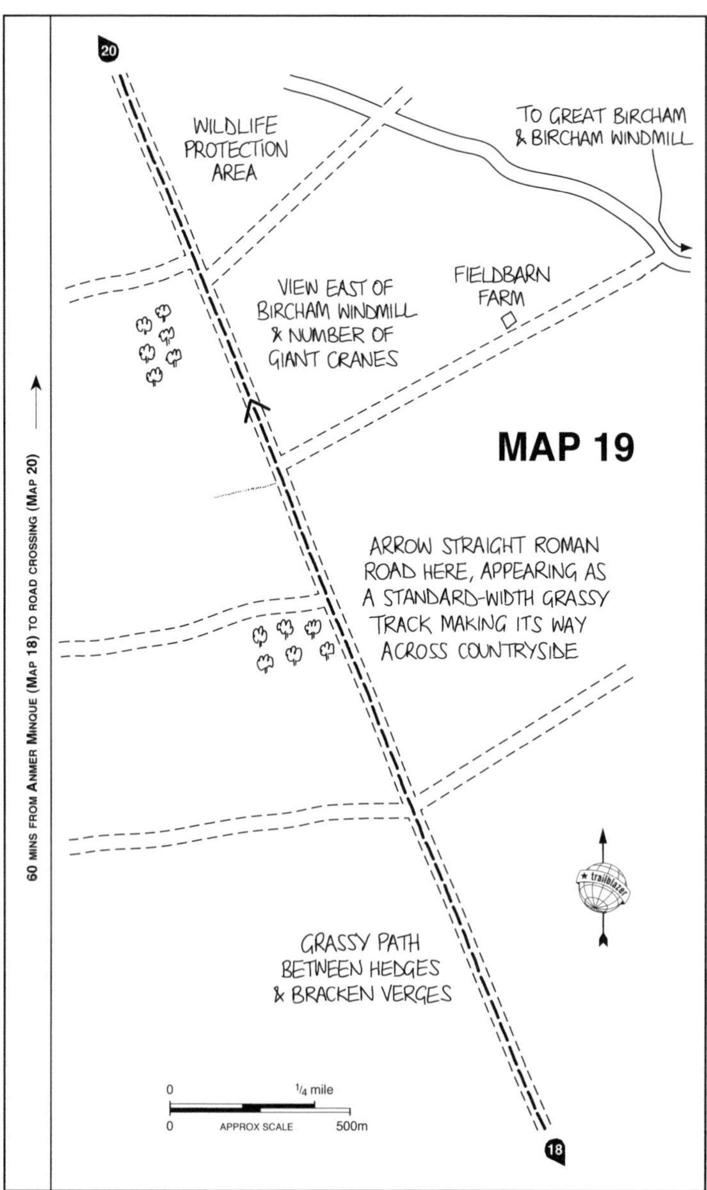

20
WILDLIFE PROTECTION AREA
TO GREAT BIRCHAM & BIRCHAM WINDMILL
FIELDBARN FARM
VIEW EAST OF BIRCHAM WINDMILL & NUMBER OF GIANT CRANES
MAP 19
ARROW STRAIGHT ROMAN ROAD HERE, APPEARING AS A STANDARD-WIDTH GRASSY TRACK MAKING ITS WAY ACROSS COUNTRYSIDE
GRASSY PATH BETWEEN HEDGES & BRACKEN VERGES
trailblazer
0
1/4 mile
0
APPROX SCALE
500m
18
60 MINS FROM ANMER MINQUE (MAP 18) TO ROAD CROSSING (MAP 20)

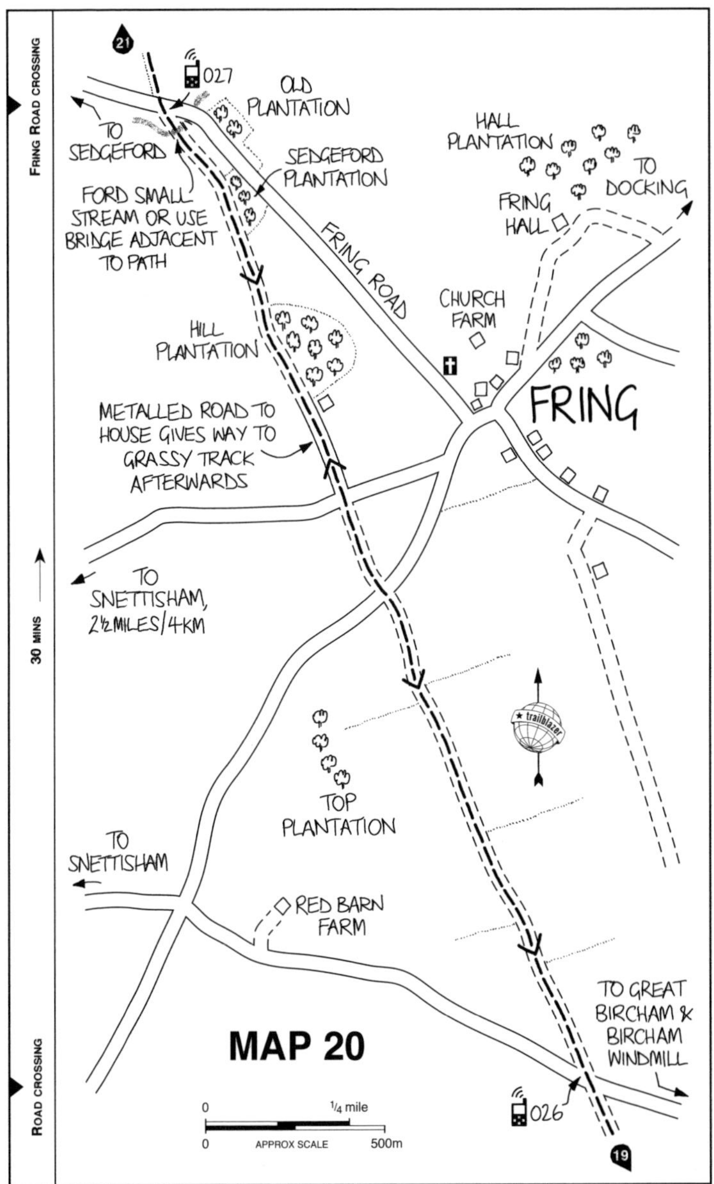

FRING ROAD CROSSING
30 MINS
ROAD CROSSING
21
027
OLD PLANTATION
TO SEDGEFORD
SEDGEFORD PLANTATION
FORD SMALL STREAM OR USE BRIDGE ADJACENT TO PATH
FRING ROAD
HALL PLANTATION
TO DOCKING
FRING HALL
CHURCH FARM
HILL PLANTATION
FRING
METALLED ROAD TO HOUSE GIVES WAY TO GRASSY TRACK AFTERWARDS
TO SNETTISHAM, 2½ MILES/4KM
trailblazer
TOP PLANTATION
TO SNETTISHAM
RED BARN FARM
TO GREAT BIRCHAM & BIRCHAM WINDMILL
MAP 20
0
1/4 mile
0
APPROX SCALE
500m
026
19

Many of the other windows were destroyed by a bomb dropped from a Zeppelin in 1915, making this the first church in England to be attacked from the air. Neither hamlet has any particular facilities for the walker, but Snettisham boasts a pretty, warm and welcoming pub, the ***Rose and Crown*** (☎ 01485-541382, 💻 www.roseandcrownsnettisham.co.uk; 10D/5D or T/1T, all en suite, bath available), near the church and opposite the cricket pitch. Complete with winding passages, low ceilings and an uneven floor, the relaxed pub-cum-restaurant-cum-boutique-hotel is quintessentially English. B&B in rooms varying in style from traditional oak panelling to contemporary pastel paints, is available from £90 (single occupancy £70), whilst the pub (Mon-Sat 11am-11pm, Sun noon-10.30pm, food served daily noon-2pm & 6.30-9pm, till 9.30 Fri & Sat) serves a mix of staples such as bangers and mash for £9.75 or beer-battered fish and chips for £10.50, as well as more exotic fare such as smoked salmon sushi and tempura red mullet. Dogs are welcome, though the charge per dog is £12.

Snettisham RSPB Reserve (see p60) faces The Wash and is sanctuary for large numbers of wading birds which, on large tides when water covers the vast mudflats, are pushed off their feeding grounds and on to the banks and islands adjacent to the RSPB hides.

A metalled road climbs past a house towards **Hill Plantation**, where it dwindles to a dirt track and descends past **Sedgeford Plantation** before crossing a small, frequently dry, stream via a ford or short bridge just before the Fring Rd. Climbing towards **Dovehill Wood**, the path switches from the east side of a hedge to the west and turns left then right to reach **Littleport**, a small string of terraced houses on a dirt track connected to the B1454. Left from here is Sedgeford.

SEDGEFORD

Listed in the *Domesday Book*, Sedgeford, lying in the fertile Heacham River valley, is an old village centred on a flint and stone church thought to be at least partly Saxon in origin. The remains of Roman villas, pottery shards and a gold torc from the Iron Age have been uncovered in the area, underlining its historical importance. There are no facilities for the walker here, although a **post office** service operates from the village hall on Tue (1.30-5.30pm), Thur (8.30am-noon) and Fri (8.30-11am).

Where to stay

The King William IV Country Inn (☎ 01485-571765, 💻 www.thekingwilliamsedgeford.co.uk; 8S, T or D/1S or D, all en suite, bath available), on Heacham Rd, has luxurious, characterful rooms; B&B from £55/95 (sgl/twin or dbl) Sun-Thur and from £65/100 (sgl/twin or dbl) Fri-Sat. Two of their rooms are suitable for dogs (£5/dog).

Sedgeford Hall (☎ 01485-572855, 💻 www.sedgefordhallestate.co.uk; 1D en suite/1D/1T share bathroom), a listed Queen Anne period property, charges £80-100 (£60-90 for single occupancy) for B&B. All the rooms, one of which has a four-poster bed, are beautifully appointed and spacious. There's also an indoor heated pool.

Where to eat and drink

The popular and often packed ***King William IV Country Inn*** (see Where to stay; bar open Mon 6-11pm, Tue-Sat 11.30am-11pm, Sun noon-10.30pm, food served Mon 6.30-9pm, Tue-Sat noon-2pm & 6.30-9pm, Sun noon-2pm & 6-8.30pm, from 6.30pm on Sun in winter) has both indoor and alfresco dining areas in which it serves sandwiches and pasta dishes at lunchtime, and classic mains such as steak and ale pie (£10.50) or Barnsley lamb chops in minted gravy (£14.50) in the evenings.

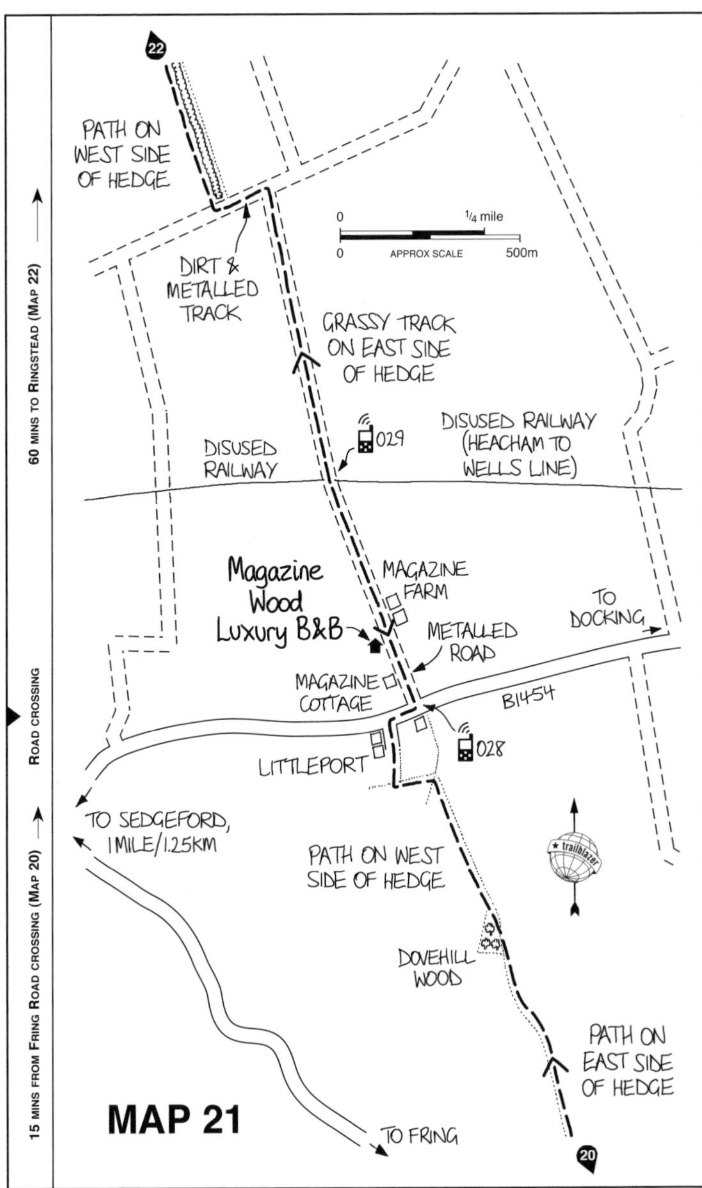

PATH ON WEST SIDE OF HEDGE
DIRT & METALLED TRACK
0 1/4 mile
0 APPROX SCALE 500m
GRASSY TRACK ON EAST SIDE OF HEDGE
029
DISUSED RAILWAY
DISUSED RAILWAY (HEACHAM TO WELLS LINE)
Magazine Wood Luxury B&B
MAGAZINE FARM
TO DOCKING
METALLED ROAD
MAGAZINE COTTAGE
B1454
028
LITTLEPORT
TO SEDGEFORD, 1MILE/1.25KM
PATH ON WEST SIDE OF HEDGE
DOVEHILL WOOD
PATH ON EAST SIDE OF HEDGE
MAP 21
TO FRING
60 MINS TO RINGSTEAD (MAP 22)
ROAD CROSSING
15 MINS FROM FRING ROAD CROSSING (MAP 20)

Join the B1454 road briefly heading right then branch left past Magazine Cottage, a Victorian folly that is occasionally claimed to have been a Civil War ammunition store, and ***Magazine Wood Luxury B&B*** (☎ 01485-570422, 💻 www.magazinewood.co.uk; 3D, all en suite with bath), which boasts rooms with king-sized beds and fitted out to the highest standard, available for around £80-110 per night (£75-90 for single occupancy). Dogs are welcome (£10 per dog per night).

After Magazine Farm the path descends to cross another disused railway line, the old Heacham to Wells line, evident as a dark cinder streak across the countryside. After a sharp zigzag, a final long gentle straight, offering you a last chance to savour the country you have been crossing, leads you past **Sedgeford Belt**, towards Ringstead where you join a road called Peddars Way South. At a roundabout turn left, then veer right shortly after a T-junction to reach the main street.

RINGSTEAD [see Map 22]

This unspoilt village, the last before Holme-next-the-Sea and the coast, used to be famous for the iron-rich spring just to the west on Ringstead Downs. Today the village is full of charm and has a number of shops selling period furniture and art. **Ringstead Gallery**, next to the Gin Trap Inn (see Where to stay), has a wide selection of material for sale by local and more widely-known artists.

Services

The **General Store** (☎ 01485-525270; Mon, Thur, Fri, Sun 8am-5.30pm, Tue, Wed, Sat 8am-1pm), at 41 High St, has a wide selection of groceries and meats, sourced from local suppliers, as well as rolls, pastries and snacks. There are also wines and a number of real ales. **Cashback** is available when you spend more than £5. There is also free **internet access** here.

Where to stay

As you approach Ringstead there are signs for ***Courtyard Farm*** (☎ 01485-525251, 💻 www.courtyardfarm.co.uk; a 4-bed and an 8-bed dorm) just over a mile to the east. A working organic farm, there is a **bunkhouse barn** with toilet/shower facilities offering basic shelter for £10 per night, although you need to supply your own bedding and cooking equipment, and **tent pitches** for £5pp. Advance booking is recommended.

In Ringstead village itself ***Gin Trap Inn*** (☎ 01485-525264, 💻 www.gintrapinn.co.uk; 2D/1T, en suite, bath available) is an award-winning, white-painted, 17th-century coaching inn offering B&B in rooms with wonky walls, low ceilings and masses of character. Rooms cost from £78 (from £100 at the weekend); single occupancy starts at £49 (£60 at the weekend). The name derives from the old gin traps, used to catch game, which used to adorn the interior of the pub. Dogs are welcome.

Where to eat and drink

Gin Trap Inn (see Where to stay; Mon-Fri 11.30am-2.30pm & 6-11pm, Sat & Sun 11.30am-11pm; food served Mon-Fri noon-2pm & 6.30-9pm, Sat noon-2.30pm & 6-9.30pm, Sun noon-2.30pm & 6.30-9pm) was one of only five restaurants in Norfolk awarded a Michelin Bib Gourmand in recognition of its kitchen. Food is served in either the rustic bar, which has an open fireplace with a wood-burning stove, or in the light, airy dining conservatory, which overlooks the beer garden. The menu changes regularly but always includes Thornham oysters (six for £8.50), a 10oz Gin Trap burger made from Sandringham Estate organic beef (£11.50), beer-battered haddock and chips (£11.25), sausages and mash (£9) and a club sandwich (£9.50).

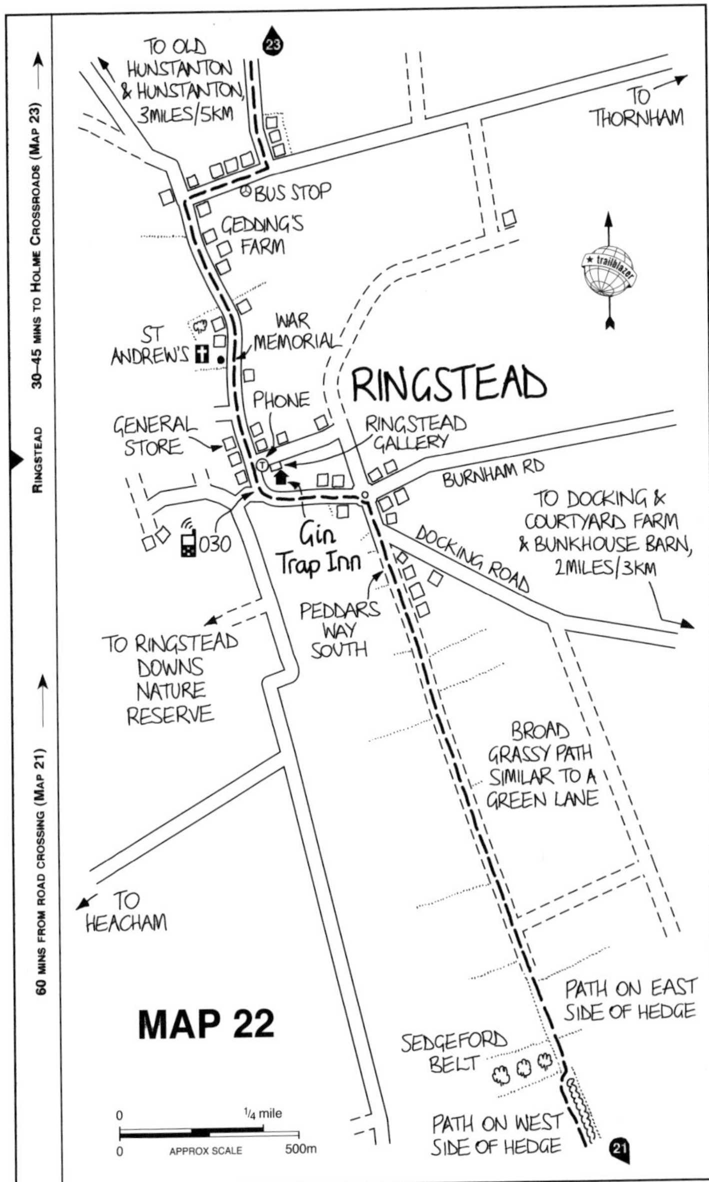
60 MINS FROM ROAD CROSSING (MAP 21)
RINGSTEAD
30–45 MINS TO HOLME CROSSROADS (MAP 23)
TO OLD HUNSTANTON & HUNSTANTON, 3MILES/5KM
23
TO THORNHAM
BUS STOP
GEDDING'S FARM
WAR MEMORIAL
ST ANDREW'S
RINGSTEAD
PHONE
GENERAL STORE
RINGSTEAD GALLERY
BURNHAM RD
TO DOCKING & COURTYARD FARM & BUNKHOUSE BARN, 2MILES/3KM
DOCKING ROAD
030
Gin Trap Inn
PEDDARS WAY SOUTH
TO RINGSTEAD DOWNS NATURE RESERVE
BROAD GRASSY PATH SIMILAR TO A GREEN LANE
TO HEACHAM
MAP 22
PATH ON EAST SIDE OF HEDGE
SEDGEFORD BELT
PATH ON WEST SIDE OF HEDGE
0
1/4 mile
0
APPROX SCALE
500m
21
trailblazer

RINGSTEAD TO HOLME-NEXT-THE-SEA (AND HUNSTANTON)
MAPS 22-23 (MAPS 23-25)

This **2½-mile (4km, ¾-1hr) walk** sees you begin to leave the farmed remoteness of the earlier days before you finish the Peddars Way when you arrive at the beach below Holme-next-the-Sea. This is also the point at which you join the Norfolk Coast Path and enter another world, where sand, sea and salt-marshes merge beneath vast skies, and small harbours, flint villages and fishing communities replace the farming hamlets you have previously passed through.

Before you bear east and start to round the top of Norfolk though, there is a decision to take, as a spur branches west to the traditional seaside town of Hunstanton (see pp127-31), a further **3 miles (5km, 1-1½hrs)** to the south-west, where you may choose to overnight. If you don't want to walk so far consider stopping in Old Hunstanton (pp124-7) where there are also places to stay and some fine restaurants.

The route from Ringstead to the coast is comfortable and straightforward. Pass **St Andrew's church** and **war memorial** on the way north out of Ringstead, then turn right at the first T junction and then first left to track past an old **windmill** at Mill Farm. Leave the road and pick up a path to the right that follows the field boundaries, giving you your first view of the sea, before passing the final **Songline sculpture** (see box p90), and developing into a green lane. This crosses the A149 between Hunstanton and Thornham, and continues to the beach on the appropriately named Beach Rd. Just before you reach the coast there is a turning right to the main part of Holme-next-the-Sea.

HOLME-NEXT-THE-SEA [Map 23]

An attractive, quiet hamlet, Holme-next-the-Sea (the 'l' in Holme is pronounced) is the gateway to the coast, where the North Sea meets The Wash. Historically this would have been the point merchant and naval vessels would have sailed to Lincolnshire and further afield.

From here to Holkham (see p146) is an interconnected series of nature reserves making the area a mecca for wildlife enthusiasts and birdwatchers in particular; the **Holme Dunes Nature Reserve** managed by Norfolk Wildlife Trust (NWT; see p55), which includes **Holme Bird Observatory** (see p60), is one such reserve rich in birdlife, insects, and plants such as marsh orchid, sea lavender. The rather harshly beautiful dunes and salt-marshes below the village are often whipped by winds, but are no less appealing or bracing because of this. Note that there are no toilet facilities at the NWT centre as the building is not connected to the mains.

There are no services of note, though the Coasthopper **bus** stops at the Holme Crossroads daily throughout the day; see public transport map and table, pp46-8, for details. Note that the road marked Peddars Way on the map is not part of the official route.

The White Horse (☎ 01485-525512; daily 11am-11pm, food served all day in July & Aug; rest of year weekdays noon-3pm & 6-9pm, Sat-Sun noon-9pm) is a good place to pause and toast your achievement in getting this far. The menu includes

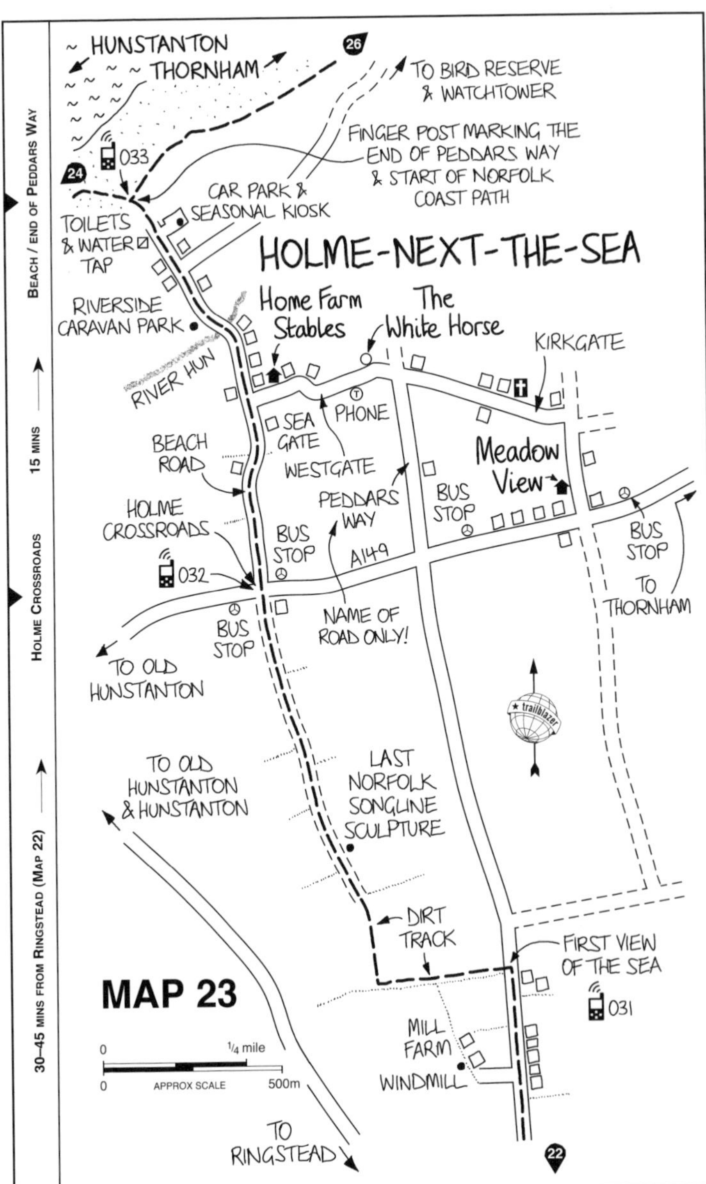
HUNSTANTON
THORNHAM
TO BIRD RESERVE & WATCHTOWER
FINGER POST MARKING THE END OF PEDDARS WAY & START OF NORFOLK COAST PATH
033
CAR PARK & SEASONAL KIOSK
TOILETS & WATER TAP
HOLME-NEXT-THE-SEA
Home Farm Stables
The White Horse
RIVERSIDE CARAVAN PARK
KIRKGATE
RIVER HUN
SEA GATE
PHONE
Meadow View
BEACH ROAD
WESTGATE
PEDDARS WAY
BUS STOP
HOLME CROSSROADS
BUS STOP
A149
BUS STOP
032
BUS STOP
TO THORNHAM
NAME OF ROAD ONLY!
TO OLD HUNSTANTON
trailblazer
TO OLD HUNSTANTON & HUNSTANTON
LAST NORFOLK SONGLINE SCULPTURE
DIRT TRACK
FIRST VIEW OF THE SEA
MAP 23
031
MILL FARM
WINDMILL
0 1/4 mile
0 APPROX SCALE 500m
TO RINGSTEAD
30–45 MINS FROM RINGSTEAD (MAP 22) → 15 MINS →
HOLME CROSSROADS
BEACH / END OF PEDDARS WAY

fisherman's pie (£8.50), tiger garlic prawns (£10.95) and a generous baked ham (£8.75); depending on the weather conditions, you can either take advantage of one of their two beer gardens or a cosy fire.

Although mainly geared up for equestrians and requiring a minimum two-night stay, ***Home Farm Stables*** (☎ 01485-525350, 💻 www.homefarmstables-norfolk .co.uk; 2D/1T/1F, all en suite with bath), on Westgate St, has accommodation in a converted barn. There's a communal, galleried sitting room, a table tennis room and two garden courtyards, a terrace and a deck overlooking a pond. Rates are £47pp for B&B; dogs (£5 per night) are welcome in one of their rooms. They also have full stable facilities for people riding sections of the route.

Alternatively ***Meadow View*** (☎ 01485-525371, 💻 www.glavenvalley.co.uk/meadowview; 2D en suite, bath available), in Manor Court on Eastgate Rd, has well-presented rooms in the barn-style family home and charges from £70 for B&B; if they are available they are happy to pick walkers up and collect luggage (they charge 50p per mile).

Beach Rd continues, crossing the River Hun and passing Riverside Caravan Park before arriving at a car park. There are public toilets and a fresh-water tap here as well as a seasonal **snack shack** (daily; hours vary) that sells drinks and ice cream. Push on to the beach, keeping a wary eye out for golf balls being hit across the path from the large course running parallel to the sea, and arrive at a finger-post just before the dunes indicating the direction of the Norfolk Coast Path. This is the finish point for the Peddars Way.

You can now either turn right and continue on to **Thornham** (see p134) and the other villages strung along the coast, or turn left and take the detour to the traditional seaside town of **Hunstanton** (see p127).

The 2½-mile (4km) route to Hunstanton begins by meandering along the top of the dunes, on the seaward side of Hunstanton Golf Course. Follow the path and allow yourself to look out over the broad expanse of beach. Although wide and generally clean, this section of sand can be windswept and is consequently often empty. Ostensibly flat it is deceptive on a calm day in that the returning tide can race in, potentially catching people who are straying far out onto the sands unaware.

The path passes behind a string of pastel-coloured beach huts and then dips inland past the golf-course clubhouse to arrive at the RNLI lifeboat shed just below Old Hunstanton.

OLD HUNSTANTON [see map p126]

Unlike its brasher, slightly contrived newer neighbour, Old Hunstanton is quieter, more traditional and retains some of its original charm.

Climbing away from the beach, there are a number of good-quality accommodation options (and a very good restaurant) that provide viable alternatives to those on offer in Hunstanton itself; this is particularly useful if you don't fancy retracing your steps all the way to Holme the following morning.

Le Strange Old Barns (☎ 01485-533402; daily Easter-Oct 10am-6pm, rest of year 10am-5pm), opposite the Ancient Mariner Inn (see Where to eat), is considered the largest collection of arts, crafts and antiques in Norfolk. Browse paintings, pottery, ceramics, jewellery, glassware and other collectables or watch craft demonstrations.

Transport

[See also pp46-8] The Coasthopper **bus** stops on Old Hunstanton Rd, the A149.

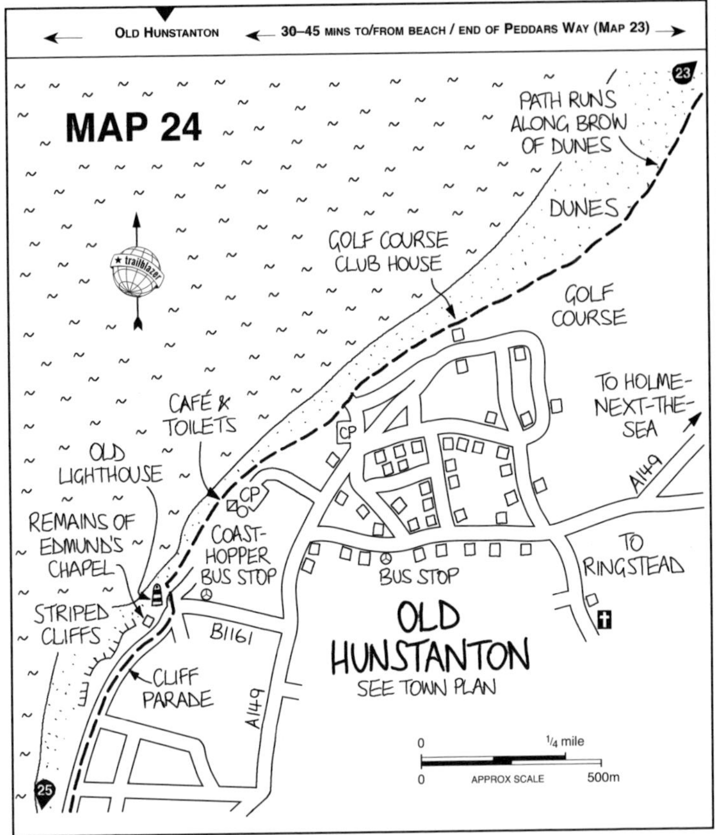

Services

There are public **toilets** next to the RNLI shed. Set back from the sea, up the hill is **Driftwood Deli and Post Office** (daily 7.30am-5.15pm, till 1pm Thur & Sun; post office facilities available daily 9am-1pm & 2-5.15pm, till 1pm Thur, till 12.30pm Sat, closed Sun) where you can pick up local produce at reasonable rates.

Where to stay

Dominating the seafront is the modern ***Best Western Le Strange Arms Hotel*** (☎ 01485-534411, 💻 www.abacushotels.co.uk; 6S/13T/14D plus some suites, all en suite, bath available), where the rooms are graded – standard, superior and suite – and come in various styles complete with mod-cons. Many of the superior rooms, which are slightly larger, and suites, which are grander still, have sea views. Standard rooms cost from £90 (from £65 for single occupancy), superior rooms start at £100 (£75 single occupancy) and suites go for upwards of £140 (£125 single occupancy). Dogs are welcome in some of the rooms.

The Lodge (☎ 01485-532896, 💻 www.thelodgehunstanton.co.uk; 7D or T/5D/1T/

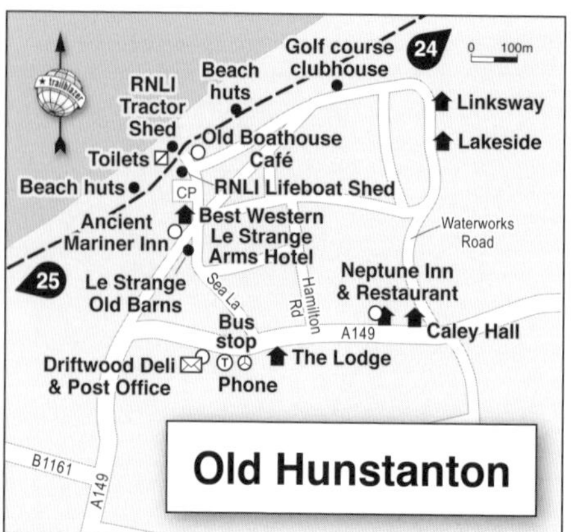

to £198 at the top end for B&B. Each room has free wi-fi, as does the bar which also boasts free wired high-speed internet access. Dogs (£5 per night) are welcome.

Lakeside (☎ 01485-533763, 💻 www.oldwaterworks.co.uk; 2D/1T, all en suite, bath available), on Waterworks Rd, is a converted Victorian waterworks that sits next to a small spring. The rooms, costing £80-90 (enquire for single occupancy rates) for bed and breakfast, have quirky shapes and are brightly decorated and have recently been refurbished. There's also an attractive airy guest lounge with stripped wood floors and a giant fireplace. If you ask in advance the hosts will prepare a packed lunch for a small charge for the following day.

Linksway (☎ 01485-532209, 💻 www.linkswayhotel.com; 2S/4D/5T/2D, T or F, all en suite, bath available), overlooking the first fairway and practice grounds of the golf course, has smart but standard rooms, a heated indoor pool, a licensed bar; evening meals are available on request. B&B costs £48pp. Single occupancy of double rooms incurs an £11/18 (low/high season) supplement.

2F all en suite, bath available), on Old Hunstanton Rd, is an imposing place at the top of Sea Lane. It has put people up since 1912 although the farmhouse the lodge was converted from has stood since 1542. A grade II listed building, it still has a number of original features and lets rooms on a B&B basis from £60/100 (sgl/dbl) during the Easter to October high season and from £85/140 (sgl/dbl) for dinner, bed and breakfast. Rates are fractionally lower outside this period. Dogs are welcome in some of the rooms. On the same road to the east is ***The Neptune Inn and Restaurant*** (☎ 01485-532122, 💻 www.theneptune.co.uk; 5D/1T, all en suite; closed three weeks in Jan and one week in Nov), which was a store for seized contraband until the 1880s when it became a coaching inn. Subsequently renovated in tasteful and fine style, it is now an exceptional restaurant with pristine rooms. Prices start at £110 for B&B, or £185 including a three-course meal from their à la carte menu (see Where to eat). Adjacent is ***Caley Hall*** (☎ 01485-533486, 💻 www.caleyhallhotel.co.uk; 6S/20D/20T, all en suite, bath available; closed Jan), which was originally a manor house dating from 1648. The house and outbuildings have been converted into a motel-style stopover and there are now masses of fairly plain rooms. Single rooms begin at £69, double and twin rooms start at £118 and both rise

Where to eat and drink

Immediately opposite the RNLI shed is the ***Old Boathouse Café*** (☎ 01485-532931; weekdays 10am-3pm, Sat-Sun 9am-3pm, longer during the summer high season), which is good for homemade cakes, hot snacks and sarnies.

For more substantial fodder, ***Best Western Le Strange Arms*** (see Where to stay) has a lounge looking out over attractive gardens, where you can have tea and coffee from 10am, take lunch (daily noon-2pm; booking essential for Sundays) or enjoy afternoon tea (Mon-Sat 2.30-5pm), evening meals are also served here (Mon-Sat 7-8.45pm). Next door and part of the Best Western is the ***Ancient Mariner Inn***

(☎ 01485-534411; Mon-Sat 11am-11pm, Sun noon-11pm, food served noon-9pm), a great sprawling place overlooking the sea, created from the barns and stables of the original Victorian hotel. It has an eclectic menu of staples – try their version of a fish pie, the Mariner's crumble (£9.75), or any of the substantial sandwiches (from £3.75) – and a good selection of cask ales. It also offers free wireless internet access.

The bar in ***The Lodge*** (see Where to stay; daily 11am-11pm, food served Mon-Sat noon-2pm & 6-9pm, Sun noon-9pm, afternoon tea available 2.30-5pm) has some original features. Food is served in the restaurant; the menu changes monthly but always includes fish and chips (£11.50) and Norfolk sirloin steak (from £17). Down the hill, ***Caley Hall Hotel*** (see Where to stay; breakfast available 8-9.30am, bar meals Mon-Sat noon-7.15pm and Sun 2.30-7.15pm, evening meals daily 6-8pm, till 9pm Fri & Sat) has a restaurant in a converted stable block that's open to both guests and non-residents. Light bites cost upwards of £4.95, more substantial lunchtime snacks start at £8.95, and evening mains such as guinea fowl, wild mushroom and artichoke pie, or medallions of pork with roasted apples, will set you back from £13.95. The popular Sunday lunch carvery is available noon-2.30pm, where generous portions go for £8.95.

Best of all though is ***The Neptune Inn and Restaurant*** (see Where to stay; Tue-Sun 7-9pm, Sun lunch noon-1.30pm), where the fine dining restaurant decorated in subtle coffee-coloured tones serves award-winning modern British food; they received a Michelin star in 2008. Start with Brancaster lobster ravioli (£11.95) or Courtyard Farm belly pork (£12), and then follow that with monkfish, white bean and mussel stew (£21.75) or a duo of Sedgeford lamb and lamb sweetbreads (£22.75). Puddings are sumptuous and cost £9.25. Appetisers, tasty breads, pre-desserts and petits fours mean you won't go away wanting. Sunday-lunch deals are available: two courses for £22 or three for £27.50. Be sure to book in advance though. There's also a cosy lounge and small bar adjacent to the understated dining room.

Passing in front of the RNLI shed and then behind another row of attractive beach huts, the path climbs on a grassy path to a car park set atop Hunstanton's famous **striped cliffs**. If the tide's out you can in fact walk along the beach all the way to Hunstanton and thereby get a great view of these 18m (60ft) high white and red walls, made of chalk and a mixture of red limestone and carrstone. Due to the lack of sea defences the cliffs are subject to a high rate of erosion, meaning that fossils, including large mussel shells, sea urchins and ammonites buried in the rocks, frequently come to light.

Follow the tarmac path along Lighthouse Close, past the out-of-service **lighthouse** and the ruins of **St Edmund's Chapel**, dating from 1272. The road turns into Cliff Parade which becomes Esplanade Gardens before finishing at the sloping Central Green in the middle of Hunstanton.

HUNSTANTON [see Map 25, p129]

Colloquially known as Sunny Hunny, the town is a traditional British family seaside resort that still has traces of Victorian sedateness about it. Lauded for being a safe, family resort it can be brash and tacky too. Originally known as Hunstanton St Edmunds in recognition of the fact that Edmund landed here in AD855, became King of East Anglia and was later martyred by the Danes, it has developed into a popular destination for day-trippers and holidaymakers although visitor numbers have declined since their peak in the 1980s. It is the only east-coast town to face west and from which you can watch the sun set over the sea, a fact the locals are particularly proud of. Weather permitting you can also see Lincolnshire and the outline of Boston's famous church, The Stump, on the far side of The Wash.

The town owes its success to Henry Styleman Le Strange who decided to develop the area as a bathing resort. In 1861 Le Strange became a director of the regional railway and arranged for the line to be extended to Hunstanton, opening up the area to tourists. Sadly he died in 1862 having never seen his dream fully realised, although his son reaped the benefits of his ambition. The remains of an ancient cross stand atop a set of tiered steps on the central Green. This was placed there by Le Strange to mark his intention and as a focal point for the town.

Along the seafront there are various **entertainment complexes** and **amusement arcades** with slot machines and computer games. The most substantial, comprising a bowling alley and arcade, stands on the site of the town's Victorian pleasure pier, which was damaged by fires in 1939 and the 1950s before being wrecked by storms in 1978. The remaining stub was finally destroyed by another fire in 2002 and it was then demolished.

Further south, on the long promenade, is a seasonal **fairground** with typical rides and **Hunstanton Sea Life Sanctuary** (☎ 01485-533576, 💻 www.sealsanctuary.co.uk; daily 10am-4pm, till 3pm in winter; adult £12.75, child £9.75); this is one of three national seal sanctuaries responsible for the rescue, rehabilitation and release of wild animals. The centre combines a seal hospital, otter and penguin sanctuary, aquarium and an underwater tunnel that allows you to come face to face with Bonnethead sharks. There's also a small gift shop and ***café*** on site.

If you want to get on to the water, **Searles Sea Tours** (☎ 0783-132 1799, 💻 www.seatours.co.uk) runs a quirky fleet of craft from Hunstanton including an amphibious landing craft used in Vietnam that still sports its distinctive shark's head livery. The Wash Monster (prices depend on the tour chosen), as it's affectionately known, is the most popular means of enjoying this stretch of coast, during the course of which you get good views of the striped cliffs, the lighthouse and even a couple of wrecks. Most trips last around half an hour. Call in the morning between 9.30 and 10am to find out which tours are available as they depend on the weather and the tides. Better though is their seal island tour (£13/7 adult/child), where you are ferried out to a boat in The Wash which takes you to see some of the 3000 common seals that live on the sandbanks here. Book in advance for this.

For a more relaxing form of entertainment **The Princess Theatre** (☎ 01485-532252 or ☎ 01553 764864, 💻 www.princesstheatrehunstanton.co.uk), by the central Green, stages plays, pantomimes, live music and comedy, and screens films.

The town also hosts a number of **annual events** including the Lifestyles Festival, the District Festival of Arts, Hunstanton Carnival and a kite festival. For more information see pp26-7.

Transport

[See also pp46-8] The Coasthopper **bus** runs from Hunstanton to Wells along the A149 coast road. Norfolk Green's No 35 links King's Lynn to Hunstanton and Old Hunstanton. First's No 40/41 bus also runs between King's Lynn and Hunstanton.

Services

Overlooking the central Green is the Town Hall dating from 1896 and designed by the eminent architect George Skipper. The town council still convenes there and it is also now home to a **tourist information centre** (TIC; ☎ 01485-532610, 💻 hunstanton.tic@west-norfolk.gov.uk; daily Apr to May 10.30am-4.30pm, late May to late Sep 10am-5pm, late Sep to Oct 10.30am-4.30pm, Nov to Mar 10.30am-3pm), which has a good supply of leaflets and flyers regarding attractions in the area as well as comprehensive accommodation listings and notes on where there are vacancies each evening. They will make bookings for you; they charge 10% of the first night's accommodation but this will be deducted from the bill you pay.

The local **library** (Mon-Wed 10am-5pm, Thur 10am-1pm, Fri 10am-7pm, Sat

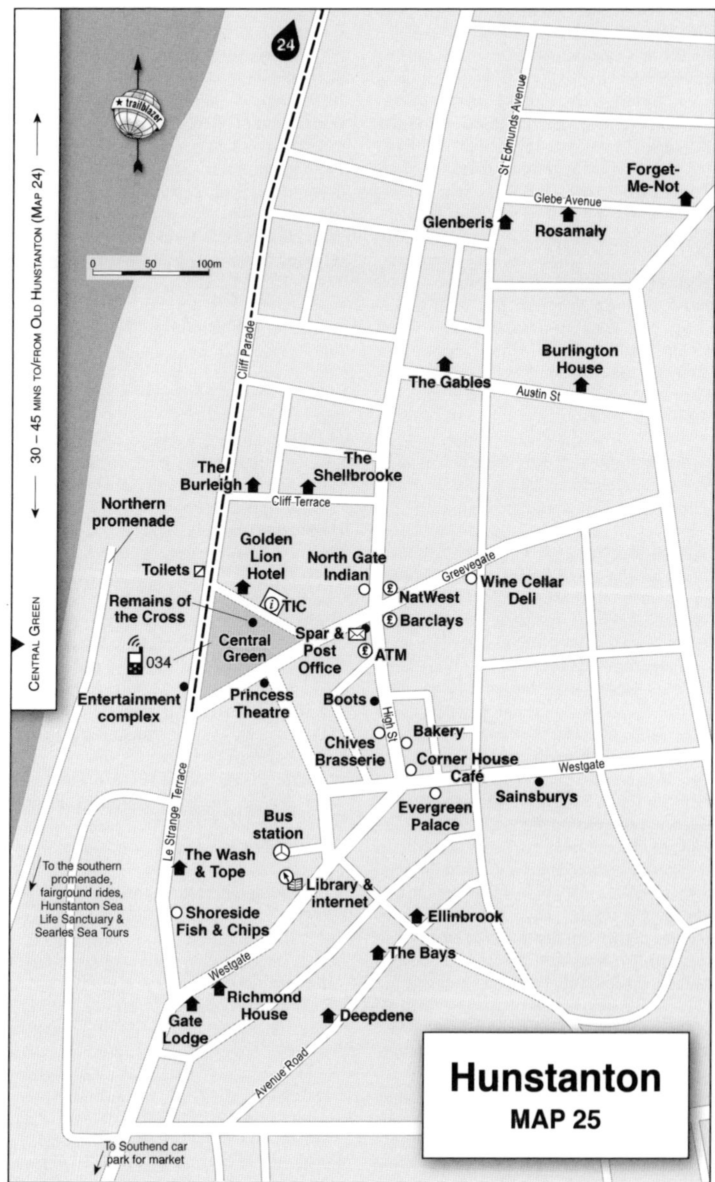
Hunstanton
MAP 25
30 – 45 mins to/from Old Hunstanton (Map 24)
Central Green
24
trailblazer
0 50 100m
Cliff Parade
St Edmunds Avenue
Glebe Avenue
Forget-Me-Not
Glenberis
Rosamaly
Burlington House
The Gables
Austin St
The Burleigh
The Shellbrooke
Cliff Terrace
Northern promenade
Golden Lion Hotel
North Gate Indian
Toilets
Greevegate
Wine Cellar Deli
Remains of the Cross
TIC
NatWest
Barclays
Spar & Post Office
Central Green
ATM
034
Entertainment complex
Princess Theatre
Boots
High St
Bakery
Chives Brasserie
Corner House Café
Westgate
Sainsburys
Evergreen Palace
Le Strange Terrace
Bus station
The Wash & Tope
Library & internet
To the southern promenade, fairground rides, Hunstanton Sea Life Sanctuary & Searles Sea Tours
Shoreside Fish & Chips
Ellinbrook
The Bays
Westgate
Richmond House
Gate Lodge
Deepdene
Avenue Road
To Southend car park for market

10am-5pm, Sun closed) is on West Gate and has free **internet access**. There are **banks** and **cashpoints** at the crossroads of High St and Greeve Gate, as well as a cashpoint on High St itself. There is also a **pharmacy**, a branch of Boots (Mon-Sat 8.30am-5.30pm, Sun 10am-3pm), on High St, as well as a Spar **supermarket** (Mon-Thur 7am-10pm, Fri-Sun 7am-11pm), inside which is a **post office** (Mon-Fri 9am-5.30pm, Sat 9am-1pm, closed Sun). There is a Sainsbury's (Mon-Sat 8am-10pm, Sun 10am-4pm), on West Gate, which is much larger than the Spar and will have everything you need to resupply. The **Wine Cellar Deli** (☎ 01485-535540; Mon 9am-4pm, Tue-Sat to 5pm, Sun 10am-4pm), 16 Greevegate, offers a vast range of cheeses, meats and wine.

On Wednesdays and Sundays (9am-5pm) throughout the year there is a **market** in the Southend car park on the seafront, selling fresh fish and general goods.

Where to stay

There are masses of B&Bs and guesthouses in Hunstanton, most of them in the quiet residential streets set back from the seafront. ***Deepdene*** (☎ 01485-532460, 💻 www.deepdenehouse.co.uk; 2D/1T, all en suite, bath available), at 29 Avenue Rd, has generously sized rooms meaning that spending time in them is peaceful and relaxing; the double rooms in particular are well turned out. Rooms cost £65 (single occupancy is £35) for B&B. ***The Bays*** (☎ 01485-532079, 💻 www.thebays.co.uk; 1S/1T/4D all en suite, bath available), next door at No 31, is a lovingly refurbished Victorian house that retains many of its original features. Two of the double rooms have king-sized beds. Rooms come with numerous extras including a fridge (stocked with soft drinks, crisps and chocolate though there is a charge for these), dressing gowns and wi-fi; rates for B&B are £40-45 (single), £60-90 (double), £70-80 (twin). Breakfast includes home-made breads and jams; they'll also provide an evening meal (three-course meal about £22) if asked in advance. Also worth a look on this street is ***Ellinbrook*** (☎ 01485-532022, 💻 www.ellinbrookhouse.com; 1D/1D or T/2D or F, all en suite), at No 37; it charges £30-39.50pp.

Richmond House (☎ 01485-532601, 💻 richmondhousehotel@xln.co.uk; 2S/10D/2T, all en suite, bath available; Apr-Oct), a large Victorian property centrally located at 6-8 Westgate offers B&B for £45/65 (sgl/dbl or twin). They also have a licensed bar and restaurant (daily 6-9pm) that caters for both guests and non-residents, though non-residents must eat here in order to have a drink. ***Gate Lodge*** (☎ 01485-533549, 💻 www.gatelodge-guesthouse.co.uk; Mar to Nov; 5D/2T, all en suite, bath available), No 2 Westgate, offers superb-value accommodation with lots of little extras. The upper rooms have sea views. Rates, which include a hearty breakfast, start from £85 (single occupancy £58.50); their luxury double, complete with king-size four-poster bed, costs £98 per night with a minimum stay of two nights.

On Cliff Terrace are two well-equipped B&Bs that have communal lounges and their own bars; the welcoming ***Shellbrooke*** (☎ 01485-532289, 💻 www.theshellbrooke.co.uk; 1S with private shower room/8D/1T/3F, all en suite with bath) has well-presented, tastefully furnished rooms (£72-85 for two sharing and £55 for the single). Evening meals (daily 6-8pm) are available if booked at least the day before. Next door is the marginally more upmarket but better-value ***Burleigh*** (☎ 01485-533080, 💻 www.theburleigh.com; 1S/4D/2T/4D, T or F, all with private facilities, bath available), which charges £30-40pp. Packed lunches are available if booked in advance. They also offer free wi-fi.

Burlington House (☎ 01485-533366, 💻 www.burlingtonhouse.info; 1T/2F, all en suite, bath available), at 3 Austin St, is a smart, well-appointed place offering tastefully decorated rooms for £75-80 for two people (£15-30 more for a third sharing). Single occupancy is £47.50-50. The rate includes a hearty breakfast, complimentary bottled water and chocolates. ***The Gables*** (☎ 01485-532514, 💻 www.thegableshunstanton.co.uk; 4D/1T/3F, all en suite, bath available), at 28 Austin St, is an attractive Edwardian House built from traditional

Norfolk carrstone, with B&B for £50-75, single occupancy £35-45.

A short walk from the town centre, ***Glenberis*** (☎ 01485-533663, 💻 www.glenberis.co.uk; 2D/1T, all en suite, bath available), at 6 St Edmunds Ave, has large, homely rooms and charges £65 for B&B (single occupancy £40). Dogs are welcome; book in advance.

Rosamaly (☎ 01485-534187, 💻 www.rosamaly.co.uk; 2D/1T/1F, all en suite), 14 Glebe Ave, is a cosy guesthouse charging £64 (single occupancy £40) for bed and breakfast. Dogs are welcome subject to prior arrangement. At No 35 on this quiet residential street is ***Forget-Me-Not Guest House*** (☎ 01485-534431; 1S or D/2D, T or F, all en suite), a Victorian house that has comfortable rooms at reasonable rates: £30-35/50-60 (sgl/dbl or twin).

Claremont Guest House (☎ 01485-533171, 💻 www.claremontguesthousehunstanton.co.uk; mid Mar to mid Oct; 1S/4D/1T/1F, all en suite, bath available), at 35 Greevegate, dates from 1873 and has large, comfortable rooms which cost from £35pp for B&B. Dogs are accepted if booked in advance.

The Golden Lion Hotel (☎ 01485-532688, 💻 www.coastandcountryhotels.com; 19D/6T/2F, all en suite with bath), built in 1846 and originally known as the Royal Hotel, was the first building in Le Strange's new town and it dominates the original centre poised as it is above the central Green and looking out to sea. For a while it stood alone and was nicknamed Le Strange's folly. Today it's a pleasant-enough place to stay. The majority of the rooms have sea views. Standard rooms start at £120, rooms with a view start from £130.

The Wash & Tope (☎ 01485-532250, 💻 www.thewashandtope.co.uk; 5D/2T/3F, most en suite, bath available), at 10-12 Le Strange Terrace, just opposite the beach, is a pub with rooms above. Most of the rooms look out over the coast and cost from £60 for B&B for two sharing.

Where to eat and drink

Surprisingly, considering the high standard of pubs and restaurants along the Peddars Way and Norfolk Coast Path, Hunstanton is bereft of good-quality eateries or places to grab a pint.

For a snack try ***Corner House Café*** (☎ 01485-532504; daily 8am-4pm; hours may vary in the winter months), on the junction of High St and Westgate, where you can pick up a good-value breakfast; scrambled eggs on toast costs £2.75 and cheap baps go from £2.20. Next door is a **bakery** if you just want to grab a loaf of fresh bread.

Fast food is available from numerous **stalls** along the seafront, otherwise pick up a portion of fish and chips from ***Shoreside Fish and Chips*** (daily) where cod and chips will set you back £5.70.

Chinese food is available from ***Evergreen Palace*** (daily 6-11pm), on Westgate, and a wide range of decent Indian dishes starting at £6.50 are on offer at ***Northgate Indian*** (☎ 01485-535005; daily noon-2pm & 5.30-11.30pm), at 8-9 North Gate Precinct. Both also offer takeaway services.

For largely Mediterranean-themed dishes try ***Chives Brasserie*** (☎ 01485-534771; daily from 9.30am, lunch Mon-Sat noon-3pm, Sun noon-4pm, and evening meals daily 6-9.30pm), at 11 High St; the menu changes weekly but always has pizza (from £8.25), pasta (from £10.50) and steaks (from £16.95). Light lunches and afternoon tea (cream tea £4) are also available, or you can simply perch at their bar to have a drink.

The Wash & Tope (see Where to stay; daily 11am-11pm, food served Mon-Fri noon-3pm & 5-9pm, Sat-Sun noon-9pm), on Le Strange Terrace, is a large town pub popular with locals and tourists alike. The main bar has a pool table, dart board and large-screen television and there's a second smaller sports bar behind this. Generic pub grub is available from £6.95.

The Golden Lion Hotel (see Where to stay; daily noon-11pm, hot food available noon-2pm & 5.30-8.15pm) has a long bar overlooking the central Green and the sea. There's a selection of cask ales and a lunchtime bar-snack menu during the low season and a more substantial lunch and evening menu during the high season. Sandwiches are available throughout the day.

(HUNSTANTON TO) HOLME-NEXT-THE-SEA TO BURNHAM OVERY STAITHE (MAPS 25-23), MAPS 23 & 26-31

This **13½-mile (21.5km, 5¼-6¼ hrs) route** is your first real experience of the North Norfolk coast. If you overnighted in Hunstanton you must return to Holme, remembering to add **3 miles (5km) and 1-1½hrs** onto the journey distance/time shown here. If you followed the path along the cliffs to reach the town, and assuming it is low tide, consider walking back under the cliffs for a change of scenery and a chance to experience this beach and admire the coloured cliffs.

❑ Seahenge

The mysterious Bronze Age monument Seahenge was discovered in 1998 close to the low-tide mark on Holme beach. Despite the similarity in names, there's no direct connection with Stonehenge and no-one really knows to what purpose it was built. Some archaeologists consider it to have ceremonial or astronomical importance; others think it was a site for excarnation, where bodies were laid out after death so that their spirits could escape as the flesh decomposed.

The site consists of a rough timber circle comprising 55 small split oak trunks centred on an enormous upturned oak-tree stump; it was the first intact timber circle discovered in Britain – usually all that remain of the circles are soil markings where the timber has crumbled away – and is the best-preserved example in Europe. One of the trunks had a narrow 'Y' in it allowing access to the circle, whilst another stood in front of this entrance, blocking the view of the interior. The trunks were set a metre below the current surface but it isn't known how high they originally stood. The trees have subsequently been dated to 2049BC using dendrochronology (tree-ring dating). Between 16 and 26 trees were used to make the monument and evidence suggests these came from nearby woodland. The central stump was hauled into place using ropes made from honeysuckle stems, which were found under the stump. It is thought to have been turned upside down as Bronze Age people are supposed to consider death an inversion of life.

Forty centuries ago the circle would have been much further inland and constructed on swampy ground rather than a beach. Having been covered by the sea and slowly hidden from sight beneath layers of soil though, the monument was only discovered as a result of the sea eroding the peat layers to reveal the ancient landscape. Since the logs had been preserved in a waterlogged state with no oxygen, they hadn't rotted. Exposure to the air immediately put them at risk though, and as the sea water that had soaked into the timbers drained away so they began to dry and crumble. The successive tides that swept Holme Beach also threatened to damage the site.

Shortly after its discovery English Heritage controversially arranged to move the site to an archaeological centre at Flag Fen, near Peterborough, in order to work on preserving the wood. Despite sit-in protests by druids and modern-day pagans who argued much of the significance of the site was its location, this went ahead. Since then a recreated Seahenge has been set-up at Lynn Museum in King's Lynn.

Subsequently, a second, older ring has been discovered a hundred metres east of the Seahenge site. Consisting of two concentric rings Holme II as it has become known dates from around 2400BC. Despite facing the same dangers, this set of posts has been left in situ, largely as a result of the controversy associated with preserving the original site.

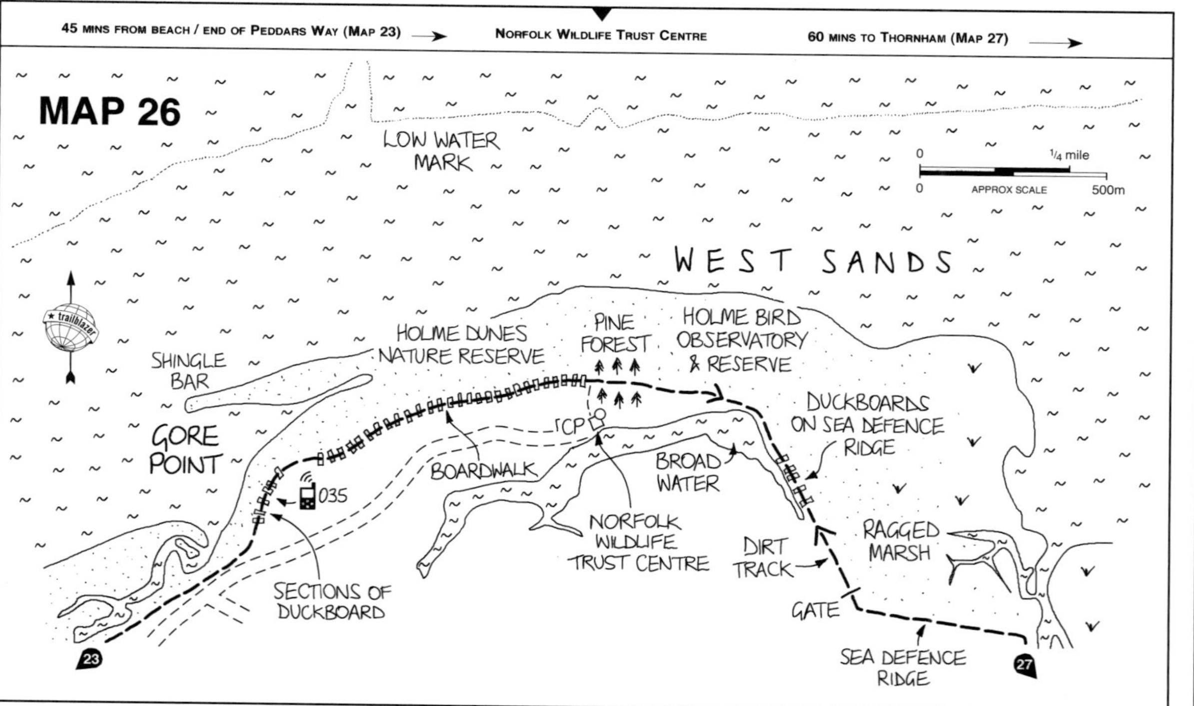
45 MINS FROM BEACH / END OF PEDDARS WAY (MAP 23) →
NORFOLK WILDLIFE TRUST CENTRE
60 MINS TO THORNHAM (MAP 27) →
MAP 26
LOW WATER MARK
0
1/4 mile
0
APPROX SCALE
500m
WEST SANDS
trailblazer
SHINGLE BAR
HOLME DUNES NATURE RESERVE
PINE FOREST
HOLME BIRD OBSERVATORY & RESERVE
DUCKBOARDS ON SEA DEFENCE RIDGE
GORE POINT
CP
BOARDWALK
BROAD WATER
035
NORFOLK WILDLIFE TRUST CENTRE
DIRT TRACK
RAGGED MARSH
SECTIONS OF DUCKBOARD
GATE
SEA DEFENCE RIDGE
23
27

Once you arrive at Holme continue to follow the finger-posts arrowing along the top of the dunes. Follow the path east towards Gore Point and Holme Dunes Nature Reserve; the latter is managed by the Norfolk Wildlife Trust (see p55) but it includes a Bird Observatory which is maintained by the Norfolk Ornithologists Association (see p55). To the seaward side are lavender marshes and shingle bars that provide refuge for roosting and migrating birds. During the autumn and spring keep an eye out for oystercatchers and knot roosting in vast numbers. A section of boardwalk ends just before Gore Point, the headland beyond which was the original location of Seahenge (see box p132).

An undulating, rolling boardwalk weaves across the dunes before entering a stand of Corsican pines, just before the **Norfolk Wildlife Trust Visitor Centre** (☎ 01485-525240; Apr-Oct daily 10am-5pm, Nov-Mar weekends 10am-5pm), which has lots of interesting information on the reserve and its inhabitants. Drinks, snacks and ice cream are available and there is a deck overlooking Broad Water and the marshes on which to enjoy them. They have an emergency telephone but note there are no toilets here.

The path then bends inland, rounding **Broad Water** and heading south past **Ragged Marsh** on a sea defence bank. Turning left at the stump of an old windmill, the path veers east and then enters Thornham.

THORNHAM [see Map 27]

Once a busy harbour (there used to be sea access via the creeks for shallow draught boats until it silted up) and a centre for trade in timber, coal and farm stuffs, Thornham went into decline with the arrival of the railways as business moved elsewhere. Nowadays it's a quiet, traditional village. Depending on how far you're hoping to walk, Thornham can make a wonderful lunch break, with three very good pubs to entice you to stop awhile. Alternatively each also offers accommodation in case you want to stay for a night.

There is a small village **shop** (daily 8am-5pm, half-day Thur & Sun) selling a variety of food and drink.

The Coasthopper **bus** stops in front of **All Saints church**; see public transport map and table, pp46-80, for more details.

The annual Midsummer Music (see pp26-7) event features classical music performances in Thornham church.

Where to stay

There is B&B at ***The Lifeboat Inn*** (☎ 01485-512236, 💻 www.maypolehotels.com/lifeboatinn; 13S, T or D, all en suite with bath), set back from the main road on Ship Lane.

This charming country pub has been operating since the 16th century when it was reputed to be a smugglers' alehouse. It's been through some changes since then but the history and character of the place have been preserved. The rooms (many of which have sea views) are spacious and bright with contemporary pine furniture and patchwork quilts. Rates for two sharing are £114-134 (Mar-Oct) but drop to £80 in winter; single occupancy is £76-86 (Mar-Oct). At the other end of town, on the High St, is the Lifeboat Inn's sister establishment, ***The Old Coach House*** (💻 www.maypolehotels.com/oldcoachhouse; 12S, T or D, all en suite, bath available). Warm and welcoming, with more of a Mediterranean vibe, the rooms here are airy and good value at £94-114 (the rate rises at the weekend), or £67-77 single occupancy.

Note that reservations for the Old Coach House are made through the Lifeboat Inn and that at both weekend stays from spring to autumn, must be for a minimum of two nights, but there is limited Saturday only availability that incurs a £10 single-night supplement. Dogs are welcome (£8 per stay) in both establishments.

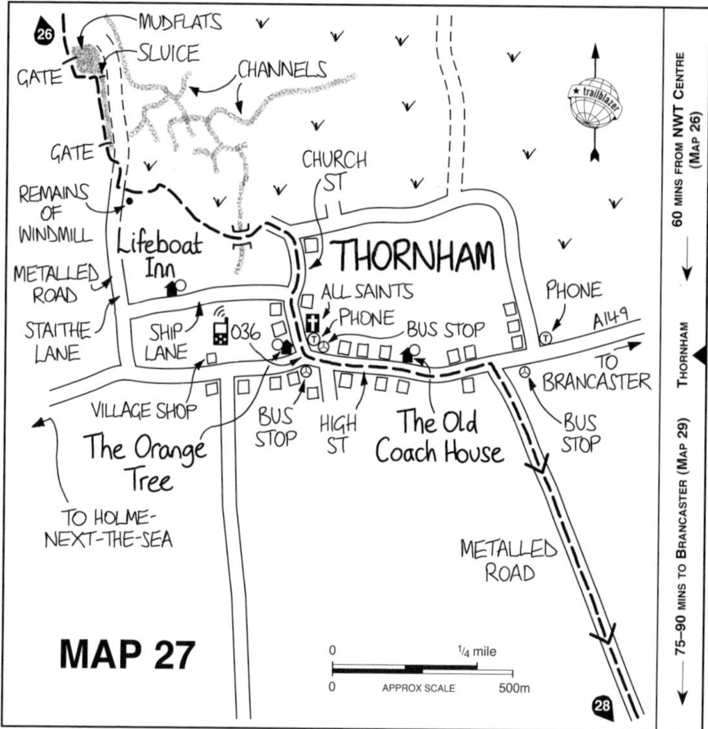

Between these two, on the High St close to the church, is ***The Orange Tree*** (☎ 01485-512213, 💻 www.theorangetree thornham.co.uk; 4D/1T/1F, all en suite, bath available), a stylish gastro pub that has contemporary rooms decorated in shades of cream and chocolate, set around a courtyard. B&B for two sharing costs £75-85; £75 for single occupancy. Dogs (£8) can be accommodated.

Where to eat and drink

The Lifeboat Inn (see Where to stay; daily 11am-11pm, food served daily noon-2.30pm & 6-9.30pm; closed Mon evening in winter) is firmly established as a local favourite. The bar area is full of guns, swords, mattocks, traditional tools and other antique equipment; you can sense the history of the place as you ease into one of the pews around the carved oak tables with a pint of one of their real ales. There are several nooks and five open fires, ideal if the weather hasn't been co-operating. The kitchen offers an extensive menu of local staples, with blackboard specials which change daily; people have been known to travel a long way for a chance to enjoy a bowl of mussels (gathered from the beds nearby), which along with perhaps partridge casserole with Guinness and mushrooms, followed by date and ginger pudding, will set you back about £25. They also serve snacks all day and cream teas (daily 3-5pm; £4.25) if you're feeling peckish.

Stiff competition is available from ***The Orange Tree*** (see Where to stay; Mon-Thur noon-11pm, till midnight Fri & Sat, to

10.30pm on Sun, food served daily noon-3pm & 6-9.30pm), which has won high praise for its exceptional cuisine. From the bar menu choose wild boar sausages (£9.50) or linguine fruits de mer using Brancaster cockles and mussels (£11). In the main restaurant, their corn-fed chicken and wild mushroom pie (£14.50) has won awards. If arranged in advance non-residents can have breakfast here (8.30-9.30am); however, it is not necessary to book for Sunday lunch (noon-5pm). During the summer months they have BBQs, using local seafood and meats, in their substantial, shady beer garden.

For something slightly less fine dining, head to ***The Old Coach House*** (☎ 01485-512229; see also Where to stay; daily 10am-11pm, food served daily noon-2.30pm & 6-9.30pm), a friendly place which has two terracotta-coloured bar areas, each with a decent atmosphere, where you can enjoy a drink from their extensive wine list and eat one of their speciality pizzas (from £5.85), pasta (from £8.60) or home-made pies (from £8). They also offer a take-away service.

About a mile west of Thornham on the A149 is Thornham Drove Orchard, a working farm with a great little farm shop selling fresh produce. On-site is also ***The Yurt*** (☎ 01485-525108, 💻 www.theyurt.co.uk; daily 9am-5pm, Tue-Sat 6-9pm; lunch noon-4pm; cakes/tea 4-5pm; booking advised for evenings), a cosy atmospheric restaurant in a traditional large, round tent. Breakfast and brunch includes a full English (£8.50); snack lunches such as well-filled sandwiches (from £3.50) and salads (£5.50-10.50) give way to an evening menu which changes regularly but may include pan-fried fillet of seabass with chive and butter sauce (£12.50) and fillet of pork with apple purée and a balsamic dressing (£10).

Assuming you can drag yourself away from Thornham's fine pubs, walk east along the High St. There is no coast path to Brancaster so you must head inland briefly. Turn right and head away from the sea along a metalled road that climbs a small hill, from the top of which, if you look back over your shoulder, you can see the large windfarm at work in The Wash. The path cuts east through farmland. At one point it crosses a road heading north towards the coast. It is two miles along this road to Titchwell and half a mile more to Titchwell Marsh Nature Reserve where you can walk past reedbeds and shallow lagoons to the beach, all the while looking for a wide variety of birds. The Peddars Way continues on before once more turning to the sea and descending to **Brancaster** along a country lane. Although sleepy and fairly quiet at first glance there's actually more to this small hamlet, set above an attractive stretch of sand, than first meets the eye, with a huge area of bird-rich salt-marsh and sandflats nearby.

To the right at the crossroads, on the A149, is ***The Ship*** (☎ 01485-210333, 💻 www.shipinnnorfolk.co.uk; 5D/4T, all en suite, bath available) run by the same Flying Kiwi chain behind The Crown in Wells (see p152). Reopened in 2010 it has had a tasteful makeover and been restored to something akin to its previous glory. Centred on an inviting bar area it also boasts a decent restaurant (daily noon-2.30pm & 6.30-9.30pm) whose wholesome menu uses local ingredients; look out for 'Howells' steaks (from £16.95), seafood linguini (£12.95), or seared sea bass fillets with crab mash (£16.95). The elegant rooms decked out in interesting and varied designs are well equipped and spotless. Room rates start at £140 for B&B during the high season (£125 for single occupancy).

The Coasthopper **bus** stops further along this road; see the public transport map and table, pp46-8, for more details.

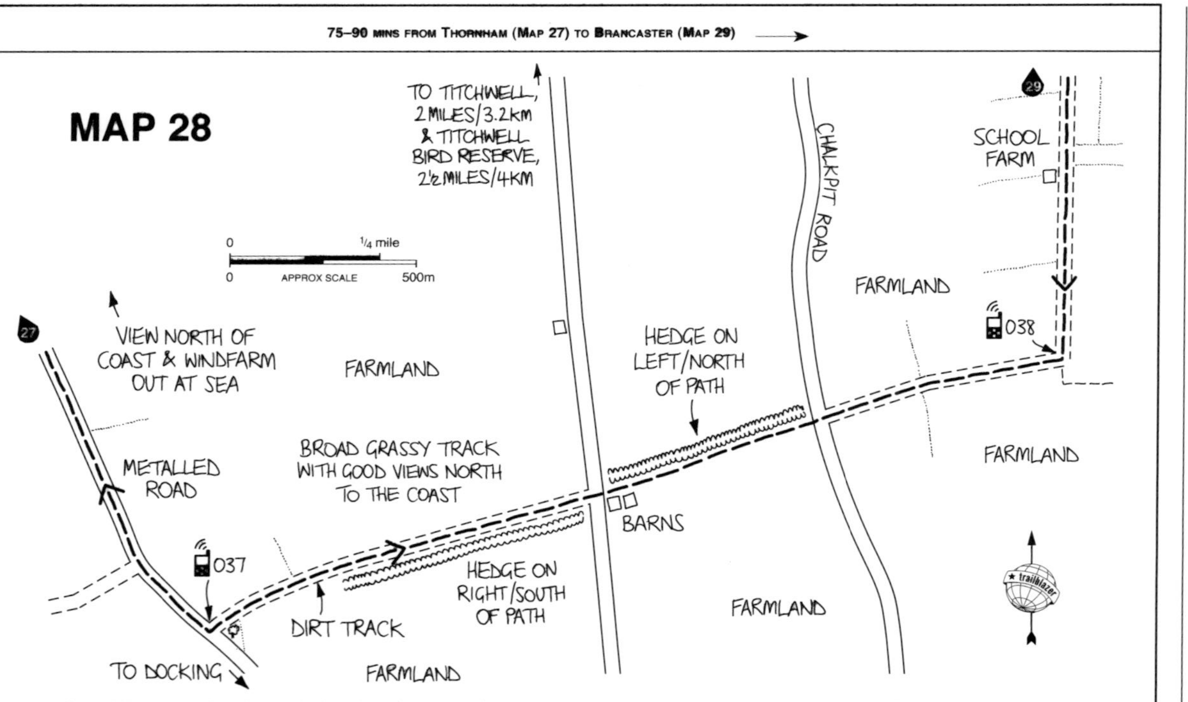
75–90 MINS FROM THORNHAM (MAP 27) TO BRANCASTER (MAP 29)
MAP 28
TO TITCHWELL, 2 MILES/3.2KM & TITCHWELL BIRD RESERVE, 2½ MILES/4KM
SCHOOL FARM
CHALKPIT ROAD
FARMLAND
038
0
¼ mile
0
APPROX SCALE
500m
VIEW NORTH OF COAST & WINDFARM OUT AT SEA
FARMLAND
HEDGE ON LEFT/NORTH OF PATH
FARMLAND
METALLED ROAD
BROAD GRASSY TRACK WITH GOOD VIEWS NORTH TO THE COAST
BARNS
037
HEDGE ON RIGHT/SOUTH OF PATH
FARMLAND
DIRT TRACK
TO DOCKING
FARMLAND
29
27
trailblazer

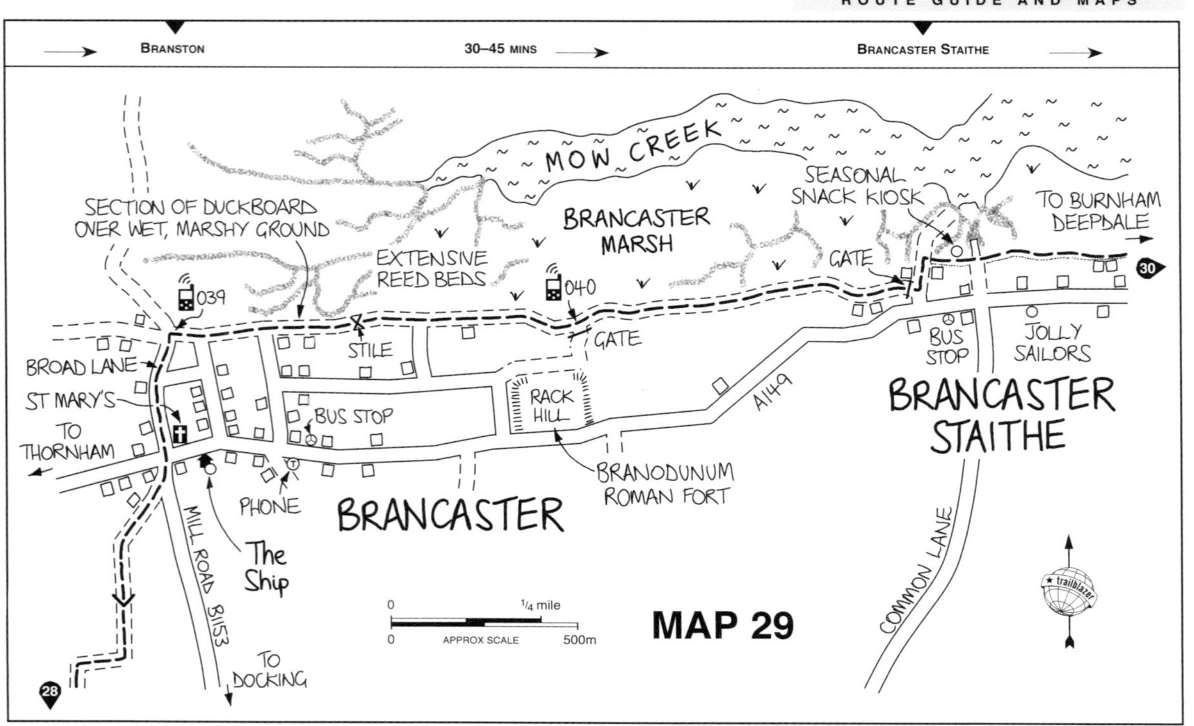

Branston
30–45 mins
Brancaster Staithe
MOW CREEK
SECTION OF DUCKBOARD OVER WET, MARSHY GROUND
EXTENSIVE REED BEDS
BRANCASTER MARSH
SEASONAL SNACK KIOSK
TO BURNHAM DEEPDALE
039
040
GATE
GATE
STILE
30
BROAD LANE
ST MARY'S
TO THORNHAM
BUS STOP
RACK HILL
A149
BUS STOP
JOLLY SAILORS
BRANCASTER STAITHE
PHONE
BRANCASTER
BRANODUNUM ROMAN FORT
MILL ROAD B1153
The Ship
COMMON LANE
0
1/4 mile
0
APPROX SCALE
500m
MAP 29
trailblazer
28
TO DOCKING

To stay on the path carry straight on over the A149, past **St Mary's church**, (where some of the concerts in Brancaster's Midsummer Music Festival, see p26, are held) and before the salt-marsh turn right onto a path running east alongside extensive reed beds and continue past the site of the Roman ruin of **Branodunum** (see box below) on Rack Hill. Branodunum is best reached from the path and is open all the time.

On the outskirts of **Brancaster Staithe** (*staithe* is the Norfolk term for quay or landing place), the path winds left then right past the yacht club and through some fishermen's sheds. The **snack kiosk** called The Crab Hut (Apr-Oct, daily 10am-5pm), sells fresh pots of prawns, whelks and cockles (£1.25/2.50 small/large), dressed crab and lobster caught from their own boat as well as mugs of tea.

During the right season you can also pick up bags of freshly collected mussels from outside fishermen's houses at very reasonable rates. If you're after something more substantial, on the main road is the 18th-century ***Jolly Sailors*** (☎ 01485-210314, 💻 www.jollysailorsbrancaster.co.uk; Mar-Oct daily noon-11pm, Nov-Mar Mon-Thur noon-3pm & 6-11pm, Fri noon-3pm & 5-11pm, Sat noon-11pm, Sun noon-10.30pm, food served Mar-Oct daily noon-9pm, Nov-Mar Mon-Fri noon-2pm & 6-9pm, Sat-Sun noon-9pm), which has local seafood (from £8.50), standard pub fare (from £7.50) and stone-baked pizzas (served till 10.45pm on Fri/Sat in the summer school holiday period; from £5.95) as well as Brancaster Brewery ales that are brewed nearby. The main bar has country charm whilst the cosy snugs are more rustic. There is also a good-sized enclosed garden and outdoor area.

The Coasthopper bus calls at the **bus** stops near the Jolly Sailors; for service details see the public transport map and table, pp46-8.

The Coast Path itself continues along the edge of the marshes and intertidal mudflats that are so popular with sea birds. After passing a path to The White Horse (see pp141-2) the coast path curves left and crosses a dirt track, The Drove, which leads to Burnham Deepdale.

❏ Branodunum

Built during the 3rd century AD, Branodunum was once part of a defensive network of 11 Roman shore forts that lined the south and east coast of Britain. Initially designed to protect and control shipping and trade, the forts were later used to repel the incursions of Angles, Saxons and German tribes, who began to harry the coast. One of the regiments to defend the position is thought to have been the Equites Dalmatae, a cavalry unit from modern-day Croatia. The site remained a garrison for 150 years until being abandoned when the Romans withdrew from Britain.

Since then the site has been plundered and much of the building material spirited away to be used elsewhere; some of the materials have been traced to St Mary's church, Brancaster. Consequently the site, which is managed by the National Trust, isn't all that impressive and it requires a little imagination to transform the grassy ramparts remaining in a field into the fort as it once would have been.

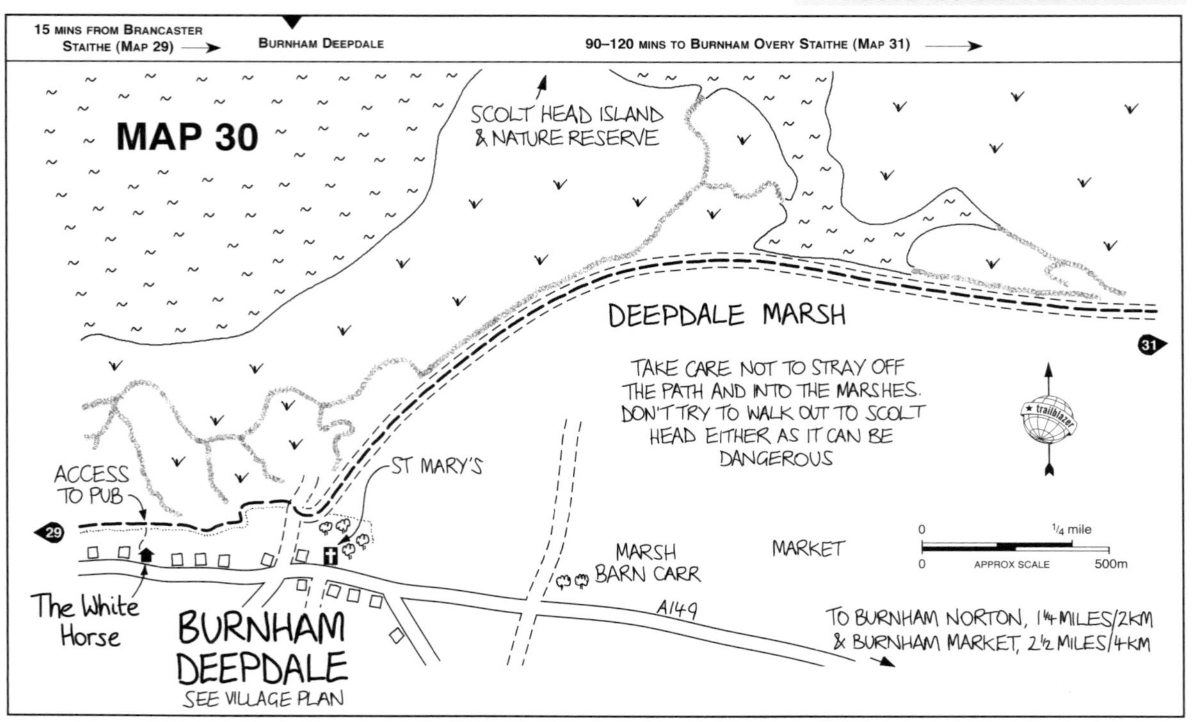
15 MINS FROM BRANCASTER STAITHE (MAP 29) →
BURNHAM DEEPDALE
90–120 MINS TO BURNHAM OVERY STAITHE (MAP 31) →
MAP 30
SCOLT HEAD ISLAND & NATURE RESERVE
DEEPDALE MARSH
TAKE CARE NOT TO STRAY OFF THE PATH AND INTO THE MARSHES. DON'T TRY TO WALK OUT TO SCOLT HEAD EITHER AS IT CAN BE DANGEROUS
trailblazer
0 1/4 mile
0 APPROX SCALE 500m
ACCESS TO PUB
ST MARY'S
MARSH BARN CARR
MARKET
A149
TO BURNHAM NORTON, 1¼ MILES/2KM & BURNHAM MARKET, 2½ MILES/4KM
The White Horse
BURNHAM DEEPDALE
SEE VILLAGE PLAN
29
31

BURNHAM DEEPDALE

[see map below]

This small village straggles along either side of the A149. Next to a petrol station is a Costcutter **supermarket** (Mon-Sat 7.30am-6pm, Sun 8am-6pm) with a wide range of groceries and food; it also offers **cashback**. Opposite is **St Mary's church**, a mostly Victorian structure with a round tower that still retains traces of its Saxon heritage. Inside is an unusual square stone font of Norman origin and a smattering of medieval glass, the best bits of which can be found in the north aisle west window.

Adjacent to the church is a stop for the Coasthopper **bus** (see the public transport map and table, pp46-8, for details) to Wells. On Docking Rd is the stop for the equivalent service going to Hunstanton.

Deepdale Backpackers and Camping Site (☎ 01485-210256, 💻 www.deepdalebackpackers.co.uk; 5D/2T/4F/dorm sleeping eight, all en suite) is a fantastic hostel-style stop centred around a covered stable courtyard. **Dorm beds**, in the carefully converted stables, cost £10.50-15pp while **double** or **twin rooms** cost £30-60 for two sharing and £45-90 for the family rooms. One of the rooms is suitable for dogs but this must be booked in advance. If you're **camping**, tent pitches cost £4.50-9pp, although from late July to late Aug you must book for a minimum of seven nights.

You can also stay in one of their six well-maintained **tipis** (for 3-6 people; £102 per tipi during the week, £114 at weekends), which come with cast-iron chimeneas for heat, and kindling, wood and fuel for the fire. There are also luxurious **yurts** that sleep 3-6 people (£115-130 per yurt during the week, £125-145 at the weekend). A strict noise policy means the site remains tranquil after 10pm. As well as a modern kitchen and lounge, eco-friendly hot showers, laundry and drying room, there is a very well-stocked **information centre** and shop (daily 10am-4pm) where you can pick up all sorts of leaflets, get advice, buy postcards and maps, as well as use their **internet** (30 mins £1, 60 mins £1.50). There is also a hostel for groups, ***The Deepdale Granary***, which sleeps up to 19 in four bedrooms with a fully fitted kitchen and dining room, and costs £150-250 per night.

Close by is ***Deepdale Café*** (☎ 01485-211055, 💻 www.deepdalecafe.co.uk; Mon-Wed 7.30am-5pm, Thur-Sun to 8.30pm, breakfast 7.30am-noon, lunch noon-3pm, teas, cakes and sandwiches 3-5pm, evening meals 5-8.30pm), an eatery that makes substantial breakfasts (book in advance at the weekends) as well as lunch snacks, good-sized sandwiches (from £3.50) and tasty salads (from £3.75) and evening meals (fish pie £10). Food is also available for takeaway. They also do a decent Sunday roast for £9.95.

About five minutes back up the road to Brancaster is ***The White Horse*** (☎ 01485-210262, 💻 www.whitehorsebrancaster.co.uk; 2S/10D/3T, all en suite with bath; Mon-Sat noon-11pm, Sun noon-10.30pm). The rooms at this splendid pub-cum-hotel are split between the main building and the surrounding grounds. Relaxed and stylish they are contemporary but classic and many boast superb views across the marshes to Scolt Head. Single rooms cost £58-78, whilst two sharing might expect to pay £68-97pp depending on the room and the season. There is a single occupancy supplement of £30 per night. The bar stocks real ales from Brancaster Brewery, including The Wreck, as well as East Anglian favourites such as Woodforde's Wherry. The

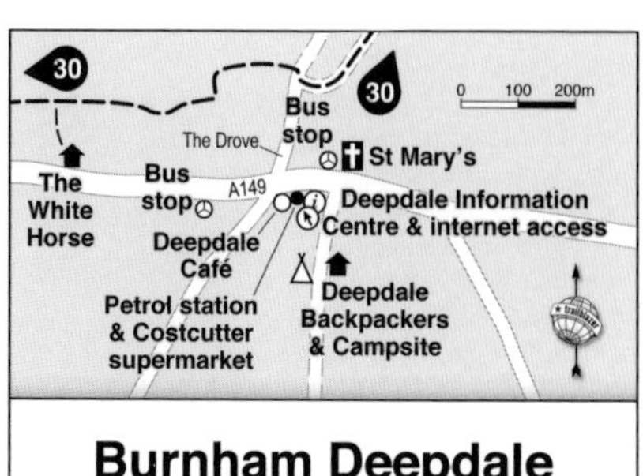

Burnham Deepdale

locals' bar has scrubbed pine furniture and old photographs from the area displayed on the walls. Food is served in the **bar** daily 9am-9pm and includes fresh-cut sandwiches (£6) at lunchtime and evening meals such as pork belly (£9.50) and deep-fried cod with pease pudding (£11.95). There is also a smart conservatory **restaurant** (food served daily noon-2pm & 6.30-9pm) that has an adjoining sundeck, from where you can see the wild salt-marshes. The extensive menu changes daily and boasts shellfish from the beds at the bottom of the garden as well as delicious local fish. Fillet of wild halibut with pickled beetroot compôte costs £16.95, as does a best end of local lamb, whilst a pan-roasted whole partridge will set you back just £14.95.

The path follows a wide sweep of shore out towards **Scolt Head**, a mass of dunes, marsh and shingle, where there is an **island nature reserve** (£3.50/2.50 adult/child) and nature trail. The reserve, just offshore, is usually cut off by an intricate pattern of salt-marsh and rivulets of sea water but is accessible by boat from Burnham Overy Staithe (see below). Weather and tide permitting, a private **ferry** (Apr-Oct) operates between the quay here and the reserve.

Curving round Deepdale Marsh the path meanders past a series of silted creeks, where the break between land and sea is poorly defined and changes all the time, before bending right and aiming inland along a bank towards a prominent six-storey windmill, **Burnham Overy Tower Mill**, now a self-catering holiday let, on the horizon. Crossing a small stream, the trail traverses a field then turns left to run parallel to the main road and enters Burnham Overy Staithe.

BURNHAM OVERY STAITHE

[see Map 31, p144]

This is yet another small hamlet strung along the A149. The Coasthopper **bus** stops here. For service information see the public transport map and table, pp46-8. The North Norfolk Music Festival (see p27) takes place annually at Burnham Norton. Burnham Norton is on the A149 midway between here and Burnham Deepdale.

The Hero (☎ 01328-738334; Apr-Sep daily noon-2.30pm & 6-10pm, Sun noon-3pm & 6-10pm, Sep-Apr Tue-Sat noon-2.30pm & 6-10pm, Sun noon-3pm), named after local man Horatio Nelson (see box opposite) is a spacious, comfortable pub, decorated in contemporary pastel colours, which serves a wide range of **food** (Apr-Sep daily noon-2.30pm & 6-9pm, Sun noon-3pm & 6-8.30pm, Sep-Apr Tue-Sat noon-2.30pm & 6-9pm, Sun noon-2.30pm) as well as cask ales and wine by the glass.

BURNHAM MARKET

[off Map 31, p144]

There's more accommodation about 1½ miles inland at Burnham Market, where there's also a host of art galleries, trendy boutiques and tempting delis huddled around a small green.

Wood Lodge (☎ 01328 730152, 🖳 philip.roll@btinternet.com; 1S or D/1D/1D or T, all with private facilities, bath available), on Herrings Lane, offers B&B for £85-90 (£60-70 single occupancy). Alternatively, ***The Old Forge*** (☎ 01328-730707, 🖳 www.theoldforgeburnhammarket.co.uk; 1D/1T, both en suite), on Creake Rd, has sunny rooms for £70 with a £5 reduction for people arriving on foot.

The Hoste Arms (☎ 01328-738777, 🖳 www.hostearms.co.uk; 32D/3T, all en suite, bath available), a 17th-century coaching inn on The Green. Nowadays the very smart, sophisticated inn has country-house-style rooms including standard doubles, four posters, suites and a penthouse. Midweek B&B rates start at £137 for a twin or double and rise to £223 for the penthouse. During the weekend in the middle of high season expect to pay upwards of £237 for a double room. The **bar** (open all day) has a good atmosphere, log fire and friendly staff. There's also a wood-panelled dining room and attractive walled garden. Lunch is served noon-2pm, afternoon tea is available 3-5pm and dinner 6-9pm. Dishes, cooked on an enormous, bespoke Aga, are interesting, inventive and where possible, ingredients are locally sourced. Chicken-liver parfait with figs costs £6.75, catch of the day starts at £16.25, whilst seared fillet of seabass with bok choy and cashews costs £15.75; saddle of Holkham venison, cauliflower purée and chocolate jus costs £16.50. An excellent and extensive wine list completes the restaurant's appeal.

❏ Lord Nelson

I am a Norfolk man and glory in being so (Horatio Nelson)

Horatio Nelson was born at Burnham Thorpe, a village some 2½ miles from Burnham Market (see opposite), on September 29, 1758. Sent to school in Norwich by his father, he went on to sign up with the navy aged just 12. However, in 1787, he retired to Burnham Thorpe with his wife. Drawn back to the sea in 1793 he proved to be a brave and courageous sailor, although the reputation came at the cost of first an eye then his right arm. The crucial victory over the French and Spanish fleets at the Battle of Trafalgar in 1805 cemented his reputation and paved the way for Britain's dominance of the high seas. Nelson himself was fatally wounded in the battle and died of gunshot wounds to the chest. Pickled in a cask of brandy in order to preserve his body on the return journey, he was eventually laid to rest in St Paul's Cathedral in London, despite his express wish to be buried in Burnham Thorpe.

Although there are any number of pubs named after or in honour of Nelson, ***The Lord Nelson*** (☎ 01328-738241, 🖳 www.nelsonslocal.co.uk; summer school holidays daily noon-11pm, rest of year Mon-Sat noon-3pm & 6-11pm, Sun noon-11pm, food served daily noon-2.30pm & 6-9pm) in Burnham Thorpe was the first. It used to be known as The Plough but changed its name around 1800 to commemorate the victory over the French at the Nile. Nelson frequented the pub and you can even sit on his high-backed settle. Upon being given his command he is reputed to have celebrated by treating the entire village to a meal in the restaurant upstairs. Real ales are served straight from the cask and the kitchen serves traditional fish broth and hearty dishes such as game stew (£15.75) in the winter; at other times look out for Cromer crab (£11) and duck with lavender sauce (£15.25). A previous landlord was the originator of Nelson's Blood, a blend of rum and spices brewed on the premises (see p18); treat yourself to a tot and toast the eponymous hero. To get there take the Coasthopper from Burnham Overy Staithe towards Burnham Market, getting off opposite Friars Lane, then walk to Burnham Thorpe along Joan Short's Lane and then Walsingham Rd. The bus journey is just over five minutes and the walk would be around 25 minutes, meaning the whole journey would take you about half an hour.

BURNHAM OVERY STAITHE TO STIFFKEY — MAPS 31-36

This is a very attractive stretch of the coast path, including as it does Holkham Beach, the gem set in the centre of the chain of beaches strung along the shore. The **10-mile (16km, 3½-4hrs) section** also sees you leave the relative calm and tranquillity of the empty Norfolk beaches for Wells-next-the-Sea, one of its bustling holiday towns and the only working port along the route.

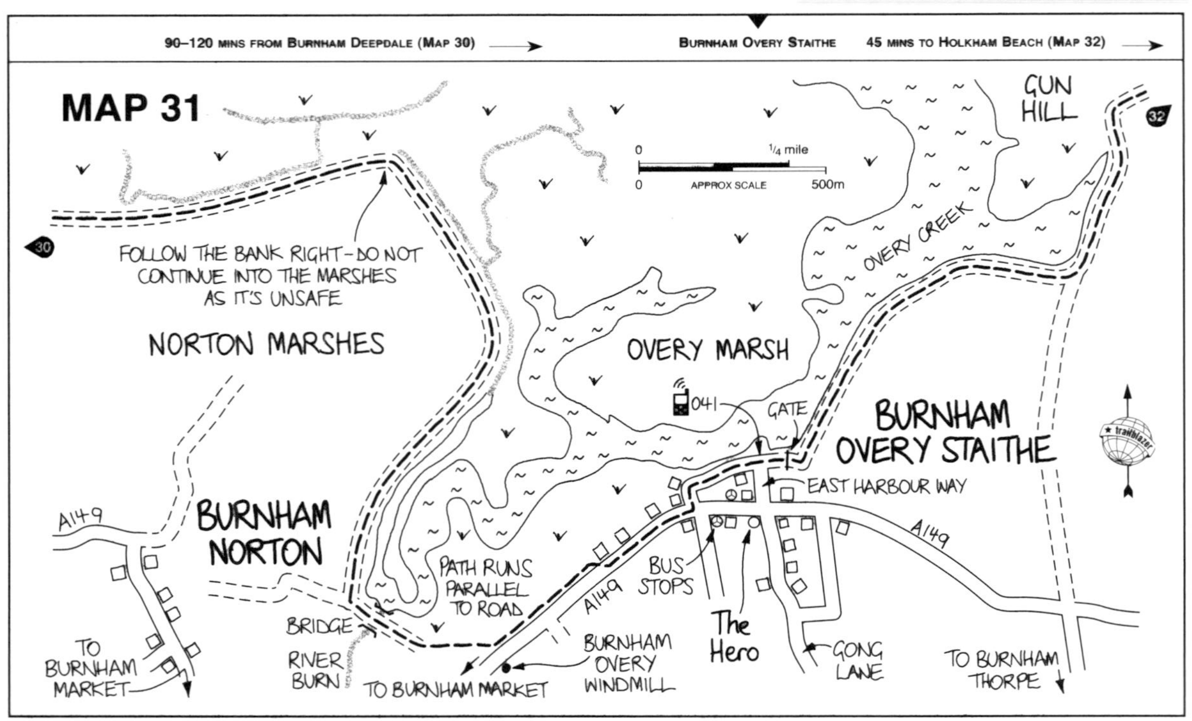
MAP 31
90–120 mins from Burnham Deepdale (Map 30) →
Burnham Overy Staithe
45 mins to Holkham Beach (Map 32) →
30
32
GUN HILL
OVERY CREEK
OVERY MARSH
0
0
1/4 mile
500m
APPROX SCALE
041
GATE
trailblazer
BURNHAM OVERY STAITHE
EAST HARBOUR WAY
A149
TO BURNHAM THORPE
GONG LANE
The Hero
BUS STOPS
A149
BURNHAM OVERY WINDMILL
TO BURNHAM MARKET
PATH RUNS PARALLEL TO ROAD
FOLLOW THE BANK RIGHT - DO NOT CONTINUE INTO THE MARSHES AS IT'S UNSAFE
NORTON MARSHES
BURNHAM NORTON
BRIDGE
RIVER BURN
TO BURNHAM MARKET
A149
TO BURNHAM MARKET

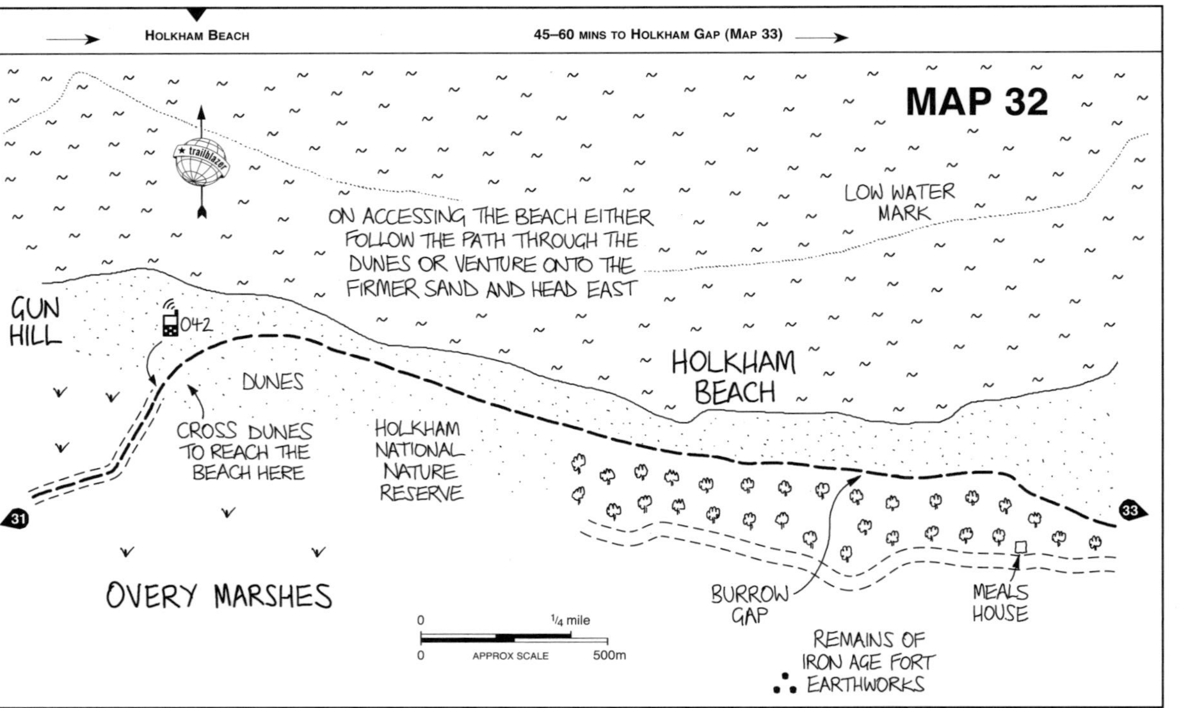
HOLKHAM BEACH
45–60 MINS TO HOLKHAM GAP (MAP 33)
MAP 32
trailblazer
LOW WATER MARK
ON ACCESSING THE BEACH EITHER FOLLOW THE PATH THROUGH THE DUNES OR VENTURE ONTO THE FIRMER SAND AND HEAD EAST
GUN HILL
042
HOLKHAM BEACH
DUNES
CROSS DUNES TO REACH THE BEACH HERE
HOLKHAM NATIONAL NATURE RESERVE
31
33
OVERY MARSHES
0
1/4 mile
0
APPROX SCALE
500m
BURROW GAP
MEALS HOUSE
REMAINS OF IRON AGE FORT EARTHWORKS

Leaving the village the path follows Overy Creek as it heads northwards alongside Overy Marshes towards Gun Hill. Cresting a row of dunes the path reaches **Holkham Beach**, a lovely, wide area of white sand comprising more than 10,000 acres. When the sea has retreated it's almost invisible from the pine-backed, wind-rippled dunes and a walk to its edge past isolated sea pools, streams and rivulets can take an age. Even on a dull day, when the colours are muted and moody, the views encompassing enormous swathes of sky, sand and sea are spectacular. On clear sunny days it is simply one of the best beaches in England. Plus there's plenty of room even at the height of summer thanks to its size and the lack of public transport to access it.

❑ Holkham Hall

Inland from the beach, the imposing stately pile Holkham Hall (☎ 01328-710227, 💻 www.holkham.co.uk; Apr-Oct Sun, Mon & Thur noon-4pm; £9/4.50 adult/child) is three miles south of Holkham Gap and can be reached on the Coasthopper **bus** (see p45) which stops at the Victoria (see below) from where you have to walk.

Built under the instruction of Thomas Coke, 1st Earl of Leicester, in homage to the buildings he saw whilst on a grand tour of Italy in the mid 18th century, and designed by the 18th-century architect William Kent, this vast sandy-coloured house has a severe Palladian exterior, concealing a much more intimate interior. There is a grand marble hall and richly decorated state rooms complete with paintings by Gainsborough, Rubens and Van Dyck as well as a selection of classical landscape pictures.

Alternatively you get access to the Hall and **Bygones Museum** (Apr-Oct, daily 10am-5pm; combined ticket £11/5.50, family ticket £28, museum only £4/2) which features a collection of steam engines. The **walled gardens** (Apr-Oct, daily noon-4pm, free admission during the restoration project) are undergoing a five-year restoration project with the help of English Heritage; the work is not likely to be completed till about 2014 or 2015 but visitors now can see the work as it progresses. The sweeping grounds of **Holkham Park** are centred on an obelisk set atop a small knoll. The lake inside the grounds is a good place to spot water fowl; there is also a resident population of about 800 fallow deer.

Stables Café and Marsh Larder Tearooms (Apr-Oct daily 10am-5pm) outside the hall and next to the Bygones Museum, has a decent range of hot food and snacks. Ideal for sitting in the courtyard with a cream tea or ice-cream made from local milk and cream, flavoured in the relevant season with lavender or plums grown on the estate.

The Victoria at Holkham (☎ 01328-711008, 💻 www.holkham.co.uk/victoria; 8D/1D or T/1D, T or F, all en suite, bath available; food served Mon-Fri noon-2pm & 7-9pm, Sat & Sun noon-3pm & 7-9.30pm) is an inn that was built close to the gates of Holkham Hall to accommodate the aristocrats that used to drop in on its residents. Nowadays the shabby chic hideaway has an interesting colonial feel to it with a collection of handsome Rajasthani furniture and intricate carved doors. The kitchen's stock in trade is modern British food, with the estate providing game and other meats whilst crab is sourced from Cromer. Booking is recommended for the evenings; the Victoria is open to non residents. If you just fancy a drink there's a good range of real ale in their two bars. You can also stay in individually decorated, opulent rooms full of exotic fabrics, colonial artefacts and furniture imported from India. If you're thinking of breaking the bank, double en suite rooms cost £120-180 from Sun-Thur, whilst compulsory two-night bookings at the weekend will set you back £300-440.

The Country Fair (see p27) is held here on odd-numbered years: 2011, 2013 etc.

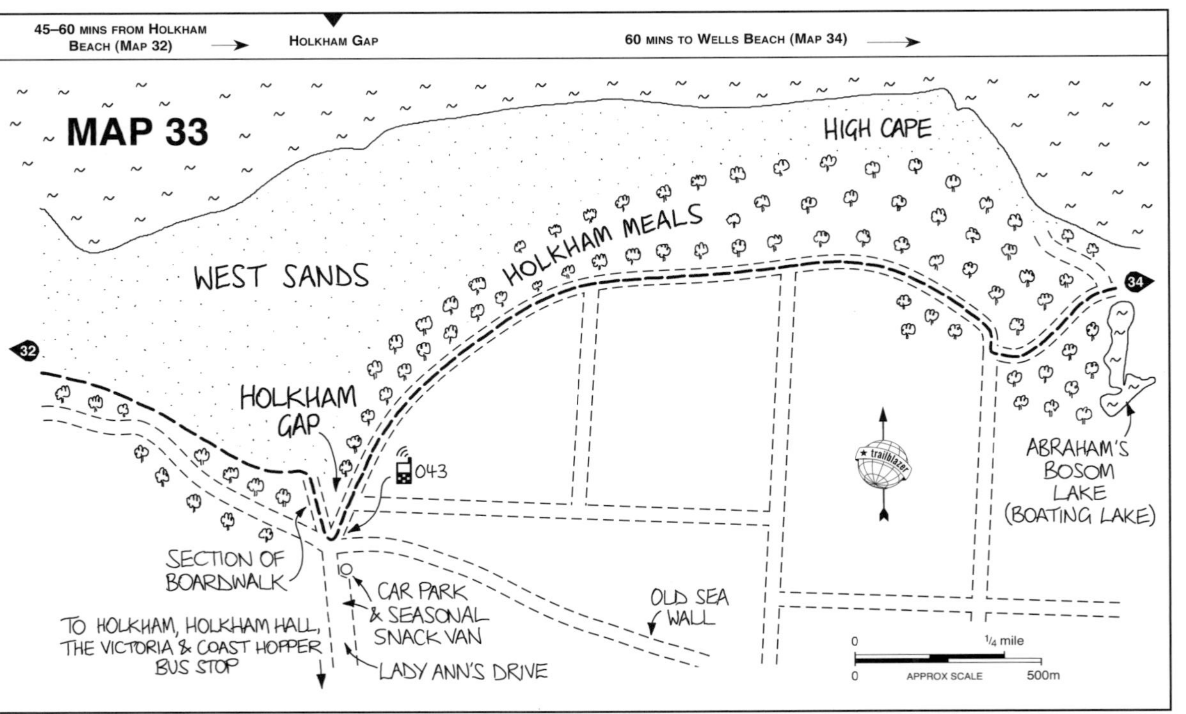

45–60 MINS FROM HOLKHAM BEACH (MAP 32) →
HOLKHAM GAP
60 MINS TO WELLS BEACH (MAP 34) →
MAP 33
HIGH CAPE
WEST SANDS
HOLKHAM MEALS
32
34
HOLKHAM GAP
043
SECTION OF BOARDWALK
CAR PARK
& SEASONAL SNACK VAN
TO HOLKHAM, HOLKHAM HALL, THE VICTORIA & COAST HOPPER BUS STOP
LADY ANN'S DRIVE
OLD SEA WALL
ABRAHAM'S BOSOM LAKE (BOATING LAKE)
trailblazer
0
1/4 mile
0
APPROX SCALE
500m

Holkham National Nature Reserve (see p60) stretches east towards the horizon. The path technically wanders amidst the dunes but it may be easier to head onto the compacted sands once the tide has gone out. The beach becomes busier as you continue towards **Holkham Gap** and Lady Ann's Drive, the main access point to the beach and one of the most impressive approaches to a beach anywhere in the UK. There is a car park but no other facilities, although you can buy upmarket snacks, such as venison sandwiches, and drinks from a **seasonal caravan**.

Beyond the car park at the end of Lady Ann's Drive the path is sheltered from the beach by a stand of pines, which shield it from the onshore breezes. Having trailed the beach east behind this screen, the path emerges next to **Abraham's Bosom Lake**, now a boating lake, and enters a car park. There is a seasonal **café** (daily 10am-5pm) here as well as public **toilets** and some steps give access to the vast, clean **beach** that you have just walked behind. The beach is backed by pine-topped dunes and a cluster of colourful beach huts, many perched on stilts, looking out to sea from the edge of West Sands. The sea here can retreat up to a mile at low tide, but returns quickly. The vast ***Pinewoods Caravan and Camping Park*** (☎ 01328-710439, 💻 www.pinewoods.co.uk; mid-Mar to late Oct) stands on the point here. Tent pitches in this large commercial outfit cost £11-29 depending on the day and time of year. There are plenty of showers, toilets and washing-up facilities in addition to a well-stocked supermarket and coffee shop (both open Mar-Oct daily). You can also rent one of the attractive **beach huts** (£13-29 per day) by the day or by the week, complete with deckchairs and windbreak; it's a good way of sampling this quirky British tradition.

The path climbs onto Beach Rd, a causeway and sea defence, from the top of which there are good views of the beach and the lifeboat station. Following a creek the path heads inland towards Wells-next-the-Sea, the only usable harbour on the North Norfolk coast. Parallel to the path runs a miniature, narrow-gauge **railway** (Easter-Oct, from 10.30am, £1.20 one way), which shuttles between the beach and the town roughly every 20 minutes.

WELLS-NEXT-THE-SEA

[see map p151]

Wells, the name derives from the clear springs found in the area, is a traditional seaside town with a split personality. It has been a harbour for more than 700 years and benefited from easy access to the sea; in its heyday it was one of eastern England's great ports and even as recently as 1986 it handled up to 200 large vessels and tons of cargo annually. Nowadays though, and despite its name, the town is actually a mile from the open water and its only connection to the sea is an inlet harbour. The town itself sits on an estuary of mudflats and saltmarsh, whilst the pristine sandy beach is at the end of a long sea defence, from the top of which you get great views of the estuary. Nonetheless Wells remains the only functioning port on this stretch of coast. Many of the granaries and maltings reminiscent of the town's heyday remain, but have been converted into luxury flats.

The waterfront unfortunately is tarnished by the familiar arcades, gift shops and chip shops that tend to blight British seaside towns. It's worth being on the quay at high tide though as this is prime time for crabbing (see box p162). Step inland from

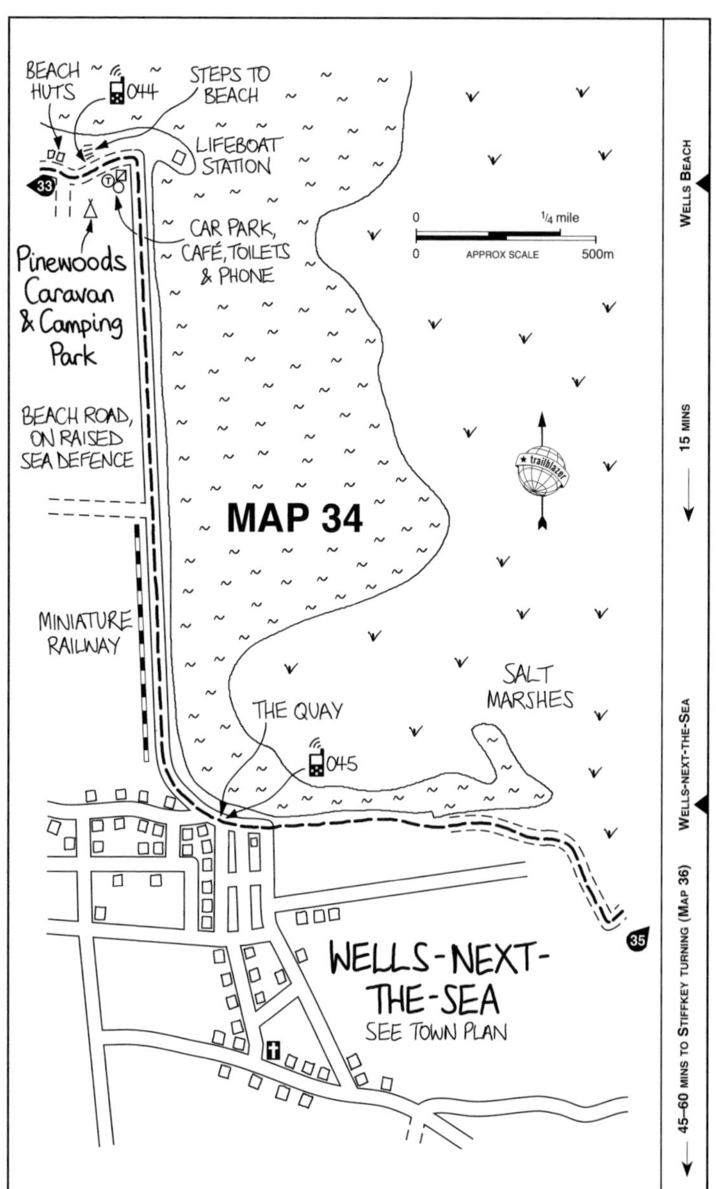
BEACH HUTS
044
STEPS TO BEACH
LIFEBOAT STATION
33
CAR PARK, CAFÉ, TOILETS & PHONE
Pinewoods Caravan & Camping Park
0
1/4 mile
0
APPROX SCALE
500m
BEACH ROAD, ON RAISED SEA DEFENCE
trailblazer
MAP 34
MINIATURE RAILWAY
SALT MARSHES
THE QUAY
045
35
WELLS-NEXT-THE-SEA
SEE TOWN PLAN
WELLS BEACH
15 MINS
WELLS-NEXT-THE-SEA
45–60 MINS TO STIFFKEY TURNING (MAP 36)

the quay, however, and the town becomes a delightful maze of narrow streets, old alleys and yards, with some impressive Georgian and Victorian housing.

The parish **church of St Nicholas** dates from 1460, although much of it was carefully rebuilt after it was struck by lightning. Set back from the quayside lies **The Buttlands**, a quiet rectangular green lined with lime trees whose name derives from the days it was used for archery practice. With several upmarket delis and shops, a couple of good restaurants serving excellent local fare and some high-quality accommodation, Wells is justifiably popular during the summer months when visitors descend in their droves to explore the haberdashery and tool shops that rub alongside more modern galleries, gift stores and eateries.

Wells also hosts an annual poetry festival and carnival (see p26 and p27).

Services

The small **tourist information centre** (☎ 0871-200 3071, 💻 wellsinfo@north-norfolk.gov.uk; daily 10am-2pm, longer in the summer months) is on Staithe St, immediately before a car park. The staff are friendly and provide an accommodation-booking service (£3 booking fee; see also box p14); the centre has masses of leaflets and information on both the town and the surrounding attractions.

Also on Staithe St is a Londis **supermarket** (Mon-Sat 7.30am-8pm, Sun 7.30am-7pm) with a good selection of groceries; it offers cashback on any purchase for a 50p charge. There is a Costcutter (Mon-Sat 8am-7pm, Sun 8.30am-2pm) on Station Rd. The renowned **Wells Deli** (☎ 01328-711171, 💻 www.wellsdeli.co.uk; July & Aug Mon-Sat 8am-6pm, rest of year daily 9am-5pm) is on the waterfront, and has a great range of well-sourced treats including cheeses, jams, chutneys, honey and ice cream. If you're just after something whilst on the move drop into the **bakery** (daily 8.30am-4.30pm), on Staithe St, where you can find fresh bread, pastries and cakes. Close by is a well-stocked greengrocer. Well-known local **butcher**, Arthur Howell's, also has a shop on Staithe St where you can pick up excellent cuts of meat and specialist sausages (try the lamb and mint) if you're self-catering or camping. The shop (Easter to end June, Sep & Oct Sat & Sun 10.30am-5.30pm; July & Aug Wed-Sun 10.30am-5.30pm) for **Whin Hill Cider** (see box p18) is in the main car park; you can pick up freshly pressed cider and perry here.

The **library** (☎ 01328-710467; Mon 2-7pm, Tue 9am-1pm, Wed 9am-6pm, Fri 9am-6pm, Sat 9am-1pm), on Station Rd, has free **internet access**. The **post office** (Mon-Fri 9am-1pm & 2-6.30pm, Sat 9am-1pm) is also on Station Rd and there is a **bank** and cashpoint on the High St.

Transport

[See also pp46-8] The Coasthopper **bus** (daily Apr-Oct) stops on the seafront where Freeman St turns into The Quay and also on Station Rd. Norfolk Green's No 29 bus links Wells with Walsingham and Fakenham.

The **Wells and Walsingham Light Railway** is a narrow-gauge steam railway (see p44; ☎ 01328-711630, 💻 www.wellswalsinghamrailway.co.uk; Apr-Oct daily 8am-5pm, up to 5/day) that connects Wells to Little Walsingham five miles east, where there is a celebrated ruined Augustinian abbey that has drawn visitors and pilgrims since medieval times; for centuries **Little Walsingham** rivalled Canterbury and Bury St Edmunds as a place of pilgrimage. The journey takes half an hour one way, stopping at Warham St Mary and Wighton; a return fare costs £8/6.50, adult/child. Wells station is three-quarters of a mile along the A149 from the edge of the town plan.

Where to stay

Wells Youth Hostel (☎ 0845-371 9544, 💻 wellsnorfolk@yha.org.uk; 31 beds), on quiet, residential Church Plain, is a converted church hall with basic dorm beds from £16 (under 18s from £12) and a handful of double rooms from £38.95. There's also a good kitchen and large communal areas.

Manor Farm Guesthouse (☎ 01328-711392, 💻 www.manorfarmguesthouse.co.uk; 1D/1T/2D or F, all en suite), on Market Lane, offers bed and breakfast from £75 for

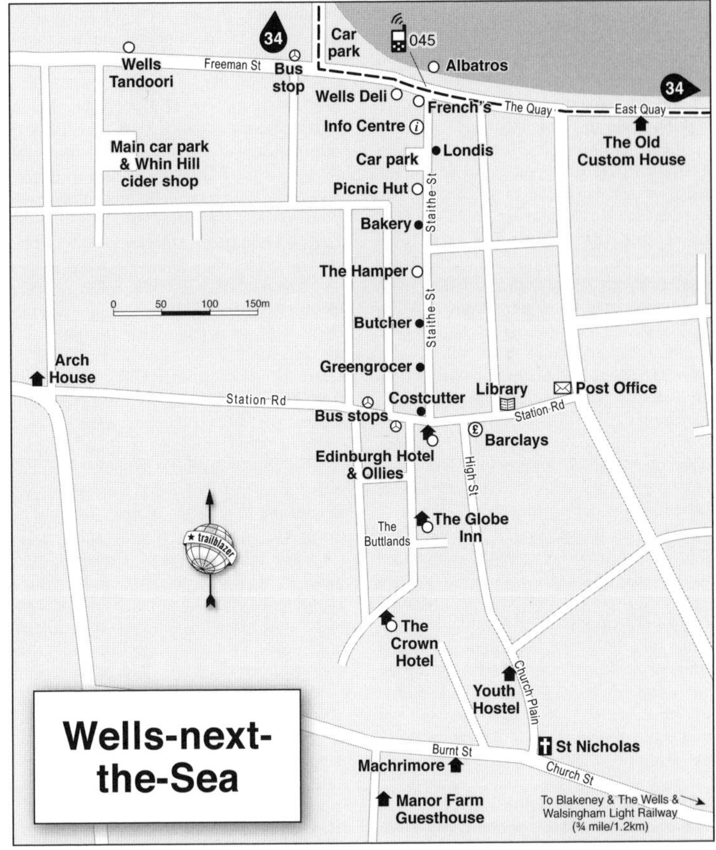

two sharing (£70 for single occupancy). Breakfast is locally sourced and includes free-range eggs. Dogs (£5) are welcome if booked in advance.

B&B is also available at ***Machrimore*** (☎ 01328-711653, 💻 www.machrimore.co.uk; 1D/2T, all en suite) set in its own peaceful, mature gardens on Burnt St. Charming rooms with their own terraces cost £76-80 for two sharing (single-night supplement £5pp); single occupancy costs £60. Remember to ask in advance if you would like kippers from the local smoke-house for breakfast.

The Old Custom House (☎ 01328-711463, 💻 www.eastquay.co.uk; 2D/1T, all with private facilities, bath available), on East Quay, was built in 1560 and served as its original incarnation until the early 1900s. Homely rooms, look out across the creeks and marshes, and start at £70; Fri-Sat night rates begin at £90. Single occupancy is charged at £10 off the standard room rate. Dogs can be accommodated in one of their rooms; book in advance.

Arch House (☎ 01328-710112, 💻 www.archhouse.co.uk; 10D/1T, all with private facilities), on Mill Rd, is a more substantial, listed house overlooking the town that charges £62-84 for two sharing or £5 discount for single occupancy. There's a £22 single-night supplement payable daily in July and August and at the weekends April to June and September to October.

The Edinburgh Hotel (☎ 01328-710120; 1S/2D, all en suite), on Station Rd, has a single room for £40 and rooms for two sharing for £70. Dogs are welcome if booked in advance. ***The Globe Inn*** (☎ 01328-710206, 💻 www.holkham.co.uk/globe; 5D/2T, all en suite, bath available) overlooking the tree-lined green known as The Buttlands is a handsome Georgian inn with bright, spacious rooms with oak flooring and decorated in a fresh contemporary style. Rates, which include a hearty breakfast, are £105-150 for two sharing (£10 discount for single occupancy). However, check their website for special offers. Dogs (£10 per night) are welcome in three of their rooms; book in advance.

Smarter though is ***The Crown Hotel*** (☎ 01328-710209, 💻 www.thecrownhotelwells.co.uk; 9D/1T/2F, all en suite, bath available), a former coaching inn also overlooking The Buttlands, has attractive contemporary rooms. B&B (a generous, locally sourced breakfast) costs £90-110 during the week and £130-160 at the weekend and in the peak season. Dogs (£10 per dog per night) can stay in some of the rooms; book in advance.

Where to eat and drink

For exceptional local produce try ***Wells Deli*** (see Services), on the quayside, where you can pick up pies, pastries, tarts and fresh bread as well as 'Builder's Tea', decent coffee and a special house hot chocolate. Sandwiches start at £3.65 whilst a panini will cost £4.50. There is also a number of cafés and coffee bars on Staithe St; try the ***Picnic Hut*** (daily summer 9am-6pm, winter 11am-3pm) for fair-trade coffee, smoothies and sandwiches priced from £3 or ***The Hamper*** (Tue-Sat 10am-4.30pm, Sun 10am-4pm, closed Mon) for a wide range of snacks available to eat in or take away.

For fast food drop into the cafés, burger bars and fish-and-chip joints along the quayside; ***French's*** (☎ 01328-710396, 💻 www.frenchs.co.uk; summer daily 11.45am-10.30pm, winter Tue-Thur 11.45am-7.30pm, Friday till 9pm, Sat 11.45am-9pm, Sun 11.45am-7pm, closed Mon) is your best bet for superior fish and chips. Alternatively try ***Wells Tandoori*** (☎ 01328-710280; daily noon-2.30pm & 6-11.30pm) on Freeman St; main dishes cost from £6.95 and chef specials such as Tandoori king prawn korai cost £10.95. They offer an eat-in and a take-away service.

Albatros (☎ 0797-908 7228) is a 33-metre, twin-masted Dutch clipper dating from 1899. Now moored permanently on the quayside, the elegant ship offers visitors Dutch pancakes from £3.50 and mussels from £6.50 (food served daily noon-9pm; winter Wed-Mon) and has a rough and ready bar (daily noon to late) below deck adorned with nautical memorabilia that sells a range of real ales. However, it can also be hired for events so may be closed to the public.

Ollie's Restaurant at The Edinburgh Hotel (see Where to stay; daily 11am-11pm; food served daily noon-2pm & summer 5-9pm, winter 6-8pm) serves good pub grub around its open fireplace or in the courtyard out the back. The menu at ***The Globe Inn*** (see Where to stay; daily 11am-11pm, food served 9-11am, noon-2.30pm & 6.30-9pm) changes seasonally and depending on the time of year may include hare ragu (£10.95), roast partridge (£13.95) or a delicious bowl of local mussels (£8.95) to be enjoyed in its spacious, well-presented bar. Rump, sirloin and rib-eye cuts of beef from cows reared at Holkham start at £12; at least one kind of steak is on the menu year-round but on Wednesday nights they have a steak night. There's also a courtyard and tables out front overlooking The Buttlands on which to enjoy a pint of Nelson's Revenge. There's live jazz on Sundays once a month in the courtyard.

You can eat casually in the bar of ***The Crown Hotel*** (see Where to stay; daily 8am-11pm, food served daily 8-10am, noon-2.30pm & 6.30-9.30pm), or more formally in their restaurant. The restored beams and open fires in the bar provide a relaxed, rustic atmosphere, whilst the upstairs dining area is a smarter venue and the orangery provides a peaceful conservatory. Start with smoked salmon with pickled beetroot and horseradish cream (£6.35) or goat's cheese mousse (£5.95), then gorge on roast venison and parsnip mash (£14.25), or char-grilled steaks with hand-cut chips (from £16.95). Good-value menus are also available with two courses for £10 and three for £12.50.

The Coast Path continues along Wells's waterfront to the far end of East Quay, where it joins a metalled road and then a grassy embankment to climb away from the town. Passing between grassy fields and salt-marshes, the path edges past Warham, after which it broadens and gives glimpses of the sea way off in the distance. Stick to the clearly defined path, ignoring trails that head into the marshes as these can be dangerous, particularly as the tide changes. Local legend has it that a giant dog, Black Shuck, haunts the marshes at night, attacking anyone who ventures out there. Put about by smugglers looking to keep people out of the marshes, Black Shuck became the inspiration for Conan Doyle's *Hound of the Baskervilles*.

At Green Way there is a car park and **campsite**, ***High Sand Creek*** (☎ 01328-830235; Apr-Oct), which has 80 tent pitches for £8.50-18.50, free hot showers, washing-up facilities and a small laundry. Booking is recommended in the summer months. Inland from here is Stiffkey.

STIFFKEY [see Map 36, p155]

Pronounced 'Stookey', this picturesque hamlet full of houses with knapped flint walls and painted woodwork, has stood since Roman times but has always remained small. Local residents included the Reverend Harold Davidson who became embroiled in a scandal involving London prostitutes in the 1930s as part of a newspaper sting. Having been defrocked, the 'prostitutes' parson' joined a circus and was later mauled to death by a lion. The author Henry Williamson, who wrote *Tarka the Otter*, used to live by the river here too and documented his daily life in *The Story of a Norfolk Farm*.

Stiffkey Marshes (see p60) are a nature reserve, a continuation of Morston Marshes. They contain some of the oldest saltmarsh on this section of coastline.

The village is on the Coasthopper **bus** route. Services stop and pick up from the bus stops opposite and adjacent to Stiffkey Stores. For details see the public transport map and table, pp46-8.

There is a superb local store, **Stiffkey Stores** (☎ 01328-830489, 💻 www.stiffkeystores.com; Mon, Tue, Thur, Fri, Sat 8am-5pm, Wed 8am-12.30pm, Sun 9am-noon; winter from 8.30am) on the main road, which doubles as a general shop, **post office**, ***café,*** gift shop and studio. Stop by to browse the kitchen wares, local organic produce and pick up one of the homemade cakes or sandwiches to snack on in their attractive outdoor terrace.

The Red Lion (☎ 01328-830552, 💻 www.stiffkey.com; 6D/3T/2F, all en suite, bath available), on Wells Rd, is an atmospheric, traditional pub; it began life as an inn during the 1600s but has also been a private house and doctor's surgery before reverting to its original purpose. The rooms on the first floor have balconies and south-facing views of the Stiffkey Valley. B&B starts at £110 for two sharing. Dogs (£5 per night) accepted by arrangement. The pub (daily 8am-11pm, food served Mon-Fri noon-2.30pm & 6-9pm, all day at weekends, winter Mon-Sat noon-2.30pm & 6-9pm, Sun all day) has bare tiled floors, exposed beams and several big open fires. There's an ever-changing menu based on seasonal ingredients. As a starter you might find red pepper and goat's cheese salad (£6), or poached mussels (£7.95 or £11.95), and then a main of Stiffkey rump steak (£15.95). Puddings cost £4.75.

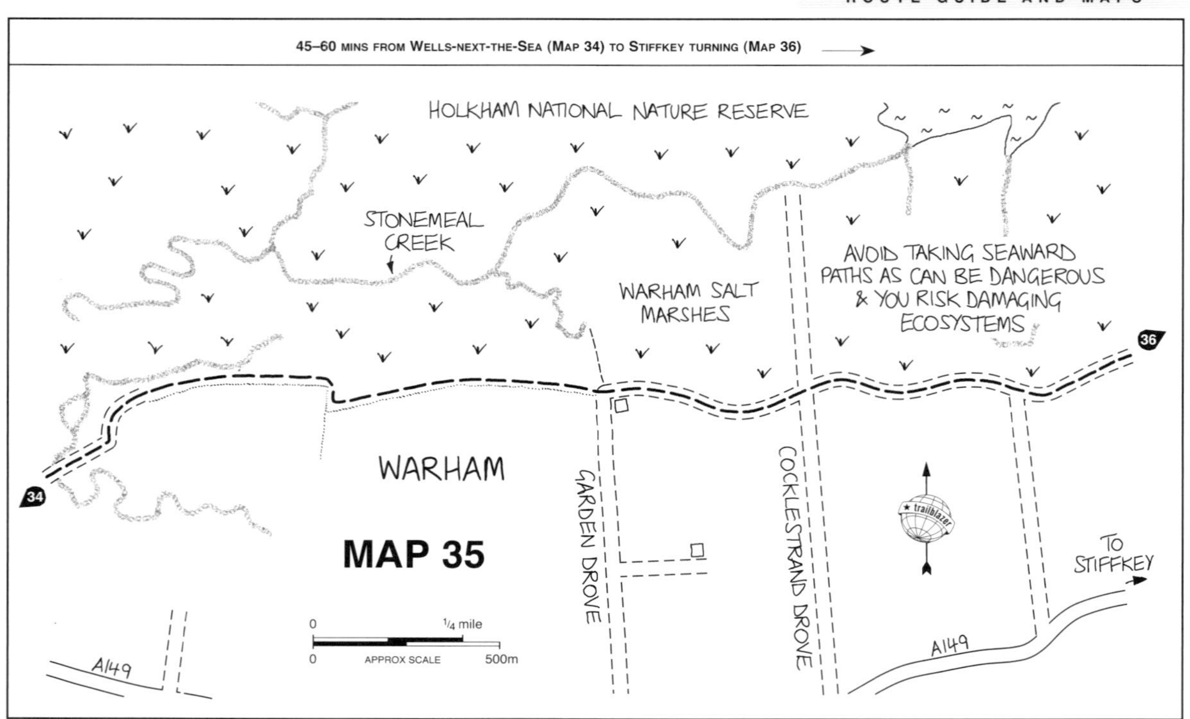
45–60 mins from Wells-next-the-Sea (Map 34) to Stiffkey turning (Map 36)
HOLKHAM NATIONAL NATURE RESERVE
STONEMEAL CREEK
WARHAM SALT MARSHES
AVOID TAKING SEAWARD PATHS AS CAN BE DANGEROUS & YOU RISK DAMAGING ECOSYSTEMS
36
34
WARHAM
GARDEN DROVE
COCKLESTRAND DROVE
trailblazer
TO STIFFKEY
MAP 35
0
1/4 mile
0
APPROX SCALE
500m
A149
A149

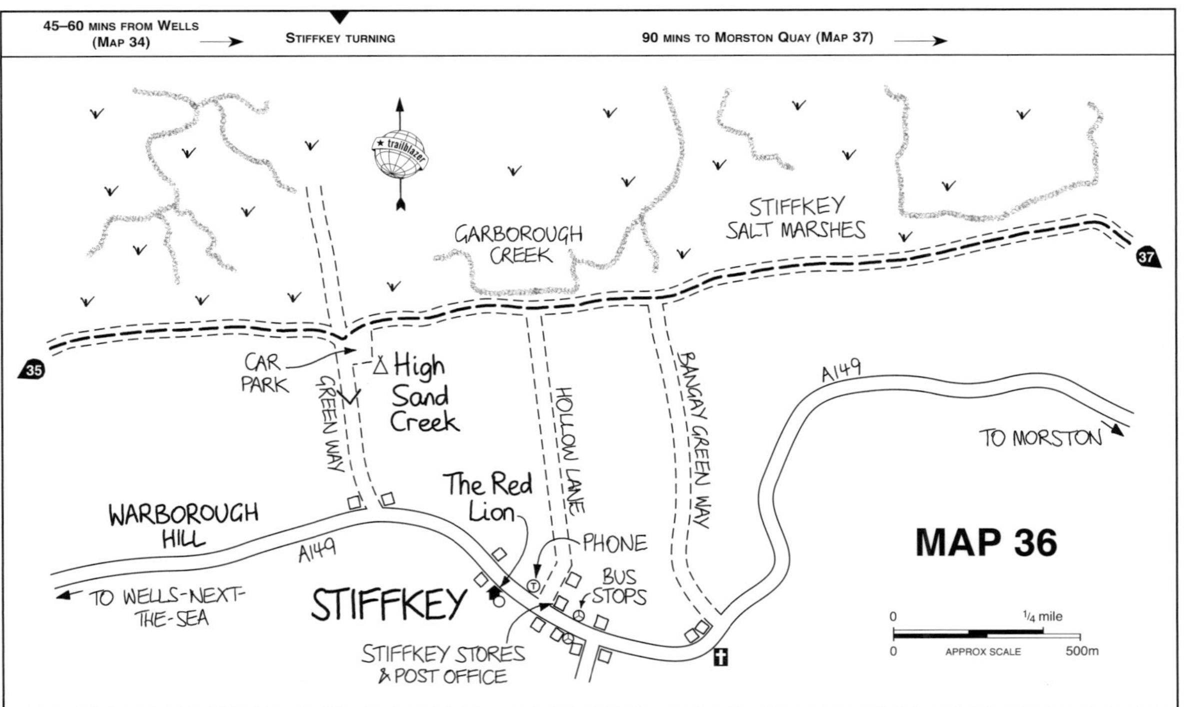
45–60 MINS FROM WELLS (MAP 34) →
STIFFKEY TURNING
90 MINS TO MORSTON QUAY (MAP 37) →
trailblazer
GARBOROUGH CREEK
STIFFKEY SALT MARSHES
37
35
CAR PARK
GREEN WAY
High Sand Creek
HOLLOW LANE
BANGAY GREEN WAY
A149
TO MORSTON
The Red Lion
WARBOROUGH HILL
A149
PHONE
BUS STOPS
MAP 36
TO WELLS-NEXT-THE-SEA
STIFFKEY
0 ¼ mile
0 APPROX SCALE 500m
STIFFKEY STORES & POST OFFICE

STIFFKEY TO WEYBOURNE MAPS 36-41

This is one of the most spectacular parts of the entire trek, with the **12-mile (19km, 5-5¼hrs) path** hugging the shoreline, skirting the marshes and connecting some of the region's most attractive, charming and reputed small towns, where you can pick up some of the freshest seafood. The coast's rich mosaic of habitats, sandy islands backed by salt-marshes, mean that it is excellent for a wide variety of birds and animals. There's access to some of the country's best birdwatching sites here as well as Blakeney Point, home to a permanent colony of seals, which you can sidle up to on organised boat tours from Morston and Blakeney, or walk to from Cley.

Beyond Green Way follow a path between more fields and marshes, home to the celebrated 'Stewkey Blue' cockles, so called for the blueish tinge they acquire living in the mud. Look out for other lanes leading inland to Stiffkey.

Blakeney Point (see box p160) begins to dominate the horizon as you approach **Freshes Creek**, after which you suddenly come across Morston.

MORSTON [see Map 37]

Set back from the coast slightly, Morston lies either side of the Blakeney Rd (the A149). A small, traditional place that's still home to working fishermen, it has a quiet charm. Look out for bags of mussels being sold outside the cottages along the road.

The Coasthopper **bus** stops here; see the public transport map and table, pp46-8, for details.

The National Trust **information centre** (☎ 01263-740241; opening times are weather dependent and vary but it's usually open two hours either side of high tide) in the car park next to Morston Quay has a small number of leaflets and local information but the staff are very friendly and helpful. Adjacent are public toilets and a small ***café*** selling sandwiches, soup and emergency rain capes for people caught unprepared.

Boat trips to see the seals and birds on and around Blakeney Point (see box p160) depart from Morston Quay throughout the year. **Bean's Boat Trips** (☎ 01263-740038, 💻 www.beansboattrips.co.uk) run up to three trips per day in the summer months, less frequently at other times, on their orange and white boats. Timings are varied as they can only operate at high tide. Seal viewings last about an hour, whilst trips that include landing on Blakeney Point last up to two hours. Crews are knowledgeable and there are plenty of opportunities to watch the seals and take photographs. Tickets cost £8/4 (adult/child); they should be reserved in advance and collected half-an-hour before departure. **Temple's Seal Trips** (☎ 01263-740791, 💻 www.sealtrips.co.uk) also offers a seal-spotting service from its red and white ferry boats; the trip duration, operating conditions and cost are the same; tickets can be booked over the phone or in the Anchor Inn (see p158).

In the village itself, there is B&B at ***Scaldbeck Cottage*** (☎ 01263-740188; 1D or F, en suite with bath; Feb-Nov), a traditional flint and brick family home. The smart but slightly old-fashioned rooms cost £100-120 for two sharing (£60 single occupancy). There's space for up to 12 people to camp in the field; £4 for a 2-man tent and £3pp. **Campers** (Apr-Nov) have access to a shower and toilet separate to the cottage.

More upmarket accommodation and fabulous food can be found at the Michelin-starred ***Morston Hall*** (☎ 01263-741041, 💻 www.morstonhall.com; 10D or T/3D, all en suite, bath available), which is run by sometime TV chef Galton Blackiston. A cosy country house, the flint-built hall has spacious, tastefully decorated rooms boasting all mod cons; some rooms include a spa bath and tile TV in the bathroom. Simple and elegant, it is familiar rather than formal and enjoys an intimate atmosphere.

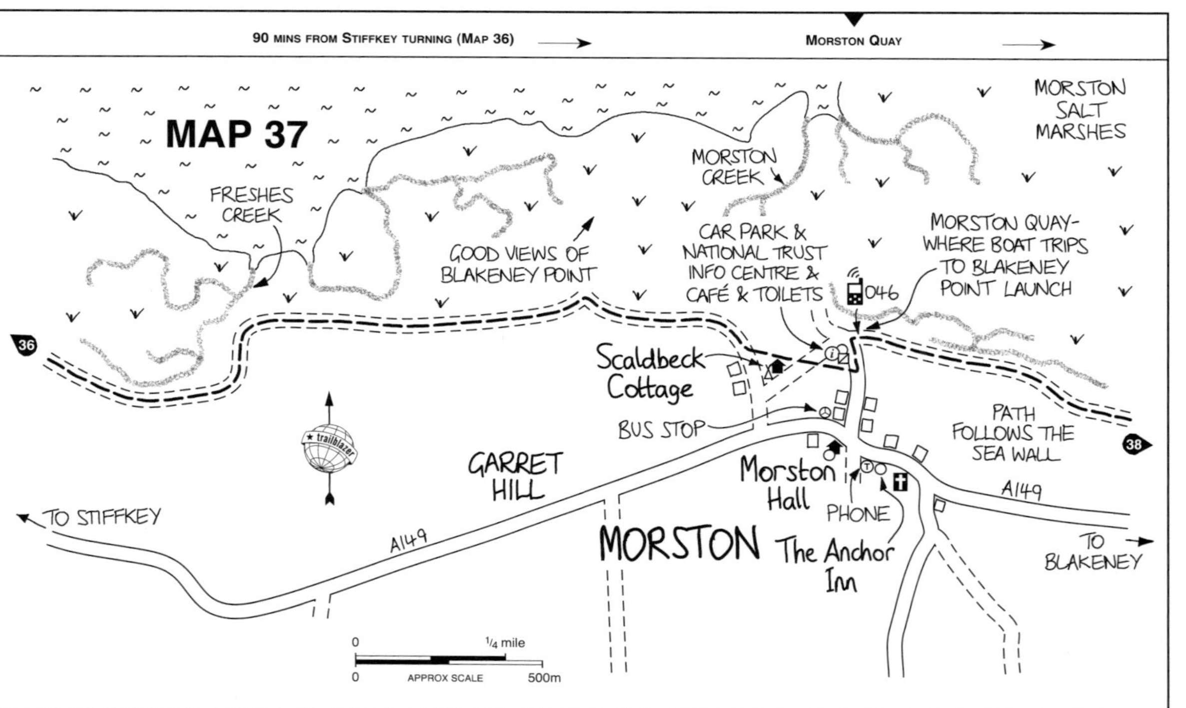
90 MINS FROM STIFFKEY TURNING (MAP 36)
MORSTON QUAY
MAP 37
MORSTON SALT MARSHES
MORSTON CREEK
FRESHES CREEK
GOOD VIEWS OF BLAKENEY POINT
CAR PARK & NATIONAL TRUST INFO CENTRE & CAFÉ & TOILETS
046
MORSTON QUAY- WHERE BOAT TRIPS TO BLAKENEY POINT LAUNCH
36
Scaldbeck Cottage
BUS STOP
PATH FOLLOWS THE SEA WALL
38
trailblazer
GARRET HILL
Morston Hall
PHONE
A149
TO STIFFKEY
A149
MORSTON
The Anchor Inn
TO BLAKENEY
0
1/4 mile
0
APPROX SCALE
500m

Standard rates are £300-360 for two sharing and include a four-course set dinner in addition to breakfast the following day. Single occupancy costs £200-260. Dogs (£5 per dog per night) are welcome; book in advance. Residents can enjoy a light lunch in their room or in the hotel lounge; on Sunday (12.30 for 1pm) a spectacular roast (£33) is put on for those who book in advance. Reservations are also taken for afternoon tea (£15) served 3.30-5pm. In the evening, non-residents can join guests for supper, which is served daily in a single sitting: 7.30 for 8pm. Booking in advance is essential and the four-course set menu costs £57pp. The menu changes nightly but is drawn from fresh local produce. Dishes might include confit leg of duck on sautéed Lyonnaise potatoes with thyme-infused jus or grilled fillet of sea bass served on fennel duxelle with sauce vierge. To finish look out for champagne jelly and the outstanding cheeseboards. The restaurant also has an exemplary wine cellar.

Alternatively, for something a little more affordable, drop into ***The Anchor Inn*** (☎ 01263-741392; daily 9am-11pm, food served Mon-Sat 9am-9pm, Sun 9am-8pm), a bustling pub filled with bric-a-brac and 1950s photographs of the surrounding coast. The menu offers sandwiches, baked potatoes, fish pie (£9.95) and haddock and chips (£10.95). The fish available on their specials board depends on the season.

Pressing on east from Morston Quay, the path hugs the edge of Morston Salt Marshes, meandering along a sea wall and following a succession of creeks and rivulets for a mile and a half until it arrives at Blakeney.

BLAKENEY [see Map 38]

Blakeney is an attractive, traditional town comprising flint fishermen's houses and narrow-winding lanes stretching back from the sea. Once an important port for goods and trade, the town thrived on its connections to the sea. A commercial seaport until the early 20th century, the harbour is now silted up so only small boats can nose their way gently out along a narrow channel, past **Blakeney Point** (see overleaf), to reach the sea. Nonetheless there is a sense of activity and bustle about the place, with children often to be seen crabbing (see box p162) on the quayside (they're guaranteed to catch plenty) and people strolling along the front. Look out for the flood high tide markers on the quayside showing where the waters reached in 1897, 1953 and 1978 – you'll have to crane your eyes upwards to spot the '53 plaque, the highest recorded water mark, some eight feet above the quay.

Increasingly dependent on tourism, the town is full of covetable second homes and is popular with visitors who are drawn to the picturesque surroundings to explore its history and revel in its atmospheric buildings.

The 14th-century **Guildhall** (opening hours daily at 'any reasonable time'; free admission), an intricate brick undercroft, or vault, that was probably the basement of a merchant's house, overlooks the quayside.

Just inland is **Mariners Hill**, a man-made vantage point thought to have acted as a look out for the harbour. On the inland edge of the village, on the hill, stands the double-towered **church of St Nicholas**. The church is incongruously large for its location; the 100ft main tower acted as a local landmark. The main chancel dates from 1296 and includes a rare stepped seven-lancet window. The church's chief feature though is its smaller octagonal tower thought to have been a lighthouse or a beacon for boats accessing the harbour even though the main tower is taller. The graveyard is filled with sailors' headstones and is also worth a visit.

Boat trips run by local families to explore Blakeney Point and see the seals and birds resident there depart from the quay. **Bean's Boat Trips** (see p156) and **Bishop's Boats** (☎ 01263-740753, 💻 www.norfolksealtrips.co.uk; daily trips early Feb-early Nov) run regular outings to the Point. Trips to simply see the seals last an hour, whilst landing on Blakeney Point

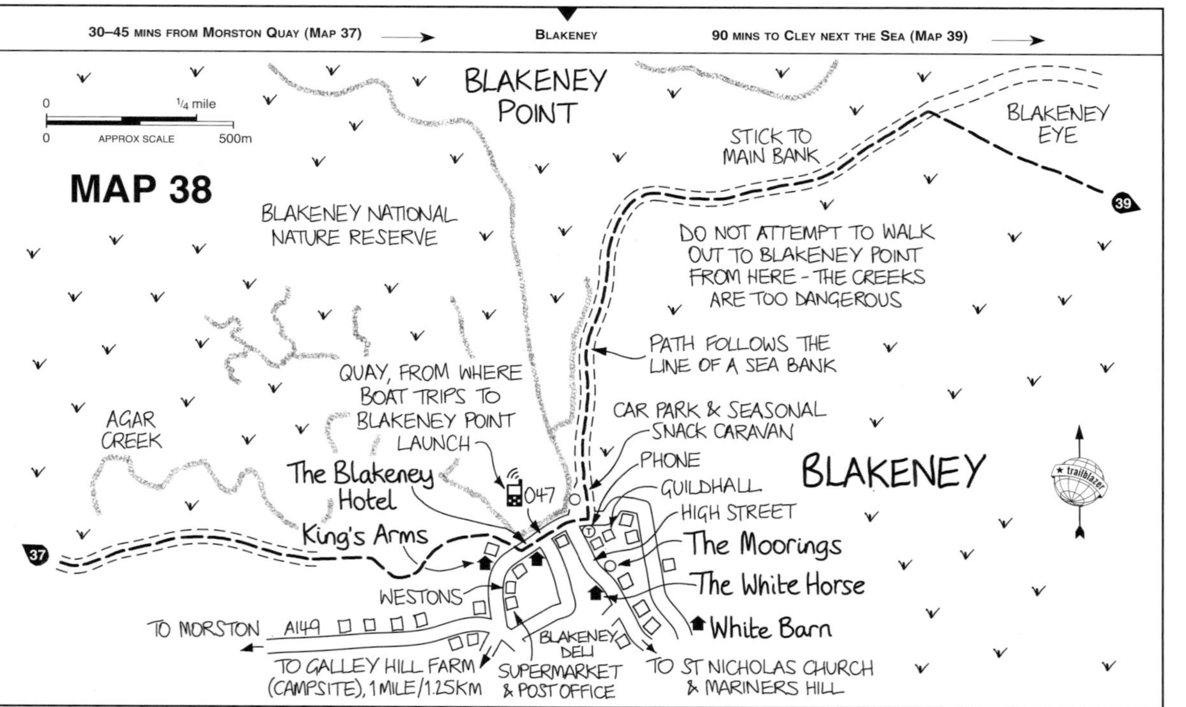
30–45 MINS FROM MORSTON QUAY (MAP 37)
BLAKENEY
90 MINS TO CLEY NEXT THE SEA (MAP 39)
0
1/4 mile
0
APPROX SCALE
500m
MAP 38
BLAKENEY POINT
BLAKENEY EYE
STICK TO MAIN BANK
BLAKENEY NATIONAL NATURE RESERVE
DO NOT ATTEMPT TO WALK OUT TO BLAKENEY POINT FROM HERE - THE CREEKS ARE TOO DANGEROUS
PATH FOLLOWS THE LINE OF A SEA BANK
QUAY, FROM WHERE BOAT TRIPS TO BLAKENEY POINT LAUNCH
AGAR CREEK
CAR PARK & SEASONAL SNACK CARAVAN
PHONE
BLAKENEY
GUILDHALL
HIGH STREET
The Blakeney Hotel
047
King's Arms
The Moorings
The White Horse
WESTONS
White Barn
TO MORSTON
A149
BLAKENEY DELI
TO GALLEY HILL FARM (CAMPSITE), 1MILE/1.25KM
SUPERMARKET & POST OFFICE
TO ST NICHOLAS CHURCH & MARINERS HILL
trailblazer
37
39

adds an extra ½-1hr to the journey time; trips cost £8/4 (adult/child) and reservations should be made in advance. You collect the tickets from the quayside. Departure times are chalked on blackboards on the quay, but are generally in the morning. However, they are dependent on the higher tides, so times vary – check the websites or call ahead for up-to-date details. The craft used are traditional clinker-build boats which offer little protection from the elements so take warm and waterproof clothing to be safe. The skippers have in-depth knowledge of the coast and its inhabitants.

❑ Blakeney Point

The horizon beyond Blakeney is dominated by the shingle ridge of Blakeney Point: a thousand acres of marram grass dunes and empty creeks. The spit runs east to west and is roughly 9½ miles (15.5km) long although this varies all the time. The shingle can be up to 65ft/20m wide and 33ft/10m high. Formed by the process of longshore drift, the shingle protects a network of creeks and salt-marshes. Gifted to the National Trust in 1912, it became the first national nature reserve in Norfolk (see box p60) and is now one of the most important breeding sites for many species of seabird.

The Point can be accessed on foot or by boat, although you shouldn't attempt to cross the marshes from Blakeney itself. Instead, it is possible to walk westwards from the car park at the end of the lane running from Cley to Cley Eye (see map p163) along the spit to Blakeney Point. The invigorating walk is three miles long and it can comfortably take you half a day to do the return journey. Alternatively, to get to the head of the spit catch one of the boats operating from Morston (see p156) or Blakeney (see p158). Bear in mind that entry to the sensitive nesting grounds on the point is restricted during the breeding season.

The Point is an internationally important breeding site for four species of tern (arctic, common, little and sandwich), which nest here between April and July. During this time you'll also be able to spot oystercatchers and ringed plovers. In the winter months look out for brent geese, wigeon, dunlin and curlew. As well as birds, the Point is an excellent spot from which to spot seals; you can't fail to see them. They are incredibly inquisitive and will often pop up alongside the boats whilst the terns, also unfazed by the boats, fuss over their chicks or dive for fish. The resident colony is made up of grey and common seals and numbers around 500, although this fluctuates during the year. The seals usually bask on the sandy banks at the far end of the spit. They are distinguishable by their size: the grey are larger and have longer pointed heads, the common seals are smaller and have a more rounded face. The common seals have their pups between June and August whilst the grey seals, which are confusingly more common, have their young between November and January. Both suckle their pups for about three weeks during which time they grow very quickly.

As you walk west along the point, you'll pass Halfway House, a hut marking the mid-point of the walk. At the far end of the curved spit is a distinctive blue-painted building that operates as a **visitor centre**, open to coincide with people arriving on the various boat trips. There are toilets next to the centre (closed Oct-Apr). Operating from Morston and Blakeney, boat trips to see the seals sometimes land about 300m to the east of the visitor centre. The building used to be a lifeboat station right on the edge of the sand, but it now stands marooned amidst a sea of dunes as a result of the sand and silt collecting on the end of the point. Inside are a number of historic black and white photographs and some general information on the Point, its flora and fauna.

(Opposite) It's well worth staying in Blakeney to give yourself time to explore the surrounding creeks, marshes and shingle spit at Blakeney Point (**bottom**).

BLAKENEY

Services

There is a small but well-equipped Spar **supermarket** (daily 8am-10pm) on Westgate St. Within the shop is a **post office** counter (Mon, Tue, Thur, Fri 9am-1pm and 2.15-5pm, Wed, Sat 9am-12.30pm, Sun closed) and a Link **cash machine**.

Also on Westgate St, **Westons** (☎ 01263-741112, Mon-Fri 9.30am-4pm, Sat till 5pm, Sun 10am-4pm, longer in the summer months) sells fabulous fresh fish, potted shrimps, fishcakes, fish pies and pre-prepared sandwiches. They also operate from a trailer at Morston quay.

Blakeney Deli (☎ 01263-740939; Mon-Sat 8.30am-5pm, Sun till 2pm; Nov to Easter from 9am) on the High St is a perfect pit-stop for upmarket treats. The family-owned establishment sources seasonal and local produce, often organic, as well as a selection of wines, but is best known for the tarts, breads and pastries produced on-site. The sausage rolls (£1.95) alone are worth the visit. They also prepare a range of frozen meals such as classic coq au vin (£5.95) and shepherds pie (£4.50) which are handy if you're self-catering.

Transport (see pp46-8)

The Coasthopper **bus** stops on New Rd.

Where to stay

A mile inland from the quay is ***Galley Hill Farm*** (☎ 01263-741201; Easter to Sep), which has 20 **tent pitches** and rather basic shower and toilet facilities. It charges £6pp.

On the quayside ***The Blakeney Hotel*** (☎ 01263-740797, 🖳 www.blakeney-hotel.co.uk; 8S/20D/34D or T/1T, all en suite, bath available), a traditional hotel, with pebble-covered walls and high gables. Some of the 60 rooms have balconies or south-facing garden views whilst others have patios leading onto the gardens. B&B starts at £87/174 (sgl/dbl) but can climb to £111/246 (sgl/dbl) for a top-end room with four-poster bed and antique furnishings in the high season. Rooms with a full view over the estuary cost an additional £12pp. Single rooms are available at no extra cost although single occupancy of a double or twin room incurs a supplementary charge of £10-60 per night depending on the season. The hotel also has a heated swimming pool, steam room, sauna and spa. Dogs (£5) are welcome in some of the rooms; book in advance.

In town there is B&B at ***White Barn*** (☎ 01263-741359, 🖳 http://northnorfolk.webs.com; 1S or D/1D/1D or T, all en suite), on Back Lane, for £60-70 for two sharing, £40 in the single. If they have time they are happy to take luggage for the cost of the diesel. ***The King's Arms*** (☎ 01263-740341, 🖳 www.blakeneykingsarms.co.uk; 4D/2T/1F, all en suite), on Westgate St, is easily identifiable by the legend 'FH+1760' tiled into its red roof although it's unclear what the initials refer to; the date was when the roof of the much older building was replaced. Most of the rooms have views of the marshes. Rates are £70-80 for two sharing and £55 for single occupancy. Dogs (£5) are welcome; book in advance.

The White Horse (☎ 01263-740574, 🖳 www.blakeneywhitehorse.co.uk; 8D/1T, en suite, bath available), a former coaching inn on the High St, is a high-quality, good-value accommodation option. Each room is individually furnished with a mix of contemporary and traditional styles and there are great additional touches. The smallest double costs £70 per night whilst the others range from £100 to £140; ask for the Harbour room if you get the chance, it's the largest and has the best view.

Where to eat and drink

The seasonal **caravan** in the car park next to the quay sells delicious snacks such as fresh crab sandwiches (£3) and oysters (£1) at remarkably cheap prices. If you have more time, visit ***The Moorings*** (☎ 01263-740054, 🖳 www.blakeney-moorings.co.uk; daily 10.30am-5pm, Tue-Sat 6.30-9pm), just up from the quay on the High St. It is an unpretentious bistro with a buzz about it. During the day drop in for a coffee and one of the tantalising home-cooked cakes. In the evenings the menu, which changes regularly, is biased towards local seafood, often

(Opposite) Blakeney's unusual twin-towered church (**top**) and tranquil waterfront (**btm**).

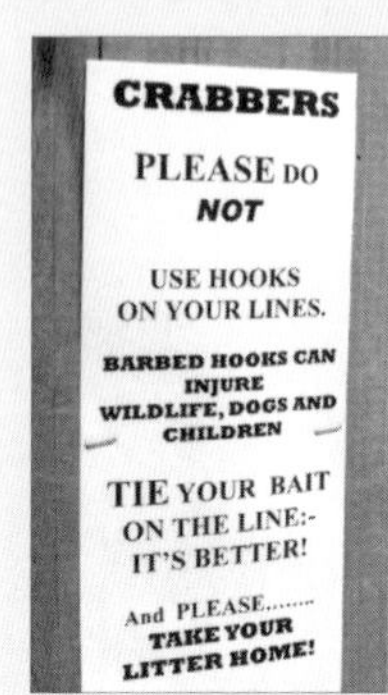

❑ Crabbing

It's a coastal tradition to hang a bit of line over the edge of a quay, strung with bait aimed at enticing crabs to grab hold. To get started, equip yourself with a bucket, crabbing line and a bag of bacon bits for bait. Set yourself up on the quay in Wells or Blakeney, watching out for boats and other traffic on the water. Fill the bucket with water, tie the bait to the line, don't use a hook as they pose a serious threat to other wildlife, then lower the line into the sea for a couple of minutes. Give it a moment and then check to see who has grabbed your bait. Pull up the line and pop your catch in the bucket. After an hour tot up the number of crabs you've caught, then put the lot back into the sea and begin again!'

bought straight from the boats that catch it, but also includes local meats and game as well as home-grown fruit and veg; try the fish soup (£4.95), Norfolk crab cakes (£6.95), local venison or partridge (£17.50) or panache of turbot and scallops (£18.50).

The King's Arms (see Where to stay; daily 11am-11pm; food available noon-9pm) serves hearty home cooking throughout the day. Dishes such as cod, prawn and bacon chowder (£5.50), homemade steak and Adnams ale suet pudding (£12.50) and lamb shank with dauphinoise potatoes (£14.50) are all well-prepared and portions are ample. Look out for the plaque halfway up the wall showing the levels of the flood that hit the area in 1953. There is also a large, child-friendly beer garden.

The White Horse (see Where to stay; daily 10.30am-11pm, food served noon-2.15pm & 6-9pm, till 9.30pm Fri & Sat) has an informal, green and red painted bar serving local real ales and a number of well-chosen wines. However, most people are here for the delicious food served either in its light and airy conservatory or more formal dining room. The bread is all home baked, and ingredients are sourced from local suppliers. The menu changes daily but often includes Morston mussels (£6.95 or £12.50). Leave room for the sumptuous desserts (£5.25); look out for the apple and fig crumble, or the white chocolate and orange cheesecake.

The Blakeney Hotel (see Where to stay; food served daily noon-2.15pm & 6.30-8.45pm) has a restaurant overlooking the quay that offers a range of breakfasts, light lunches and seasonal à la carte evening menus for guests and non-residents alike. If you can, pause here to drink in the views across the marshes and estuary before moving on. Flaked Cley kiln-roasted smoked salmon sandwiches cost £5.75 whilst fish pie will set you back £9.95 and twice-baked Norfolk dapple cheese soufflé costs £8.95. The three-course supper using regional and seasonal produce costs £27.50.

From the quayside in Blakeney cross the car park and step onto the sea bank curving north towards Blakeney Eye. The path affords excellent views of the vast expanse of marsh and sky before bending south again and aiming inland towards the distinctive **windmill** of Cley next the Sea. Although drawn towards the mill you can't access it from this side of the marshes and must circle around to reach the village and its centrepiece. When the path finally joins the Blakeney to Cley road turn left, cross a sluice and climb down from the bank. At a T-junction on the edge of the village follow the road round to the left.

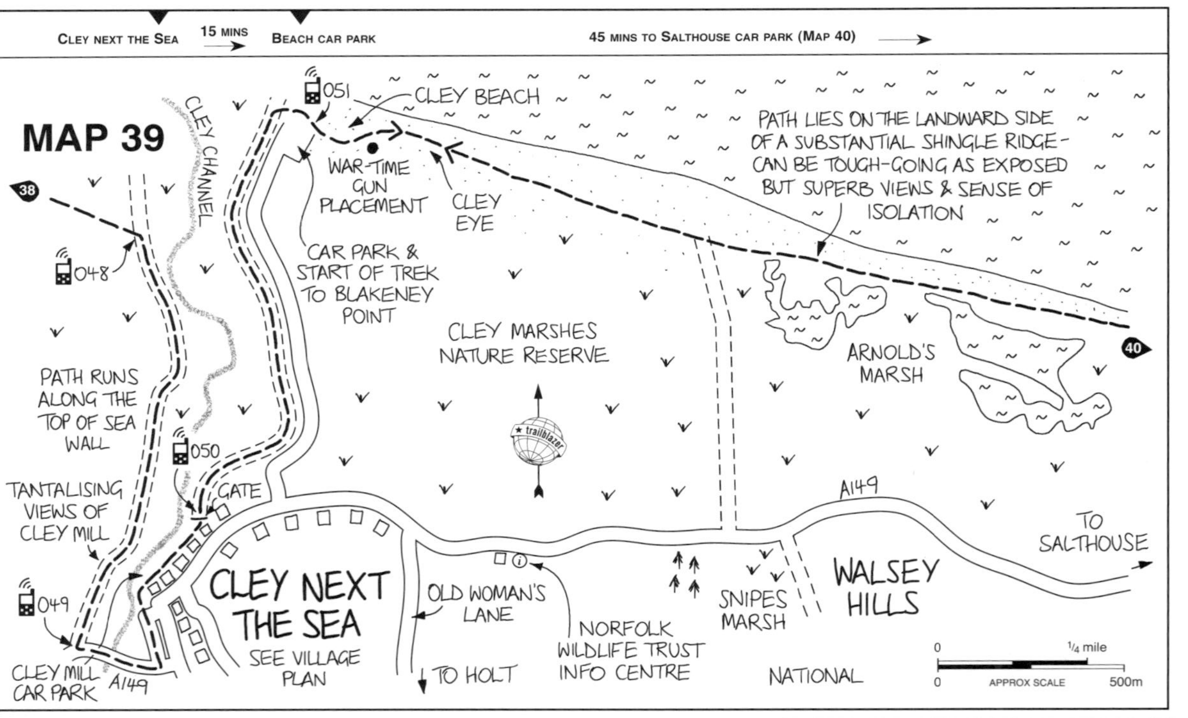
Cley next the Sea
15 mins
Beach car park
45 mins to Salthouse car park (Map 40)
MAP 39
38
CLEY CHANNEL
051
CLEY BEACH
WAR-TIME GUN PLACEMENT
CLEY EYE
PATH LIES ON THE LANDWARD SIDE OF A SUBSTANTIAL SHINGLE RIDGE - CAN BE TOUGH-GOING AS EXPOSED BUT SUPERB VIEWS & SENSE OF ISOLATION
048
CAR PARK & START OF TREK TO BLAKENEY POINT
CLEY MARSHES NATURE RESERVE
ARNOLD'S MARSH
40
PATH RUNS ALONG THE TOP OF SEA WALL
trailblazer
050
TANTALISING VIEWS OF CLEY MILL
GATE
A149
TO SALTHOUSE
049
CLEY NEXT THE SEA
SEE VILLAGE PLAN
OLD WOMAN'S LANE
TO HOLT
NORFOLK WILDLIFE TRUST INFO CENTRE
SNIPES MARSH
WALSEY HILLS
NATIONAL
CLEY MILL CAR PARK
A149
0
1/4 mile
0
APPROX SCALE
500m

If you go right at the T-junction and follow the road for half a mile you will come to **Newgate Green** and ***The Three Swallows*** (☎ 01263-740526, 💻 www.thethreeswallows.co.uk; 4D, all en suite; daily noon-11pm, food served Mon-Sat noon-2pm & 6-9pm, all day on Sun; these hours may change in the winter months). This rustic pub's rooms are in converted outbuildings and cost £70 (£40 for single occupancy). Dogs are welcome; booking is advisable. The pub has pine tables and log fires at which to relax, and black and white photographs of Cley over the years. The food – from sandwiches up – is reasonably priced, with local seafood a speciality.

By turning left at the T-junction after crossing the sluice you enter Cley.

CLEY NEXT THE SEA

During medieval times Cley (rhymes with 'sky') was a prosperous port, one of East Anglia's principal export points. In the early 17th century the River Glaven began to silt up and access to the sea became impossible for large boats. These days the village is little more than a row of Georgian houses and flint cottages alongside a marshy inlet that just about offers access to the sea.

Further inland, at the site of the original village green, stands the medieval church of **St Margaret**. The arrival of the Black Death meant construction of the church ceased suddenly, which is why the unassuming chancel and spectacular nave are so wildly different in design and detail. Look out for the fine figures of musicians, a lion and St George facing down a dragon depicted here.

To the north of the village is a mile long track (see Map 39, p163) that leads to the sea, a car park and **Cley Beach**. This is the start point for the four-mile walk west to Blakeney Point (see box p160). Make sure you stick to the low-water mark for the firmest track and to avoid nesting birds.

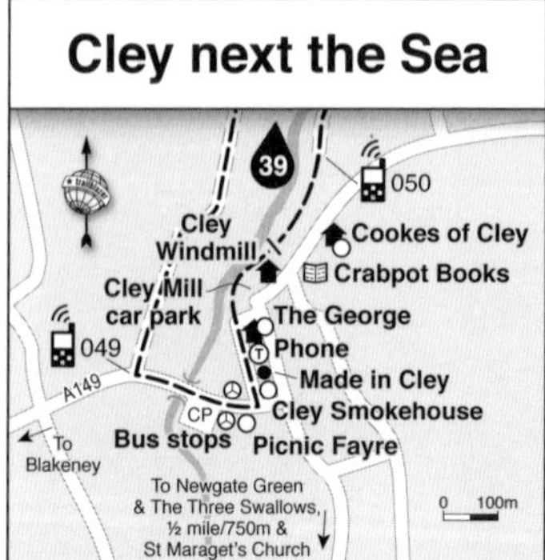

Cley Marshes Reserve (see p60) hugs the coast here. Established in 1926 it is one of the oldest nature reserves in England; more than 300 species of bird have been spotted here. Half a mile east of Cley on the A149 coast road is the Norfolk Wildlife Trust **information centre** (see Map 39, p163; ☎ 01263-740008, 💻 www.norfolkwildlifetrust.org.uk; April-Oct daily 10am-5pm, Nov-March 10am-4pm) associated with the reserve. In the exhibition building is a remote-controlled wildlife camera and audio-visual presentations about the coastline. The centre has fabulous views over the bird reserve. There is also a ***café*** (daily 10am-4.30pm, to 3.30pm in winter, lunch 11.30am-2.30pm) serving delicious food and a gift shop on site. Admission to the nature reserve costs £4 for adults (children go free) and allows you access to a series of hides dotted amidst the marshes; trails for children are also available at various times in the year. An audio tape detailing the reserve's history through reminiscences of people who have worked there as well as about the wildlife can be hired free of charge from the centre subject to payment of a returnable deposit.

Made in Cley (☎ 01263-740134, 💻 www.madeincley.co.uk; Mon-Sat 10am-5pm, Sun 11am-4pm) occupies the old general store and many of the old Regency fittings and wooden features are still present, creating a charming space to display the hand-thrown pottery, prints and jewellery on sale.

Transport

[See also pp46-8] The Coasthopper **bus** stops in the village near Picnic Fayre.

Services

Picnic Fayre (☎ 01263-740587, 🖳 www.picnic-fayre.co.uk; Mon-Sat 9am-5pm, Sun 10am-4pm) set in an old forge on the T-junction as you enter the village, sells a wide variety of fruit and veg from the local area as well as take-away hot drinks, ice creams, homemade lavender bread and cakes, venison pies, local chutneys and preserves. **Cley Smokehouse** (☎ 01263-740282, 🖳 www.cleysmokehouse.com; Mon-Sat 9am-5pm, Sun 9.30am-4.30pm), a little further up the road, has been working for more than thirty years, producing traditionally cured and smoked fish, shellfish and meats as well as homemade patés. If nothing else, buy some of the traditional North Norfolk kippers – herring, slit in two, gutted, cleaned, brined and then smoked over oak. Simply delicious, though remember they need to be cooked.

Crab Pot Books (☎ 01263-740218; daily 10am-5.30pm) is a second-hand bookshop specialising in antiquarian and natural history books; it also carries a number of local history titles.

Where to stay, eat and drink

The smartest accommodation option is ***Cley Windmill*** (☎ 01263-740209, 🖳 www.cleymill.co.uk; 8D, all en suite, bath available), a stylish converted windmill dating from the 18th century. With its restored sails, cap and wooden galleries the mill has become a well-known local landmark, easily identifiable across the marshes and commanding breathtaking views of the surroundings. Converted into a guesthouse with masses of character, the mill boasts antique furniture, comfortable sofas and, in winter, a large open fire. The rooms are spotless and B&B costs £112-165 per room, £20 discount for single occupancy. An evening meal (£32.50) is available most nights and is served at 7.30pm. Featuring seasonal and local produce the menu is a fixed three-course event. Available to non-residents as well, it must be booked in advance though.

More affordable is ***Cookes of Cley*** (☎ 01263-740776, 🖳 www.cookes-of-cley.co.uk; 3D/1T or D/1F, all with private facilities) offering B&B for £65-75 (single occupancy £55). They offer packed lunches (£5). The homely **tea room** (Fri-Sun 10am-5pm and during school holidays Wed-Mon 10am-5pm, closed Tue) serves coffee and homemade cakes as well as light lunches between noon and 3pm; try the deeply flavoursome homemade soups, and depending on the season devilled crab (£6.95), Morston mussels (£7.25) or lobster salad (£7.75/14.50). Where possible they use fresh, local produce.

The George (☎ 01263-740652, 🖳 www.thegeorgehotelatcley.co.uk; 12D/1T, all en suite, bath available; daily 11am-11pm, food served Mon-Sat noon-2.15pm & 6.30-9pm, Sun noon-3pm & 6.30-8.30pm) is a good-sized inn with a cosy public bar and two larger dining rooms. Dark wood and green-painted furniture provide an attractive backdrop to the photographs of local scenes and a large stained-glass window depicting St George fighting the dragon. Good sandwiches, ploughman's and soup are available as light snacks alongside a Cley Smokehouse platter of prawns and salmon (£7.95), half a dozen Blakeney oysters (£7.25) as well as pub grub such as sausages and mash (£9.95) and fish and chips (£10.95). There is a grassy beer garden on the opposite side of the road that backs onto the marshes.

The rooms above the pub are modern and well-furnished, and cost from £55 to £115 (£10 discount for single occupancy) depending on the size, view, season and day of the week required. Dogs (£10 per night per dog) can stay in some of the rooms; book in advance.

The onward path enters the Cley Mill car park and goes through a gate before climbing onto a sea bank. Head north towards the sea, passing alongside **Cley Marshes Nature Reserve**, one of the foremost bird-spotting grounds in the

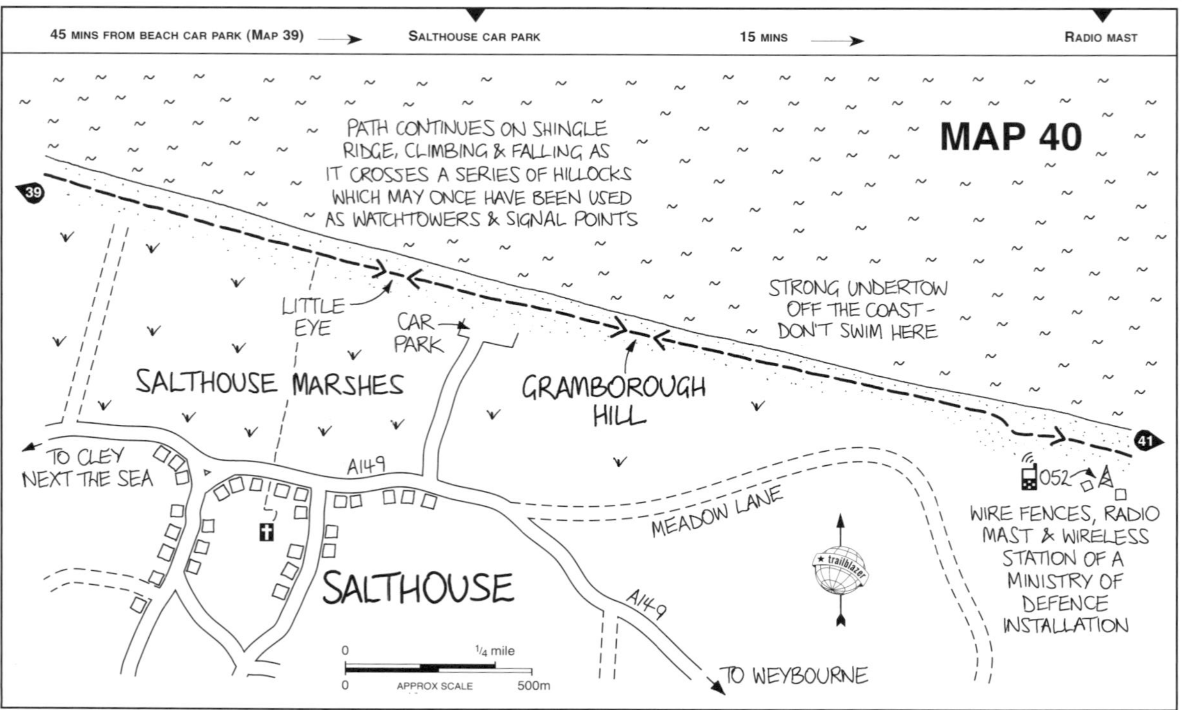

45 MINS FROM BEACH CAR PARK (MAP 39) ⟶
SALTHOUSE CAR PARK
15 MINS ⟶
RADIO MAST
MAP 40
PATH CONTINUES ON SHINGLE RIDGE, CLIMBING & FALLING AS IT CROSSES A SERIES OF HILLOCKS WHICH MAY ONCE HAVE BEEN USED AS WATCHTOWERS & SIGNAL POINTS
39
LITTLE EYE
CAR PARK
STRONG UNDERTOW OFF THE COAST - DON'T SWIM HERE
SALTHOUSE MARSHES
GRAMBOROUGH HILL
41
TO CLEY NEXT THE SEA
A149
052
WIRE FENCES, RADIO MAST & WIRELESS STATION OF A MINISTRY OF DEFENCE INSTALLATION
MEADOW LANE
trailblazer
SALTHOUSE
A149
0
1/4 mile
0
APPROX SCALE
500m
TO WEYBOURNE

country. At the end of this stretch is another car park. Here sand gives way to a shingle beach. Turn right past a war-time gun placement and begin an enervating four-mile walk along the landward side of a substantial shingle ridge, stumbling up and over **Cley Eye**, **Little Eye** (where you can turn right for Salthouse and the Coasthopper bus stop) and **Gramborough Hill** in turn. In places the ridge will have been flattened and knocked across the path by the storms that occasionally lash this stretch of coast. High tides and bad weather can mean that the path becomes flooded. The trade off for the tiring walk and the exposure to the elements is stunning views across the marshes and along the coast.

Wire fences and sturdy faceless buildings beneath a radio mast signal are a sign you are approaching a Ministry of Defence installation. Beyond this is the approach to **Weybourne Hope**, where sea-anglers can often be spotted casting from the beach. Inland a little under half a mile from here lies Weybourne.

WEYBOURNE [see Map 41, p168]

Weybourne is mentioned in the *Domesday Book* as Wabrunna. An old **Augustinian priory** dating from around 1200 stands on the site of an earlier, simpler Saxon church, whilst well-preserved 17th century brick and flint cottages line its streets. The town has a history of military defence and has been a base for repelling invasion from the time of the Spanish Armada in 1588. The old rhyme 'He who would old England win, must at Weybourne Hoop (Hope) begin' recognises that, because of the deep sea-water, access to Weybourne Hope was simple and invading armies could put ashore. In 1914 the area became a front-line defence with the construction of pill boxes and other armaments and the billeting of large numbers of troops. An anti-aircraft artillery base and training station from 1936 it finally ceased action in 1958. Thirty years later many of the buildings were demolished and the town turned over to tourism. The memory of its past lives on though in the **The Muckleburgh Collection** (☎ 01263-588210, 🖳 www.muckleburgh.co.uk; Easter-Oct daily 10am-5pm, Feb half-term week, weekends only till Easter; adult/child £6/4) which is housed in the site's original NAAFI building. The Collection is the UK's largest privately owned military museum; it includes more than 120 tanks, guns and military vehicles from all around the world as well as a large number of operational radios. Some of the attractions, such as tank demonstrations and rides in vehicles are available only in the summer months; contact them for details. There's also a small ***café*** and gift shop on site.

Weybourne hosts the North Norfolk Country Fair (see p26).

Services

On Beach Lane there is a small village **shop** (☎ 01263-588219; Mon-Sat 8am-6pm, Sun 8.30am-5pm) selling basic provisions and household items as well as local produce, sandwiches, coffee/tea to eat in or takeaway. There is a **post office** (Tue & Thur 9.30-11.30am) in the village hall.

Transport

[See also pp46-8] The Coasthopper **bus** stops just outside Foxhills (see Where to stay) gate as well as near the church.

Weybourne station (a mile inland from the town centre) is also one of the four stopping points for the **North Norfolk Railway** (The Poppy Line; ☎ 01263-820800, ☎ 01263-820808 for a talking timetable, 🖳 www.nnrailway.co.uk; daily Feb half-term and Mar to end of Oct, Nov weekends only, Dec Santa trains, 4-11/day) connecting Sheringham to Holt. Services operate with steam locomotives and occasionally diesel. A Rover ticket allowing unlimited travel for a day costs £10.50/7.

Where to stay

Campers can head to ***Foxhills*** (☎ 01263-588253), adjacent to the Muckleburgh

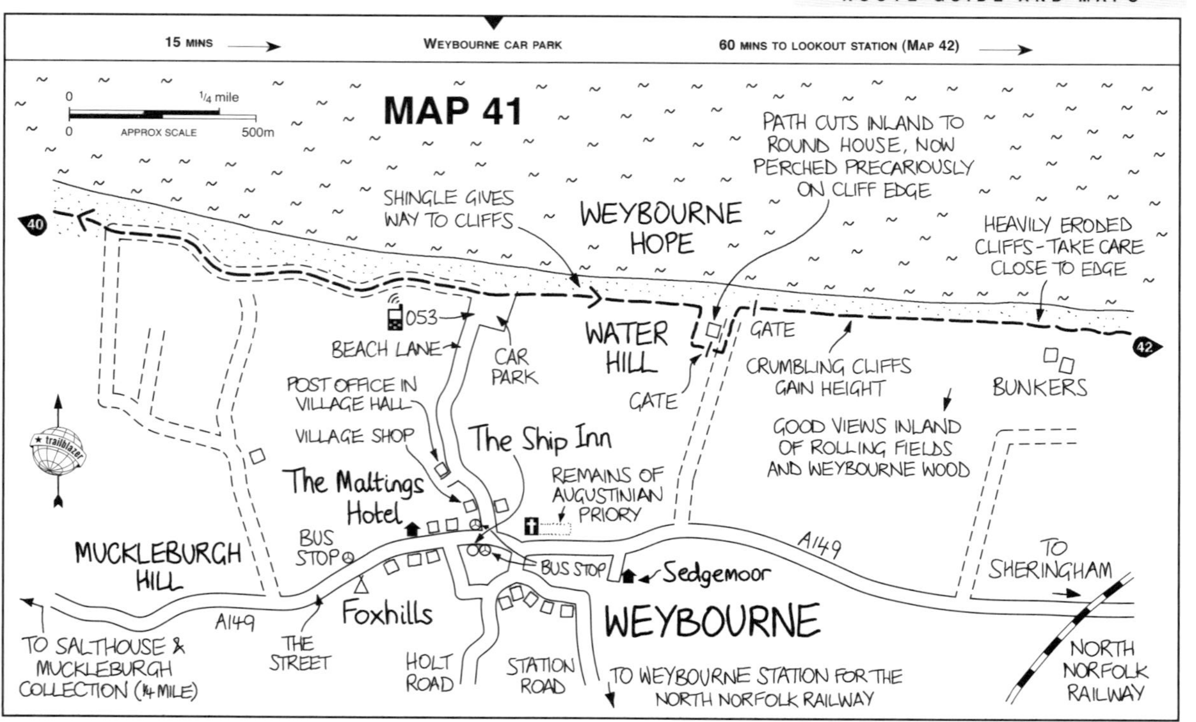

15 MINS
WEYBOURNE CAR PARK
60 MINS TO LOOKOUT STATION (MAP 42)
MAP 41
0
1/4 mile
APPROX SCALE
0
500m
40
42
SHINGLE GIVES WAY TO CLIFFS
WEYBOURNE HOPE
PATH CUTS INLAND TO ROUND HOUSE, NOW PERCHED PRECARIOUSLY ON CLIFF EDGE
HEAVILY ERODED CLIFFS - TAKE CARE CLOSE TO EDGE
053
BEACH LANE
CAR PARK
WATER HILL
GATE
GATE
CRUMBLING CLIFFS GAIN HEIGHT
BUNKERS
POST OFFICE IN VILLAGE HALL
VILLAGE SHOP
The Ship Inn
GOOD VIEWS INLAND OF ROLLING FIELDS AND WEYBOURNE WOOD
The Maltings Hotel
REMAINS OF AUGUSTINIAN PRIORY
trailblazer
BUS STOP
MUCKLEBURGH HILL
A149
BUS STOP
Sedgemoor
TO SHERINGHAM
Foxhills
A149
WEYBOURNE
TO SALTHOUSE & MUCKLEBURGH COLLECTION (1/4 MILE)
THE STREET
HOLT ROAD
STATION ROAD
TO WEYBOURNE STATION FOR THE NORTH NORFOLK RAILWAY
NORTH NORFOLK RAILWAY

Collection, a small **campsite** with 20 pitches for £10 per tent with two people staying. Hot and cold water and toilet/shower facilities are available. They do not take bookings so there are no guaranteed pitches; just turn up and try your luck but the owner will try to accommodate walkers, especially if they have called in advance to inform him.

On Sheringham Rd, B&B is available at ***Sedgemoor*** (☎ 01263-588533; 2D, shared bathroom facilities) for £40. ***The Maltings Hotel*** (☎ 01263-588731, 🖳 www.maltingshotel.activehotels.com; 2S/8D/5T/2F, all en suite, bath available), on The Street, has slightly old-fashioned-looking rooms from £84 (£56 for a single).

Where to eat and drink

The Maltings Hotel (see Where to stay; bar daily noon-2.30pm & 6.30-11pm, food served Sun noon-2pm, daily 7-8.15pm, till 9pm with reservation; closed mid Dec to end Jan) offers hearty pub meals in its bar and restaurant. Service is friendly and the menu extensive. Alternatively, drop in to ***The Ship Inn*** (☎ 01263-588721, 🖳 www.shipinnweybourne.co.uk; daily 11am-3pm & 5-11pm; food served noon-2pm & 6.30-9pm during the week, till 9.30pm at weekends), a cheerful pub on The Street, identifiable by the attractive hanging baskets at the front. The large bar is comfortable and accommodating and has a wood-burning stove for those chilly evenings. A changing selection of real ales is on offer as are decent wines by the glass. The bar food menu includes meat they butcher themselves and fish they catch from their own boat. Fresh Weybourne crab sandwiches cost £5.75 whilst a Weybourne surf and turf £12.95.

WEYBOURNE TO CROMER — MAPS 41-45

This short final **8½-mile (13.5km, 2¾-3¾hr) stretch** sees you explore the sea cliffs before Sheringham, the largest town encountered so far along the trek, after which you detour inland via the highest point anywhere on the Peddars Way or Norfolk Coast Path to finally descend once more to the sea and the finish point at Cromer pier.

Beyond Weybourne Hope the shingle gives way to crumbling **sea cliffs**. Although not especially substantial they are cliffs nonetheless and the most impressive so far seen along the coast! These fragile defences are constantly eroding and in places the path has had to be re-routed as the edge crumbles away; a good example is at **Water Hill** where the path now has to pass to the landward side of a house precariously perched on the edge of the fast-eroding cliff and destined to slip into the sea.

The path undulates as it gains height above the beach. Passing a golf course it climbs steeply to the summit of **Skelding Hill** and the old coastguard lookout station from where there are spectacular views out to sea, along the beaches and over the town below. Descending the easterly shoulder of the hill, the path passes a boating pond and descends to the promenade below Sheringham.

SHERINGHAM [see map p172]

Sheringham is an appealing, traditional place. Historically the upper part of the town, set further inland, was for farming families whilst fishermen lived in the lower section. However, these days it's mostly full of tourists, drawn by the safe swimming and huge expanse of sand exposed at low tide. You'll still see a handful of crabbing boats dragged high and dry on the sand and pebble beach though and the slipway by the quay is often festooned with nets and buoys. The town centre is busy and packed with independently owned specialist shops selling second-

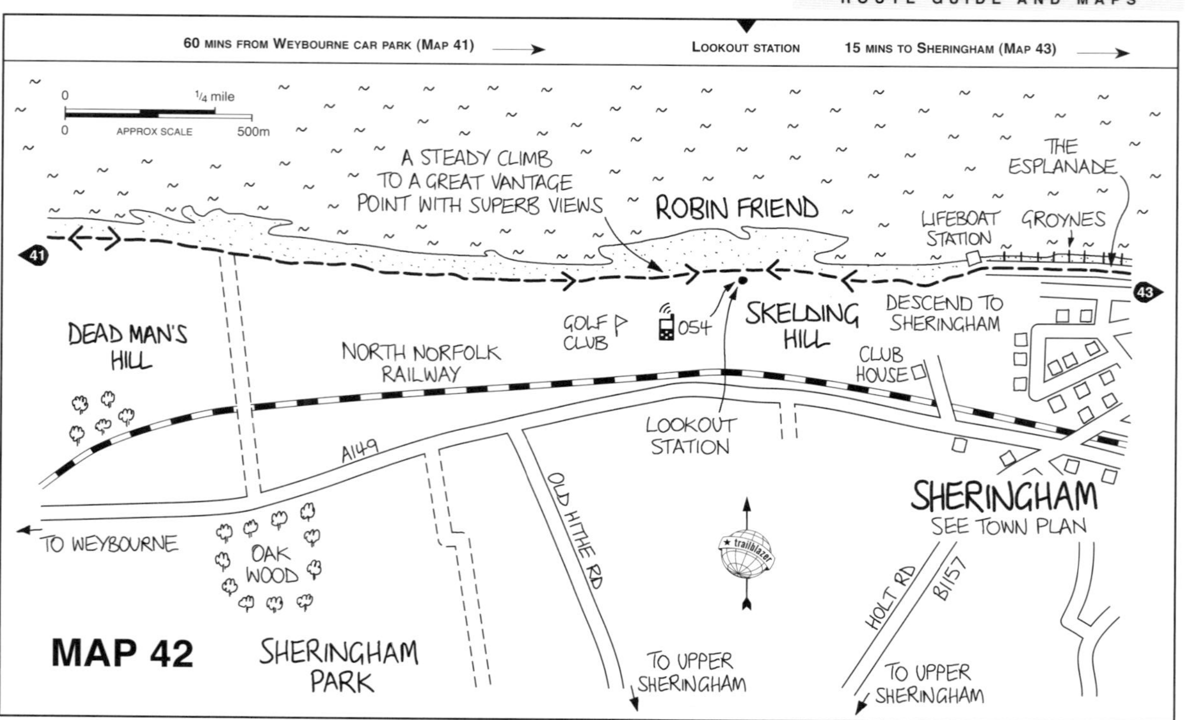
60 MINS FROM WEYBOURNE CAR PARK (MAP 41)
LOOKOUT STATION
15 MINS TO SHERINGHAM (MAP 43)
0
1/4 mile
0
APPROX SCALE
500m
A STEADY CLIMB
TO A GREAT VANTAGE
POINT WITH SUPERB VIEWS
ROBIN FRIEND
THE
ESPLANADE
LIFEBOAT
STATION
GROYNES
41
43
DESCEND TO
SHERINGHAM
GOLF
CLUB
054
SKELDING
HILL
DEAD MAN'S
HILL
NORTH NORFOLK
RAILWAY
CLUB
HOUSE
LOOKOUT
STATION
A149
OLD HITHE RD
SHERINGHAM
SEE TOWN PLAN
TO WEYBOURNE
OAK
WOOD
HOLT RD
B1157
MAP 42
SHERINGHAM
PARK
TO UPPER
SHERINGHAM
TO UPPER
SHERINGHAM

hand books, antiques and bric-a-brac as well as arts and crafts.

The unusual red-brick church of **St Joseph** on Cromer Rd was designed by Sir Giles Gilbert Scott, the man responsible for Battersea Power Station and Liverpool Cathedral. It towers over its neighbours and has a high rose window set in the east wall.

The **Fisherman's Heritage Centre** (Wed-Fri noon-4pm, during high summer, Tue-Sat noon-4pm provided volunteers are available to man it) is housed in part of the historic Fishing Sheds on West Cliff and is dedicated to demonstrating the history of the town's lifeboats. There is also information about, and a photographic record of, some of the fishermen who crewed the rescue boats. Admission is free.

Some of the original lifeboats are preserved at **Sheringham Museum** (☎ 01263-824482, 💻 www.sheringhammuseum.co.uk; Feb-Oct Tue-Sat 10am-4.30pm, Sun and bank hol Mon noon-4pm; £3.50/1.50 adult/child), affectionately known as The Mo, is set above the promenade, and underwent a major renovation in 2010. It tells the story of Sheringham and its people, looking at the past, present and future for the town to show how it has evolved from fishing village to tourist destination. Stroll through the galleries and walk amongst an historic fleet of lifeboats and fishing vessels. There are good views across the seafront from an elevated viewpoint and a small shop on-site.

In 2011 the **Sheringham Shoal Windfarm Visitor Centre** (💻 www.scira.co.uk; same hours as museum; free) is expected to open in the same building.

A couple of miles south-west of the town is **Sheringham Park** (see Map 42; daily dawn to dusk, visitor centre Mar-Oct daily 10am-5pm; free), a large tract of woodland covering 770 acres that erupts into colour in May-June when hordes of azaleas and rhododendrons flower. There is a series of walks through the park, including a path that connects to the North Norfolk railway station at Weybourne, and some specially constructed towers to scale for dramatic views.

For entertainment try the **Little Theatre** (☎ 01263-822347, 💻 www.sheringhamlittletheatre.com), on Station Rd; it presents an eclectic programme of drama, comedy, films and pantomimes and has a small coffee bar.

Sheringham hosts the Crab and Lobster Festival and the Lobster Potty Morris Festival (see p26 and p27), which celebrate crustacea and traditional dancing respectively.

Transport

[See also pp46-8] The Coasthopper **bus** stops on Station Approach. Several of Sanders Coaches' services call here.

The North Norfolk Railway (The Poppy Line, see p44) connecting Sheringham to Holt via Kelling Heath and Weybourne, departs from a restored 1950s station on Station Approach; stepping onto the platform here is like being transported back in time. The steam and diesel trains

❑ Sheringham Shoal offshore wind farm

The Sheringham Shoal offshore wind farm is set to be completed in 2011, at which point up to 88 turbines, each 80m high, will stand a minimum of 9 nautical miles (17km) from the coast and up to 13 nautical miles (23km) offshore. Although this massive farm, which will cover a total area of approximately 14sq miles, will generate power for around 220,000 average UK homes, it will undoubtedly affect the view and natural appearance of the North Norfolk coastline. The first turbines will be installed in early 2011 with a view to all 88 being in place by the end of the year, and the farm fully operational by early 2012. To take advantage of a view and wild expanse that has lain untroubled and untouched by human hand for several millennia, head to the coast now and take to the trail before the work gains further momentum.

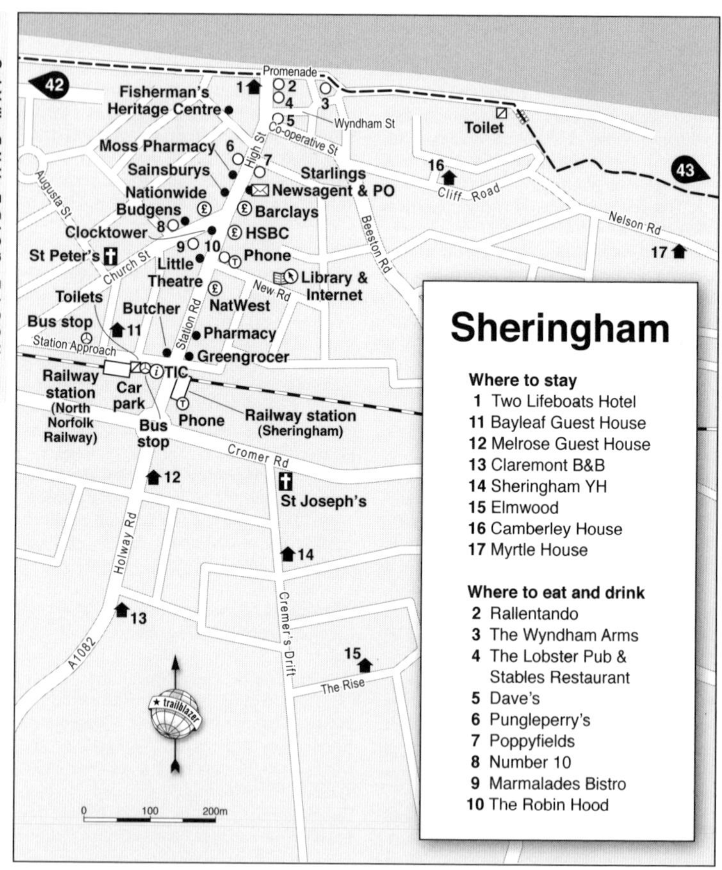

chug along five miles of track allowing you to soak up the views. Return fares (a Rover ticket) from Sheringham to Holt cost £10.50/7 (adult/child).

There are also regular **trains** from Sheringham Station, which can be found on the opposite side of Station Approach, to the east. This is the terminus for the Bittern Line (see p44) on which almost hourly trains connect Sheringham, Cromer and Norwich. There are frequent National Express East Anglia (see p43) connections from here to London Liverpool St.

National Express's NX496 **coach service** (London Victoria to Cromer) drops (and picks up) passengers on Station Approach.

Services

Sheringham Tourist Information Centre (☎ 0871-200 3071, 🖳 sheringhamtic@north-norfolk.gov.uk; Jun-Aug Mon-Sat 10am-5pm, Sun 10am-4pm; Sep-Nov & Mar/Apr-May daily 10am-2pm), on Station Approach, is a mine of information with pleasant and helpful staff. There are several **banks** and cashpoints on High St and

Station Rd. The local **library** (Mon & Thur 9.30am-7pm, Tue & Fri 9.30am-5pm, Wed 9.30am-1pm, Sat 9.30am-12.30pm) is on New Rd, and has free **internet access**. There is a **post office** counter (Mon & Thur 8.30am-5.30pm, Tue, Wed & Fri 9am-5.30pm, Sat 9am-1pm) in Starlings Newsagent on High St.

There are two **supermarkets** (Sainsbury's and Budgens), one at the southern end of High St and the other on Church St. Additionally, there is a **butcher** and a **greengrocer** on Station Rd. The **market** takes place in the car park by the North Norfolk railway station every Saturday throughout the year and on Wednesdays between March and the end of October. Lloyd's **pharmacy** is at 31 Station Rd, whilst Moss **pharmacy** is at 46 High St.

For **cycle hire**, see box p35.

Where to stay

Sheringham Youth Hostel (☎ 0845-371 9040, 🖳 www.yha.org.uk; 101 beds inc 10T; open all year), at 1 Cremer's Drift, is in a large rambling Victorian building and has a common room, games room, TV lounge, dining room and small self-catering kitchen. A bed costs from £14 though expect to pay £22 in the summer months.

The friendly, family-run ***Melrose Guest House*** (☎ 01263-823299, 🖳 www.themelrosesheringham.co.uk; 4S/4D/1T, all en suite, bath available) is centrally located at 9 Holway Rd and charges £38 per person for B&B for two sharing and £30pp for two nights or more. On the same street, the charming ***Claremont Bed & Breakfast*** (☎ 01263-821889, 🖳 www.claremont-sheringham.co.uk; 1D/1T, en suite), at No 49, lets its generously proportioned rooms for £60-80 depending on the time of year, or £45 for single occupancy. The smart ***Bayleaf Guest House*** (☎ 01263-823779, 🖳 www.bayleafbandb.co.uk; 3D/ 2T/2F, all en suite), at 10 St Peter's Rd, charges £35-50 for single occupancy and £52-70 for two sharing.

A short stroll from the centre is ***Camberley House*** (☎ 01263-823101, 🖳 www.camberleyguesthouse.co.uk; 2S/3D/ 2T or D, most en suite, bath available), perched precariously at 62 Cliff Rd. Rooms cost £56-72; the single room is £35-40. During the high season, particularly at the weekend, they are reluctant to take bookings for just one night.

Elmwood (☎ 01263-825454; 1D en suite/1T shared bathroom), at 6 The Rise, has B&B for £50 but charges a £10 single-night supplement. ***Myrtle House*** (☎ 01263-823889, 🖳 www.myrtlehouse-sheringham.co.uk; 2D/1T, all with private facilities, bath available) stands at 27-29 Nelson Rd, some five minutes' walk from the town centre, and has rooms for £70 (from £40 for single occupancy). Bikes are available for guests to use free of charge and they will prepare a packed lunch for a small charge.

The Two Lifeboats Hotel (☎ 01263-822401; 2S/4D/1T/1F, all with private facilities, bath available), at the northern end of High St, is a small, unpretentious place with rooms, many with sea views, available for £27.50-35/70/85 (sgl/dbl/family). The building dates from 1728 and the hotel is named after the *Augusta* and *Duncan* lifeboats, which saved the crew of the Norwegian brig *Caroline* when it was wrecked offshore in December 1882. Dogs (£5) are welcome.

Where to eat and drink

For a snack try ***Rallentando*** (☎ 01263-820011; daily 9.30am-5pm, slightly later in high summer), on the promenade. For good-quality fresh fish and chips there's ***Dave's*** (☎ 01263-823830; daily 11.30am-9pm, during the winter closed 2-4.30pm and shuts at 8.30pm), on Co-operative St. There's a second branch with a wider menu at 50 High St (Mon-Fri 9am-4pm, Sat & Sun 9am-5pm, until 7pm in summer).

Pungleperry's (☎ 01263-822078; daily 9am-5pm, in winter to 4.30pm), on High St, is a funky espresso bar serving freshly made pancakes, homemade pasties and quiche as well as smoothies and good coffee. Over the road, ***Poppyfields*** cooks up burgers (£6.50), lasagne (£7.25) and three-bean chilli (£7.50). ***Marmalades Bistro*** (☎ 01263-822830; food served daily noon-2pm & 6-9pm, in winter from 6.30pm), on Church St, is a venerable wood-beamed cottage serving a variety of English and

European dishes depending on seasonal produce. Start with local cider-pickled herrings (£5.95) before ordering roast pork with caramelised pears in cider, honey and wild garlic sauce (£13.95).

Number 10 (☎ 01263-824400; Wed-Sat 10am-2pm & 6.30-9pm; tea and coffees served 10am-noon, lunch noon-2pm, supper 6.30-9pm; August also open Mon/Tue, contact them for details), at 10 Augusta St, is the pick of the local eateries. Guests dine in an intimate room decorated with candles, mirrors and chapel chairs, and select from a menu that changes every four weeks. Dishes might include poached smoked haddock with spinach and dill (£8.50), sea bass fillet with anchovy sauce (£14.50), Italian cheese tart with roasted Mediterranean vegetables (£10.95) or Gressingham duck breast with Savoy cabbage and port sauce (£14.95). Booking in advance is recommended.

The Two Lifeboats Hotel (see Where to stay; bar daily 11am-11.30pm, food served Mon-Sat noon-3pm & 6-9pm, Sun noon-9pm) serves meals from an extensive menu in both of their bars and in their cosy restaurant. ***The Robin Hood*** pub (☎ 01263-820291; bar daily 11am-11pm; food Mon-Fri noon-2.45pm & 6-8.45pm, Sat & Sun noon-8.45pm as long as there is demand) offers everything from sandwiches and snacks through to mixed grills for £13. ***The Lobster Pub and Stables Restaurant*** (☎ 01263-822716, 💻 www.the-lobster.com; Mon-Thur 10am-midnight, Fri-Sat 10am-1.30am, Sun noon-midnight, food served weekdays 11.30am-2.30pm & 5.30-9.30pm, weekends all day), at 13 High St, is a traditional family pub that serves sandwiches, jacket potatoes, light bites, great seafood (from £8) and steaks (from £16.50) in smart, contemporary surroundings. They have 5-10 real ales as well as an extensive wine list.

Overlooking the promenade and with views of the sea, ***The Wyndham Arms*** (☎ 01263-822609; Mon-Fri noon-11.30pm, Sat noon-midnight, Sun noon-10.30pm), on Wyndham St, just behind the High St, serves excellent ales in a friendly and welcoming atmosphere that is full of vintage character; it also serves Greek- and British-influenced food (daily noon-2.30pm & 6.30-9pm).

Follow the promenade above the beach, past the town and towards a line of beach huts. When you come to a toilet block, turn right and begin to climb a series of steps. Continue up a concrete incline and turn left adjacent to a putting green before winding your way to the top of **Beeston Hill** (see box opposite), affectionately known as Beeston Bump, marked by an old Ordnance Survey triangulation point. The panoramic views from this 63m/207ft vantage point are spectacular and you can readily see the impact of coastal erosion on the cliffs below the summit.

Descend the eastern side of Beeston Hill towards Beeston Regis Caravan Park. Unless planning to stay in West Runton turn right before actually reaching the caravan park and walk along the Beeston Regis Nature Trail, which meanders like a river, heading inland. Look out for the interpretation board describing the flora and fauna here.

WEST RUNTON [Map 43, p176]

Beeston Regis Caravan Park (☎ 01263-823614, 💻 www.beestonregis.co.uk; Mar-Oct) has 43 tent pitches overlooking the sea as well as shower blocks with hot water and laundry rooms; a pitch for a tent with two people costs £16-27; booking is advised.

Half a mile east of here and right in this unspoilt village B&B is available at ***Homefield Guest House*** (☎ 01263-837337, 💻 www.homefieldguesthouse.co.uk; 4D/2T, all en suite, bath available), a refurbished Victorian house on Cromer Rd. The rate for two sharing is £60-80; single occupancy is £40-60.

West Runton is served by local **trains** operated by National Express East Anglia

❑ Beeston Bump Y-Station

The dominant landmark of Beeston Hill has a secret history. During the Second World War this innocuous mound, little more than a giant rounded molehill, was the site of a top-secret military listening post, known as a 'Y-station', that was vital to Britain's success in the fight against Germany. Nazi ships would patrol the coast off Sheringham, and the British command would spy on them from a series of listening posts such as Beeston Hill, which required height in order to maximise the distance they could listen. Today there is little physical evidence of the site but, when in use, the listening posts would have consisted of wooden towers almost 4m/12ft wide, and around 10m/30ft tall, set on large concrete bases. The structures would have been double-skinned, with the cavity filled with shingle in an attempt to make it bullet or at least splinter proof.

The outline of the concrete octagonal base is actually all that still remains on the summit of Beeston Hill. Radio signals and code intercepted at Beeston would have been passed on to military command and the codebreakers at Bletchley Park. In this sense, the listening stations provided the raw material for the codebreakers and played an essential role. The nine listening stations along the Norfolk coast would also relay the co-ordinates of the signals intercepted to one another in order to triangulate the location of the ship or plane sending them and thereby pinpoint the position of the craft.

After the war the listening stations were deliberately dismantled to maintain their secrecy and their location and role has since become a forgotten piece of history.

on the Bittern Line (see p44) from Norwich to Cromer and Sheringham.

The Coasthopper **bus** stops here as do several of Sanders Coaches' services; see the public transport map and table, pp46-8, for details.

The daily National Express **coach** (NX496; see p44) coming from London Victoria to Cromer, via Sheringham, pauses briefly in West Runton, at the bus stop near the post office.

Cross a railway line and then the A149 to pick up the path heading east on an old tarmac road. Turn right off this and join a gravel track heading south past Beeston Hall School and Hall Farm.

The path climbs gently, joining Calves Well Lane briefly and entering a patch of forest before it curves eastwards to pass above the earthworks at the **Roman Camp**, managed by the National Trust. Pass Roman Camp Caravan Park to reach the brow of Beacon Hill, where a mast marks the highest point in Norfolk (102m/338ft). The hill is part of the Cromer Ridge, a mass of old moraines that marks the edge of the ice sheet at the last glaciations. A mile south of here is **Felbrigg Hall** (mid-Mar to Oct, Mon-Wed, Sat and Sun 1-5pm; £7.90/3.70, adult/child; NT members are free), a Jacobean mansion surrounded by parklands. The house is full of art and paintings and the extensive walled gardens feature attractive flowering borders and a dove house whilst the stables have been converted into a tearoom. The entrance is off the B1436 – it is signposted from the A148.

Take the downhill road on the far side of sunken Sandy Lane and descend through the trees to emerge alongside a series of fields. Continue east past

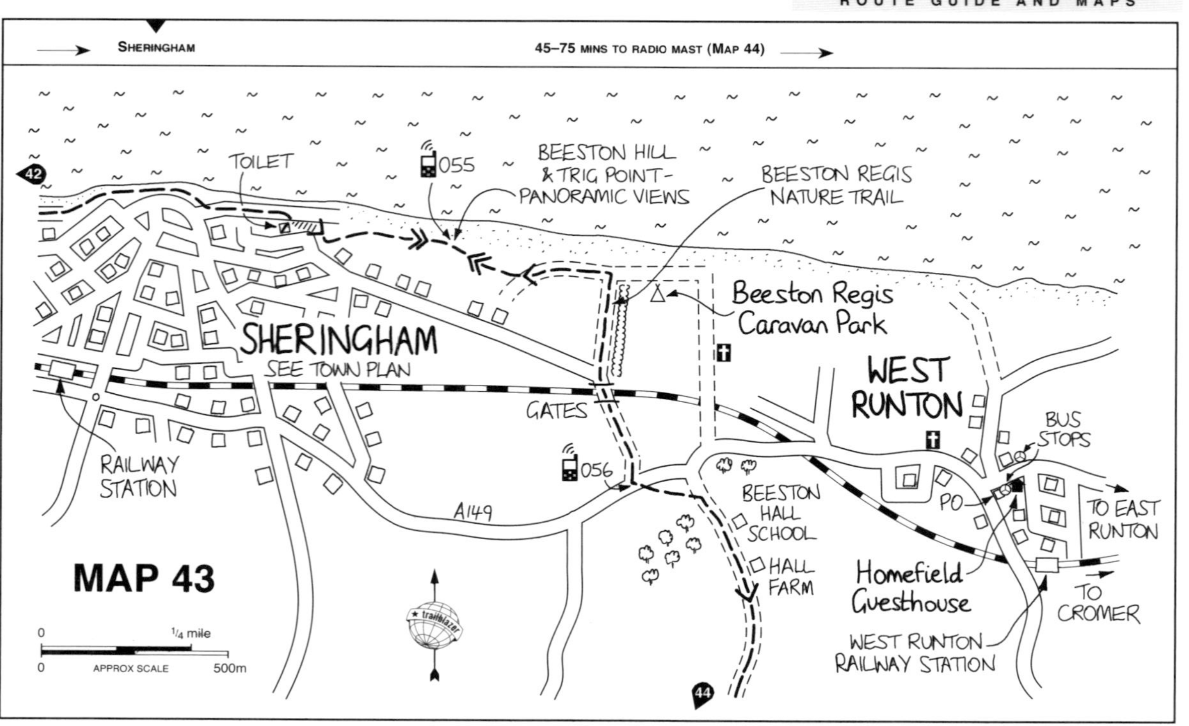
SHERINGHAM
45–75 MINS TO RADIO MAST (MAP 44)
42
TOILET
055
BEESTON HILL & TRIG POINT- PANORAMIC VIEWS
BEESTON REGIS NATURE TRAIL
Beeston Regis Caravan Park
SHERINGHAM
SEE TOWN PLAN
WEST RUNTON
GATES
BUS STOPS
RAILWAY STATION
056
A149
BEESTON HALL SCHOOL
HALL FARM
PO
TO EAST RUNTON
Homefield Guesthouse
TO CROMER
WEST RUNTON RAILWAY STATION
MAP 43
trailblazer
0
1/4 mile
0
APPROX SCALE
500m
44

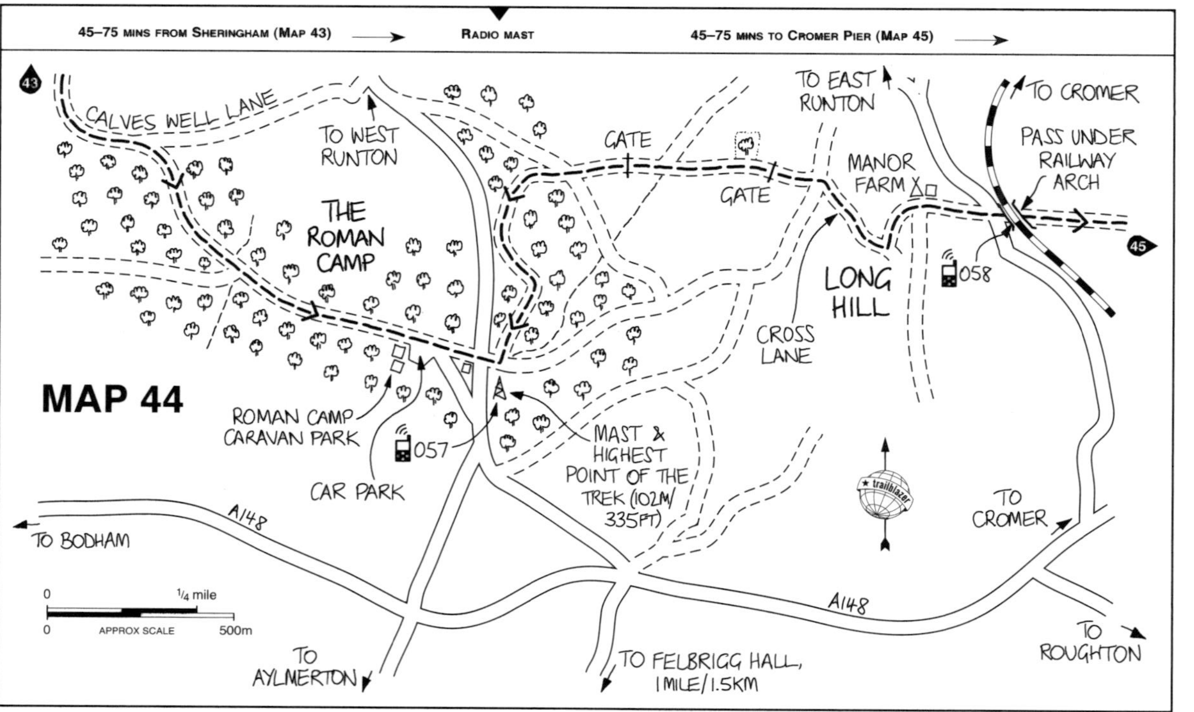
MAP 44
45–75 MINS FROM SHERINGHAM (MAP 43) →
RADIO MAST
45–75 MINS TO CROMER PIER (MAP 45) →
43
45
CALVES WELL LANE
TO WEST RUNTON
THE ROMAN CAMP
ROMAN CAMP CARAVAN PARK
CAR PARK
057
MAST & HIGHEST POINT OF THE TREK (102M/335FT)
GATE
GATE
TO EAST RUNTON
MANOR FARM
LONG HILL
CROSS LANE
058
PASS UNDER RAILWAY ARCH
TO CROMER
TO CROMER
TO ROUGHTON
A148
A148
TO FELBRIGG HALL, 1 MILE/1.5KM
TO AYLMERTON
TO BODHAM
trailblazer
APPROX SCALE
0
1/4 mile
0
500m

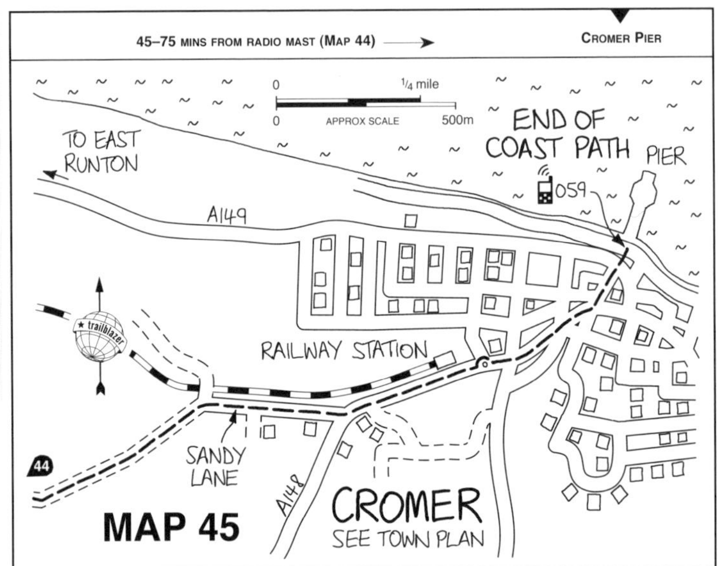

Manor Farm, passing under a substantial brick arch supporting a railway line. The path climbs gently to ease past ***Manor Farm Caravan and Camp Site*** (☎ 01263-512858, 💻 www.manorfarmcaravansite.co.uk; Apr-Oct) which has space for masses of tents with clean, well-maintained facilities including showers and toilets, coin-operated washing machines and tumble driers, as well as freezers. A pitch for a tent and two people costs £13-16.

The path meets a metalled road and then a main tarmac road. Join the pavement and turn left to walk downhill past a cemetery opposite the large Cromer Crab company building, then Cromer railway station and a large supermarket. Follow the road towards the sea, entering the main part of Cromer and making your way to the seafront where you will find the end of the Coast Path marked by a sign on a lamp post above Cromer **pier**, with the waves breaking onto the beach below.

CROMER [see map p180]

The gentrification of North Norfolk has meant that Cromer, once a fairly trashy, workaday seaside town full of amusements arcades and novelty shops is now more closely associated with local art, independent shops and, of course, Cromer crab. Nonetheless, there's a certain shabbiness to the place, what Paul Theroux described as an 'atrophied charm' (*Kingdom by the Sea*).

The **Church of St Peter and St Paul** dominates the centre of Cromer and recalls the town's prestige and wealth. During the summer months the 160ft/49m steeple, the tallest in the county, can be climbed via 172 steps to enjoy excellent views of the town and surrounding area. The interior is mostly Victorian, having been rebuilt in the late 1880s, but the sheer scale of the arches and aisles make it impressive. Lofty windows depicting some of Cromer's seafaring characters line the walls.

Tourists have been drawn to the town for more than a century to stroll on the blustery cliff tops and relax on the beach, a long stretch of sand and shingle interrupted by groynes, which is popular with all sorts, particularly a growing number of surfers. There has been a jetty or **pier** in Cromer since 1391. The 70ft wooden jetty was so badly damaged by storms that it had to be replaced by a new pier in 1901. Yet more storms wrecked this in 1953, destroying the pavilion. Two years later the **Pavilion Theatre** (☎ 01263-512495, 💻 www.cromer-pier.com) reopened though; it hosts comedy, music, dance, opera and community performances throughout the year as well as the Seaside Special, an end-of-the-pier variety show that runs through the summer and at Christmas.

There are two museums in town: **Cromer Museum** (☎ 01263-513543; Mar to end Oct Mon-Sat 10am-5pm, Sun 1-4pm, Nov to end Feb Mon-Sat 10am-4pm; £3.20/1.80 adult/child) displays local history, geology and archaeology and is housed in a row of fishermen's cottages adjacent to the church. The **RNLI Henry Bloggs Museum** (☎ 01263-511294; Apr-Sep Tue-Sun 10am-5pm, Feb-Mar & Oct-Nov to 4pm, Dec weekends only 10am-4pm; admission free) dedicated to the life of Henry Blogg, who served as a lifeboatman for 53 years, launching 387 times and saving 873 lives around the Cromer coast, is in the old lifeboat house at the foot of The Gangway. The current lifeboat, which launches from the new **Cromer Lifeboat station** at the end of the pier, can also be visited. **Cromer Lighthouse** stands half a mile from the cliff edge at Foulness to the east. The present structure dates from 1833 and the light can be seen for 23 nautical miles (26½ miles).

The **Regal Movieplex** (☎ 01263-510151, 💻 www.merlincinemas.co.uk), on Hans Place, shows the latest film releases.

Cromer is home to an annual Crab and Lobster Festival (see p26) and a Carnival (see p27).

Transport

[See also pp46-8] The Coasthopper **bus** stops on Cadogan Rd (see Services); several of Sanders Coaches' services also call here.

Cromer is one of only a few points on the north coast accessible by **rail**. The train station is on Holt Rd, a short walk west of the centre, with a regular service operating on the Bittern Line (💻 www.bitternline.com) to and from Norwich, on which almost hourly trains connect Sheringham, Cromer and Norwich. There are frequent National Express (💻 www.nationalexpresseastanglia.com) rail connections from Norwich to London Liverpool St. National Express's NX496 **coach** to London runs daily from the bus terminus on Cadogan Rd.

Services

The large, well-equipped, eco-friendly **North Norfolk Information Centre** (☎ 0871-200 3071, 💻 cromerinfo@north-norfolk.gov.uk; June-Aug Mon-Sat 10am-5pm, Sun 10am-4pm, rest of year Mon-Sat 10am-4pm) is on Louden Rd; the staff can answer questions, arrange accommodation (see box p14) and provide inspiration for things to do in the area. There is also free **internet access** in the centre.

There are **banks** and cashpoints on Tucker St, Church St and Chapel St. Cromer **Library** (Mon, Tue, Thur, Fri 9.30am-7pm, Wed & Sat 9.30am-1pm) is on Canada St and has free **internet access**. Both a Boots **chemist** (daily 8.45am-6pm) and Lloyds **Pharmacy** can be found on Church St. Cromer **Hospital** is to the east of town off Mill Rd. The **police station** stands immediately opposite the train station on Holt Rd.

There is a **post office** counter (Mon-Fri 9am-5.30pm, Sat 9am-noon) within the Budgens **supermarket** on Tucker St. There is also a large **supermarket** (Mon-Sat 8am-8pm, Sun 10am-4pm) adjacent to the train station. For dressed crab, lobsters, cockles, whelks, and fish of all description head to Richard and Julie Davies' (☎ 01263-512727; summer Mon-Sat 9am-5pm & Sun 10am-4pm, winter Mon 9am-2pm till Dec, Wed 9am-2pm, Tue, Thur, Fri & Sat 8.30am-4.30pm) **fishmonger** on Garden St.

For **cycle hire**, see box p35.

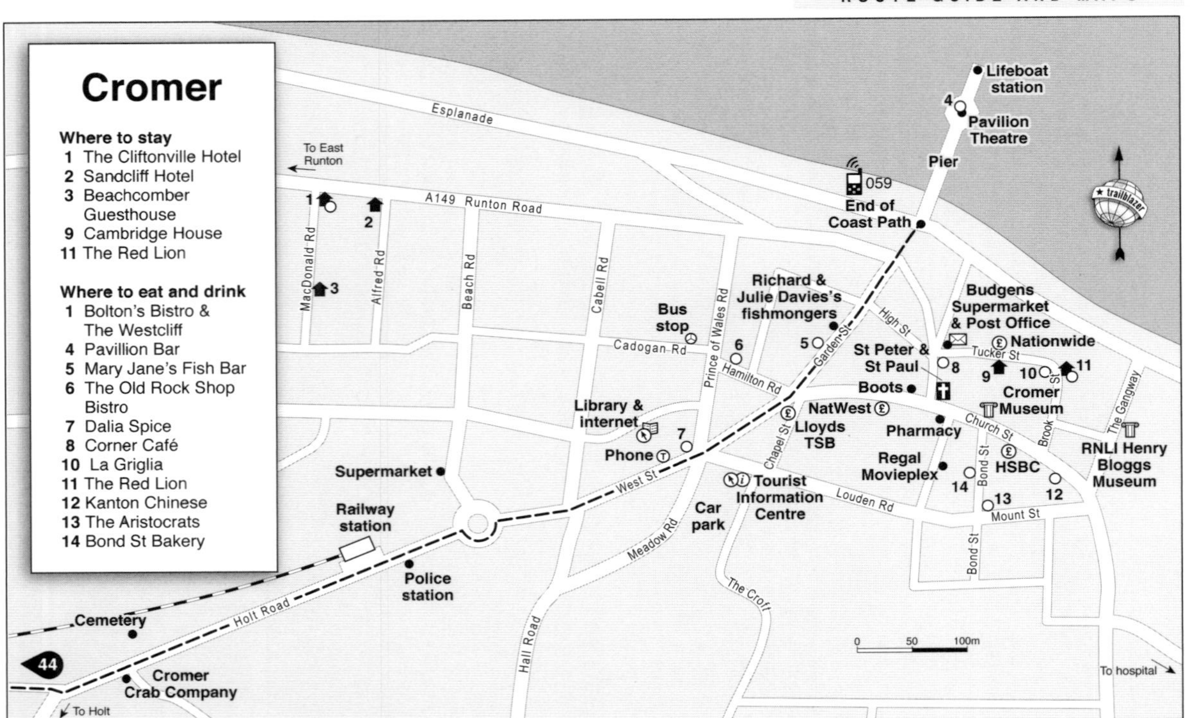
Cromer
Where to stay
1 The Cliftonville Hotel
2 Sandcliff Hotel
3 Beachcomber Guesthouse
9 Cambridge House
11 The Red Lion
Where to eat and drink
1 Bolton's Bistro & The Westcliff
4 Pavillion Bar
5 Mary Jane's Fish Bar
6 The Old Rock Shop Bistro
7 Dalia Spice
8 Corner Café
10 La Griglia
11 The Red Lion
12 Kanton Chinese
13 The Aristocrats
14 Bond St Bakery
Esplanade
To East Runton
A149 Runton Road
MacDonald Rd
Alfred Rd
Beach Rd
Cabell Rd
Cadogan Rd
Bus stop
Prince of Wales Rd
Hamilton Rd
Richard & Julie Davies's fishmongers
Garden St
High St
059
End of Coast Path
Pier
Lifeboat station
Pavilion Theatre
Budgens Supermarket & Post Office
Nationwide
Tucker St
St Peter & St Paul
Boots
Cromer Museum
The Gangway
Brook St
Church St
RNLI Henry Bloggs Museum
NatWest
Lloyds TSB
Pharmacy
Chapel St
Regal Movieplex
HSBC
Bond St
Louden Rd
Mount St
Library & internet
Phone
West St
Tourist Information Centre
Car park
Meadow Rd
The Croft
Supermarket
Railway station
Police station
Holt Road
Hall Road
Cemetery
Cromer Crab Company
44
To Holt
To hospital
0
50
100m
trailblazer

Where to stay

There's a wide range of relatively inexpensive accommodation. For B&B head to ***Beachcomber Guest House*** (☎ 01263-513398, 🖳 www.beachcomber-guesthouse.co.uk; 4D/1T or D, all en suite), at 17 Macdonald Rd, is a charming Victorian house with rooms for £60-64 (single occupancy £40-45). Note that they do not accept credit/debit cards.

Slightly more expensive, ***Cambridge House*** (☎ 01263-512085, 🖳 www.cambridgecromer.co.uk; 2S or D/4D, T or F, most en suite, bath available), on East Cliff, Tucker St, was built in 1887 and retains much of its original character. Ideally located overlooking the beach and pier, there are steps to the promenade opposite the front door. B&B is £35-40pp.

The Red Lion (☎ 01263-514964, 🖳 www.redlion-cromer.co.uk; 9D/2T/1F, all en suite, bath available), on Brook St, charges £50-90pp for B&B; many of the rooms have sea views. There's also a first-floor residents' lounge that overlooks the beach as well as a sauna, solarium and snooker room. Well-behaved dogs (£5) are welcome; booking recommended.

The Sandcliff Hotel (☎ 01263-512888, 🖳 www.sandcliffhotel.com; 4S/ 10D/4T/5F, most en suite, bath available) overlooking the sea on Runton Rd, lets its rooms on a B&B basis: £52.50-55 for a single and £75-95 for two sharing; the rate depends in part on whether rooms have a sea view. Check their website for special deals and discounts. Popular with group bookings there is a bar and restaurant (three-course evening meal £13 served summer 6-7.30pm, winter to 7pm) on site. Dogs are welcome.

The Cliftonville Hotel (☎ 01263-512543, 🖳 www.cliftonvillehotel.co.uk; 9S/18D/3T, all en suite, bath available), also on the seafront, has rooms with spectacular sea views. Many of the hotel's Edwardian features are intact including attractive stained-glass windows and doors. B&B costs from £67pp midweek and from £72pp at weekends. Dogs (£5 inc meal) are welcome.

Where to eat and drink

With some of the best views in Cromer, the ***Pavilion Bar*** (daily all day) on the pier is a good place to pop in to for a coffee, smoothie or snack.

On the seafront, at the Cliftonville Hotel (see Where to stay) is ***Bolton's Bistro*** (🖳 www.boltonsbistro.co.uk; daily noon-2pm & 6-10pm), a popular eatery offering freshly prepared dishes including Cromer crab, locally caught lobster and a range of changing specials such as fish and penne pasta (£11.95) and medallions of beef and crayfish tails topped with ginger, chilli and lime butter (£14.95). The hotel's restaurant, ***The Westcliff*** (summer daily 6-9pm) is a grand Edwardian affair with a Minstrel's gallery, marble fireplace and stained-glass windows. The à la carte menu provides a more formal and consequently pricy experience, though there is a 3-course set menu for £28.50.

For fantastic fish and chips to eat on the seafront head to ***Mary Jane's Fish Bar*** (☎ 01263-511208), on Garden St, which is open daily (summer 11.30am-7pm, winter hours vary). For more international flavours try ***Kanton Chinese Takeaway*** (☎ 01263-517171; daily noon-2pm & 5-11pm), on Church St, or ***Dalia Spice*** (☎ 01263-519700; daily noon-2pm & 5-11pm), on Prince of Wales Rd, for good Indian dishes.

Bond St Bakery makes good cakes, filled rolls and fresh bread if you just want a snack. On the same street is ***The Aristocrats*** (☎ 01263-512320, 🖳 www.aristocratrestaurant.co.uk; summer Tue-Sat 9am-4pm, to 2pm in winter, Sun 11.30am-2pm for Sunday lunch only) serving cakes, snacks, sandwiches and simple lunch specials; main courses are about £10.50. ***The Corner Café*** (☎ 01263-512860; summer daily 9am-6pm winter 9am-4pm), at 11 High St, does a decent all-day breakfast (£3.20-6.75) and later good fish dishes and simple steaks. ***West St Café*** also does all-day breakfasts (£5.50) and good-value sandwiches from £2.50. On Hamilton Rd you'll find ***The Old Rock Shop Bistro*** (☎ 01263-511926, 🖳 www.theoldrockshop bistro.co.uk; Mon-Thur 8am-6pm, Fri-Sun till 9pm), a café-cum-bistro that does decent homemade cakes and savouries as well as reasonably priced light lunches.

Within the Victorian quarter, where Brook St meets Tucker St, is ***La Griglia*** (☎ 01263-519619, 🖳 www.lagriglia.co.uk; Tue-Sat 10am-9pm), on Brook St, a relaxed café-restaurant with a Mediterranean flavour. Open for coffee and snacks from 10am, they also serve seasonal main meals (noon-2pm & 6-9pm) including squash risotto (£11), meatballs and spaghetti (£12) and pizzas from £9. The two-course set lunch menu for £11 is particularly good value. Close by, ***The Red Lion*** (see Where to stay; daily 11am-11pm, food served daily noon-2.30pm & 6-9.30pm) is an Edwardian-era pub that still has most of its rich mahogany fittings. The pub serves a wide range of real ales, an ideal way (though clearly only for those who like real ale!) to toast the completion of the walk. You can either eat in the bar (pies and curries available from £9.25) or the smarter Galleons Restaurant, which offers dishes such as grilled pollock and tomato salsa (£11.50), or lamb shank and mash (£11.95).

APPENDIX – GPS WAYPOINTS

Each GPS waypoint was taken on the route at the reference number marked on the map as below. This list of GPS waypoints is also available to download from the Trailblazer website (🖳 www.trailblazer-guides.com)

MAP	REF	WAYPOINTS (N/E)	DESCRIPTION
1	001	52° 23.433' / 00° 51.318'	Finger-post – start of the Peddars Way
1	002	52° 23.800' / 00° 51.411'	Bridge over Little Ouse River (Suffolk/Norfolk border)
1	003	52° 24.648' / 00° 51.386'	A1066 road crossing
2	004	52° 25.289' / 00° 51.254'	Bridge over River Thet
3	005	52° 26.845' / 00° 50.688'	A11 road crossing
4	006	52° 28.783' / 00° 50.152'	Stonebridge
5	007	52° 30.019' / 00° 49.856'	Junction – take dirt track branching right along edge of Stanford Military Training Zone
5	008	52° 31.066' / 00° 49.099'	Thompson Water
7	009	52° 33.413' / 00° 48.217'	Crossroads – take dirt track left
7	010	52° 33.891' / 00° 47.425'	Dirt track meets B1108 – turn left
8	011	52° 33.933' / 00° 45.791'	Little Cressingham
8	012	52° 34.804' / 00° 45.647'	Crossroads – go straight over
9	013	52° 36.290' / 00° 44.874'	Crossroads – South Pickenham
10	014	52° 36.719' / 00° 44.886'	Path leaves road and continues behind hedge
10	015	52° 37.522' / 00° 44.869'	Join road and turn right – North Pickenham
11	016	52° 39.122' / 00° 43.532'	A47 crossroads
12	017	52° 39.779' / 00° 42.851'	Sporle Road junction – dog leg right
13	018	52° 41.110' / 00° 41.305'	A1065 crossing – take dirt track heading north-west
13	019	52° 41.904' / 00° 41.140'	Bridge over River Nar
13	020	52° 42.210' / 00° 41.267'	Castle Acre, Stocks Green
14	021	52° 43.547' / 00° 40.456'	Crossroads, Old Wicken Cottages; the path rejoins the road
15	022	52° 44.947' / 00° 39.468'	Trig Point, Shepherd's Bush
16	023	52° 46.293' / 00° 38.517'	Crossroads, dirt track to right goes to Great Massingham
17	024	52° 47.892' / 00° 37.530'	A148 road crossing
18	025	52° 50.000' / 00° 36.182'	B1153 road crossing by Anmer Minque
20	026	52° 51.973' / 00° 34.945'	Snettisham–Great Bircham road crossing
20	027	52° 53.402' / 00° 33.972'	Sedgeford–Fring road crossing
21	028	52° 54.081' / 00° 33.547'	B1454, join road and turn right then immediately left by Magazine Cottage
21	029	52° 54.424' / 00° 33.419'	Disused railway crossing
22	030	52° 56.018' / 00° 32.316'	Ringstead
23	031	52° 56.840' / 00° 32.305'	Junction, leave road to take dirt track branching left
23	032	52° 57.404' / 00° 31.736'	Holme crossroads
23	033	52° 57.973' / 00° 31.449'	Finger-post on Holme Dunes – end of Peddars Way and point where route joins Norfolk Coast Path
25	034	52° 56.382' / 00° 29.258'	Hunstanton Central Green – start of Norfolk Coast Path

26	035	52° 58.408' / 00° 32.374'	Gore Point, Holme Dunes (duckboards)
27	036	52° 57.588' / 00° 34.752'	Thornham
28	037	52° 56.646' / 00° 35.924'	Junction, leave road to take dirt track branching left
28	038	52° 57.022' / 00° 37.949'	Dirt track, turn left towards coast
29	039	52° 57.962' / 00° 38.234'	Broad Lane meets dirt track along coast, turn right
29	040	52° 57.964' / 00° 39.008'	Gate to Branodunum Roman fort
31	041	52° 57.893' / 00° 44.715'	Burnham Overy Staithe
32	042	52° 58.706' / 00° 46.003'	Holkham Beach entrance
33	043	52° 58.167' / 00° 48.838'	Holkham Gap; path doglegs
34	044	52° 58.360' / 00° 50.851'	Abraham's Bosom Lake and access to Wells Beach via steps
34	045	52° 57.440' / 00° 51.070'	Path joins The Quay in Wells-next-the-Sea
37	046	52° 57.448' / 00° 59.158'	Quay – where the boat trips to Blakeney Point launch
38	047	52° 57.345' / 01° 00.984'	Blakeney quay
39	048	52° 57.804' / 01° 02.545'	Path meets dirt track, turn right
39	049	52° 57.173' / 01° 02.369'	A149, join road and turn left – Cley
39	050	52° 57.310' / 01° 02.656'	Raised sea defence, bear left
39	051	52° 57.927' / 01° 02.870'	Car park and access to shingle beach, turn right
40	052	52° 57.087' / 01° 07.317'	Ministry of Defence installation
41	053	52° 56.933' / 01° 08.395'	Car park at bottom of Beach Lane – Weybourne
42	054	52° 56.732' / 01° 11.816'	Lookout station
43	055	52° 56.597' / 01° 13.498'	Beeston Hill
43	056	52° 56.286' / 01° 13.858'	A149, cross road and pick up tarmac path bearing left
44	057	52° 55.478' / 01° 15.021'	Mast – highest point of the trek
44	058	52° 55.665' / 01° 16.272'	Arches under railway line
45	059	52° 55.955' / 01° 18.028'	Cromer Pier – end of Norfolk Coast Path

INDEX

Page references in **bold** type refer to maps

Map key

Symbol	Meaning	Symbol	Meaning	Symbol	Meaning
	Where to stay		Library/bookstore	●	Other
○	Where to eat and drink		Internet	CP	Car park
	Campsite		Museum/gallery		Bus station
	Post Office		Church/cathedral		Bus stop
	Bank/ATM		Telephone		Rail line & station
	Tourist Information		Public toilet		Park
		□	Building	082	GPS waypoint

Symbol	Meaning	Symbol	Meaning	Symbol	Meaning
	Peddars Way/ Norfolk Coast Path		Gate		Water
	Other path		Stile		River
	4 x 4 track		Duckboards		Beach
	Tarmac road		Bridge		Salt marsh
	Steps		Hedge		Conifer trees
	Slope		Fence		Deciduous trees
	Steep slope		Disused railway line	24	Map continuation

Adventure Cycle-Touring Handbook	2nd edn out now
Adventure Motorcycling Handbook	5th edn out now
Australia by Rail	5th edn out now
Australia's Great Ocean Road	1st edn out now
Azerbaijan	4th edn out now
Coast to Coast Path (British Walking Guide)	4th edn out now
Cornwall Coast Path (British Walking Guide)	3rd edn out now
Corsica Trekking – GR20	1st edn out now
Cotswold Way (British Walking Guide)	1st edn out now
Dolomites Trekking – AV1 & AV2	2nd edn out now
Inca Trail, Cusco & Machu Picchu	4th edn Jan 2011
Indian Rail Handbook	1st edn mid 2011
Hadrian's Wall Path (British Walking Guide)	2nd edn out now
Himalaya by Bike – a route and planning guide	1st edn out now
Japan by Rail	2nd edn out now
Kilimanjaro – the trekking guide (inc Mt Meru)	3rd edn out now
Mediterranean Handbook	1st edn out now
Moroccan Atlas – the trekking guide	1st edn out now
Morocco Overland (4WD/motorcycle/mountainbike)	1st edn out now
Nepal Mountaineering Guide	1st edn mid 2011
Nepal Trekking & The Great Himalaya Trail	1st edn Dec 2010
New Zealand – The Great Walks	2nd edn out now
North Downs Way (British Walking Guide)	1st edn out now
Norway's Arctic Highway	1st edn out now
Offa's Dyke Path (British Walking Guide)	3rd edn Apr 2011
Overlanders' Handbook – worldwide driving guide	1st edn Feb 2011
Peddars Way & Norfolk CP (British Walking Guide)	1st edn out now
Pembrokeshire Coast Path (British Walking Guide)	3rd edn out now
Pennine Way (British Walking Guide)	3rd edn Mar 2011
The Ridgeway (British Walking Guide)	2nd edn out now
Sahara Overland – a route and planning guide	2nd edn out now
Scottish Highlands – The Hillwalking Guide	2nd edn out now
The Silk Roads – a route and planning guide	3rd edn out now
South Downs Way (British Walking Guide)	3rd edn out now
Tour du Mont Blanc	1st edn out now
Trans-Canada Rail Guide	5th edn out now
Trans-Siberian Handbook	7th edn out now
Trekking in the Annapurna Region	5th edn Mar 2011
Trekking in the Everest Region	5th edn out now
Trekking in Ladakh	3rd edn out now
Trekking in the Pyrenees	3rd edn out now
Walker's Haute Route – Mont Blanc to Matterhorn	1st edn out now
West Highland Way (British Walking Guide)	4th edn out now

The Inca Trail, Cusco & Machu Picchu
Alexander Stewart, 4th edn, £12.99
ISBN 978-1-905864-15-7, 352pp, 74 maps, 40 colour photos
The Inca Trail, from Cusco to Machu Picchu, is South America's most popular trek. Practical guide including detailed trail maps, plans of Inca sites, plus guides to Cusco and Machu Picchu. Route guides to other trails in the area: the Santa Teresa Trek and the Choquequirao Trek as well as the Vilcabamba Trail plus the routes linking them. This entirely rewalked and rewritten fourth edition includes a new history of the Incas by Hugh Thomson.

New Zealand – The Great Walks
Alexander Stewart, 2nd edn, £12.99
ISBN 978-1-905864-11-9, 272pp, 60 maps, 40 colour photos
New Zealand is a wilderness paradise of incredibly beautiful landscapes. There is no better way to experience it than on one of the nine designated Great Walks, the country's premier walking tracks which provide outstanding hiking opportunities for people at all levels of fitness. Also includes detailed guides to Auckland, Wellington, National Park Village, Taumarunui, Nelson, Queenstown, Te Anau and Oban.

Kilimanjaro – the trekking guide to Africa's highest mountain *Henry Stedman*, 3rd edn, £12.99
ISBN 978-1-905864-24-9, 368pp, 40 maps, 30 photos
At 19,340ft the world's tallest freestanding mountain, Kilimanjaro is one of the most popular destinations for hikers visiting Africa. It's possible to walk up to the summit: no technical skills are necessary. Includes town guides to Nairobi and Dar-Es-Salaam, and a colour guide to flora and fauna. Includes Mount Meru.

Nepal Trekking and the Great Himalaya Trail
Robin Boustead, 1st edn, £14.99, ISBN 978-1-905864-31-7
256pp, 8pp colour maps, 40 colour photos
This guide includes the most popular routes in Nepal – the Everest, Annapurna and Langtang regions – as well as the newest trekking areas for true trailblazers. This is the first guide to chart The Great Himalaya Trail, the route which crosses Nepal from east to west. Extensive planning sections.

Trekking in the Everest Region
Jamie McGuinness, 5th edn, £12.99, ISBN 978-1-873756-99-7
320pp, 30 maps, 30 colour photos
Fifth edition of this popular guide to the Everest region, the world's most famous trekking region. Planning, preparation, getting to Nepal; detailed route guides with 30 route maps and 50 village plans; Kathmandu city guide: where to stay, where to eat, what to see.

The Walker's Haute Route – Mt Blanc to the Matterhorn
Alexander Stewart, 1st edn, £12.99
ISBN 978-1-905864-08-9, 256pp, 60 maps, 30 colour photos
From Mont Blanc to the Matterhorn, Chamonix to Zermatt, the 180km (113-mile) Walkers' Haute Route traverses one of the finest stretches of the Pennine Alps – the range between Valais in Switzerland and Piedmont and Aosta Valley in Italy. Includes Chamonix and Zermatt guides.

TRAILBLAZER'S BRITISH WALKING GUIDES

We've applied to destinations which are closer to home Trailblazer's proven formula for publishing definitive practical route guides for adventurous travellers. Britain's network of long-distance trails enables the walker to explore some of the finest landscapes in the country's best walking areas. These are guides that are user-friendly, practical, informative and environmentally sensitive.

'The same attention to detail that distinguishes its other guides has been brought to bear here'.
THE SUNDAY TIMES

● **Unique mapping features** In many walking guidebooks the reader has to read a route description then try to relate it to the map. Our guides are much easier to use because walking directions, tricky junctions, places to stay and eat, points of interest and walking times are all written onto the maps themselves in the places to which they apply. With their uncluttered clarity, these are not general-purpose maps but fully edited maps drawn by walkers for walkers.

● **Largest-scale walking maps** At a scale of just under 1:20,000 (8cm or 3¹/₈ inches to one mile) the maps in these guides are bigger than even the most detailed British walking maps currently available in the shops.

● **Not just a trail guide – includes where to stay, where to eat and public transport** Our guidebooks cover the complete walking experience, not just the route. Accommodation options for all budgets are provided (pubs, hotels, B&Bs, campsites, bunkhouses, hostels) as well as places to eat. Detailed public transport information for all access points to each trail means that there are itineraries for all walkers, for hiking the entire route as well as for day or weekend walks.

Coast to Coast Path *Henry Stedman*, 4th edition, £11.99
ISBN 978-1-905864-30-0, 256pp, 110 maps, 40 colour photos

Cornwall Coast Path *Edith Schofield*, 3rd edition, £9.99
ISBN 978-1-905864-19-5, 256pp, 112 maps, 40 colour photos

Cotswold Way *Tricia & Bob Hayne*, 1st edition, £9.99
ISBN 978-1-905864-16-4, 192pp, 60 maps, 40 colour photos

Hadrian's Wall Path *Henry Stedman*, 2nd edition, £9.99,
ISBN 978-1-905864-14-0, 208pp, 60 maps, 40 colour photos

North Downs Way *John Curtin*, 1st edition, £9.99
ISBN 978-1-873756-96-6, 192pp, 80 maps, 40 colour photos

Offa's Dyke Path *Keith Carter*, 3rd edition, £11.99 (due Apr 2011)
ISBN 978-1-905864-35-5, 226pp, 98 maps, 40 colour photos

Peddars Way & Norfolk Coast Path *Alexander Stewart*, £11.99
ISBN 978-1-905864-28-7, 192pp, 54 maps, 40 colour photos

Pembrokeshire Coast Path *Jim Manthorpe*, 3rd edition, £9.99
ISBN 978-1-905864-27-0, 224pp, 96 maps, 40 colour photos

Pennine Way *Keith Carter & Chris Scott*, 3rd edition, £11.99 (due Mar 2011)
ISBN 978-1-905864-34-8, 272pp, 135 maps, 40 colour photos

The Ridgeway *Nick Hill*, 2nd edition, £9.99
ISBN 978-1-905864-17-1, 192pp, 53 maps, 40 colour photos

South Downs Way *Jim Manthorpe*, 3rd edition, £9.99
ISBN 978-1-905864-18-8, 192pp, 60 maps, 40 colour photos

West Highland Way *Charlie Loram*, 4th edition, £9.99
ISBN 978-1-905864-29-4, 192pp, 60 maps, 40 colour photos

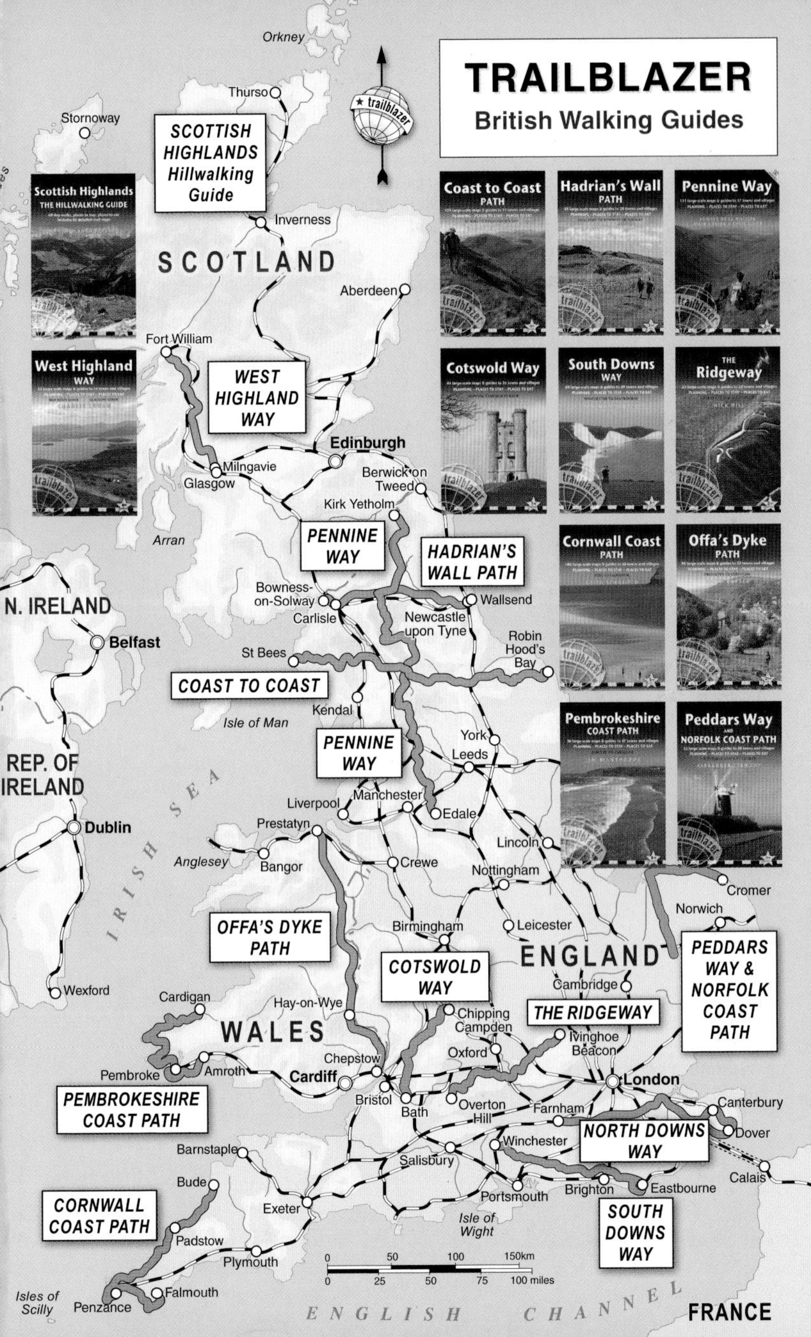
TRAILBLAZER
British Walking Guides
SCOTTISH HIGHLANDS Hillwalking Guide
WEST HIGHLAND WAY
PENNINE WAY
HADRIAN'S WALL PATH
COAST TO COAST
OFFA'S DYKE PATH
COTSWOLD WAY
THE RIDGEWAY
PEDDARS WAY & NORFOLK COAST PATH
NORTH DOWNS WAY
SOUTH DOWNS WAY
PEMBROKESHIRE COAST PATH
CORNWALL COAST PATH
SCOTLAND
ENGLAND
WALES
N. IRELAND
REP. OF IRELAND
FRANCE
IRISH SEA
ENGLISH CHANNEL
Orkney
Thurso
Stornoway
Inverness
Aberdeen
Fort William
Edinburgh
Milngavie
Glasgow
Berwick-on Tweed
Kirk Yetholm
Arran
Bowness-on-Solway
Carlisle
Wallsend
Newcastle upon Tyne
Belfast
Robin Hood's Bay
St Bees
Kendal
Isle of Man
York
Leeds
Liverpool
Manchester
Edale
Dublin
Prestatyn
Anglesey
Bangor
Crewe
Lincoln
Nottingham
Cromer
Norwich
Birmingham
Leicester
Cambridge
Wexford
Cardigan
Hay-on-Wye
Chipping Campden
Ivinghoe Beacon
Oxford
Chepstow
Pembroke
Amroth
Cardiff
London
Bristol
Bath
Overton Hill
Farnham
Canterbury
Dover
Winchester
Barnstaple
Salisbury
Calais
Bude
Brighton
Eastbourne
Exeter
Portsmouth
Isle of Wight
Padstow
Plymouth
Falmouth
Isles of Scilly
Penzance
0 50 100 150km
0 25 50 75 100 miles
Scottish Highlands THE HILLWALKING GUIDE
West Highland WAY
Coast to Coast PATH
Hadrian's Wall PATH
Pennine Way
Cotswold Way
South Downs WAY
THE Ridgeway
Cornwall Coast PATH
Offa's Dyke PATH
Pembrokeshire COAST PATH
Peddars Way AND NORFOLK COAST PATH
trailblazer

Peddars Way & Norfolk Coast Path